PR
Ver

M000086473

HOUGHTON MIFFLIN

WORLD REGIONAL STUDIES

Unless we know about the traditions and ways of life of people in other nations, we cannot develop an adequate understanding of the present-day world. The goal of the World Regional Studies series is to provide a well-rounded picture of human experience in six major areas of the world:

The Middle East

Africa

China

India

Japan

Russia

Using history as the organizing principle, the books in this series incorporate concepts and skills from the social sciences and from the humanities. Political and economic systems, geography, social organization and human values, the fine arts, and religion are all discussed in depth.

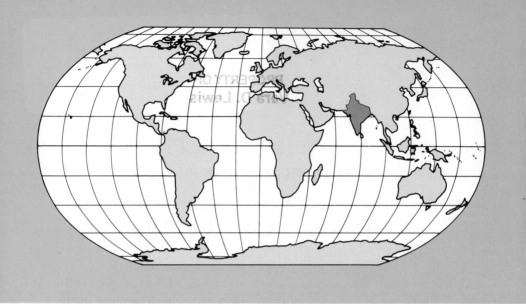

WORLD REGIONAL STUDIES

India

Third Edition

Michael Kublin

Hyman Kublin

HOUGHTON MIFFLIN COMPANY / Boston

Atlanta / Dallas / Geneva, Illinois / Palo Alto / Princeton / Toronto

Michael Kublin

Dr. Kublin received his Ph.D in History from New York University. He also has an MBA from Pace University. He is currently Assistant Professor of International Business at the University of New Haven and taught history previously at Kingsborough Community College in Brooklyn, New York. Dr. Kublin is also general editor for the Houghton Mifflin World Regional Studies series.

Hyman Kublin

A specialist in non-Western history, the elder Dr. Kublin received his Ph.D from Harvard University. Formerly Associate Dean of Graduate Studies of the City University of New York, he taught history at Brooklyn College, the University of California (Berkeley), the University of Delaware, and the University of Hawaii. He was a Fulbright Research Professor at Waseda University in Japan.

Howard R. Anderson

Dr. Anderson, consulting editor, taught social studies in Michigan, Iowa, and New York. He also taught at the University of Iowa and at Cornell University, and served as President of the National Council for the Social Studies.

Special thanks to Alison Lipski and Christine Walnycky, reference librarians at the University of New Haven Library, for their unflagging cooperation. My wife, Janet Blaustein Kublin, provided research and editorial and typing support as well as unending encouragement.

Cover photo: The Taj Mahal

The chapter opener art on the first page of every chapter shows a detail from the decoration over the main entrance to the Taj Mahal.

Printed in the U.S.A.

ISBN: 0–395–47080–3

ABCDEFGHIJ-M-99876543210

CONTENTS

MAPS

CHARTS, GRAPHS, AND TABLES

PHOTO ESSAYS

INTRODUCTION

Next to China, South Asia ranks highest in the world in terms of population and length of historical tradition. The subcontinent has a record of 5,000 years of civilized life. Foreign influences, especially those from the Aryans, Muslims, Mongols, and British, have played a large part in developing the diversity that characterizes the subcontinent.

A Land of Extremes

The subcontinent has snow-capped mountain peaks and steamy tropical areas. It is affected by wet seasons that bring flooding and by seasons of drought that cause famine. It has areas with too much water or not enough water to sustain a productive agricultural economy. It has people with great wealth, but the majority live in poverty. Most of the people follow Islam or Hinduism, yet these religions are a source of conflict that has caused the death of many thousands of people and influenced the present-day political divisions of the subcontinent.

Early Heritage

In the 1920's, scholars thrilled to the discovery of an advanced civilization that existed in the subcontinent about the same time as the civilizations of Sumer in Mesopotamia. Located in the Indus River Valley of present-day Pakistan, the remains of the civilization of Harappa and Mohenjo–Daro showed a high degree of organization and technical knowledge.

South Asia, although rimmed on the northwest and north-east by the high ranges of the Himalayas, has often been invaded since this first civilization. The invaders have come through mountain passes, bringing with them their cultures, languages, and traditions, which have enriched the culture of the subcontinent in many ways and given the region its great diversity.

Home of Great Religions

As beliefs from Aryan invaders mixed with beliefs of people native to the subcontinent, Hinduism developed—a religion practiced today by the majority of people in India. Buddhism also developed in the subcontinent as a result of the search for peace and enlightenment undertaken by Siddartha Gautama. While Buddhism declined in importance in the subcontinent, it spread to other regions of Asia, where it has remained an important religion. Although Islam was brought to the subcontinent by invaders, it attracted many followers in the region, especially in Pakistan and Bangladesh where it is the majority religion. Other religions of the subcontinent include Jainism, Sikhism, and Christianity.

South Asia Today

In 1947, after decades of seeking freedom from the British, the people of the subcontinent were divided into the predominantly Muslim nation of Pakistan and the predominantly Hindu nation of India. In 1970 the people of East Pakistan rebelled against the central government in West Pakistan and, aided by India, won their independence in 1971 as the nation of Bangladesh. Just off the coast of India's southern tip lies Sri Lanka, an island nation that received its independence in 1948.

India, a republic with a prime minister and a democratically elected legislature, has shown the most stability in its government, having had the benefit of effective leadership from Jawaharlal Nehru; his daughter, Indira Gandhi; and his grandson, Rajiv Gandhi. Pakistan and Bangladesh also have democratic constitutions that declare them to be republics. The military, however, has often interrupted the term in office of democratically elected governments to impose a form of military rule that amounts to a dictatorship.

Independent India

India is strategically located, bordering two great powers—the Soviet Union and China. It lies astride three important bodies of water—the Arabian Sea, the Bay of Bengal, and the Indian Ocean. Because of its strategic location and stable government, India has become a regional superpower. No country in the region dares act without considering India's response. India has also come to play a major role in world affairs.

Contemporary India inhabits two worlds. Economists frequently use the term "dual economy" to describe India's condition. Urban areas are often modern and cosmopolitan. Rural areas where the majority of Indians live, however, offer a sharp contrast to the urban image. Villagers live in much the same type of housing as their ancestors. Villagers who farm use agricultural methods that were devised hundreds of years ago. Except for the movie theater and radio, the people of rural India have few modern conveniences.

In recent decades, however, the gap between rural and urban life in India has narrowed somewhat and a more integrated national economy has begun to emerge. The nation's transportation system has improved, literacy levels have risen, and many new jobs have been created in the cities. Some villagers now commute to the cities to work. Many others have moved to more industrialized parts of the country in search of opportunity and an improvement in their standard of living.

Pakistan and Bangladesh

Pakistan can justly take credit for some of the subcontinent's most significant developments. It was in Pakistan that the remnants of Harappa and Mohenjo–Daro were uncovered, revealing the subcontinent's earliest civilization. It was also this region that gave birth to the Muslim way of life in South Asia. When the people of the subcontinent began to develop nationalist goals, Muslim leaders were afraid that their people would be submerged in the Hindu majority if the whole of the subcontinent was made into a united independent India. To avoid dominance by a Hindu majority, Muslims agitated for a separate nation of their own. Bitter feelings between Hindus and Muslims, which had been smoldering for several centuries, erupted into near warfare before and immediately after the two nations were created in 1947. Independence has not lessened the tensions between India and Pakistan. They have fought three wars and continue to regard each other as mortal enemies. Indeed, the foreign policy of each nation centers around the objective of improving its military and diplomatic posture against the other.

Despite considerable foreign aid from nations such as the United States, Bangladesh ranks among the poorest countries in the world. Since gaining independence in 1971, the country has had scant success in expanding its economy. Part of the problem stems from its location in the region drained by the Ganges and Brahmaputra rivers to an area subject to great flooding during the wet monsoon season.

Third World Economic Development

Experts from such fields as history, economics, and sociology have carefully studied the nature of economic development in Third World nations. These are nations of Africa and Asia that received independence after World War II and found themselves forming a third bloc between the superpowers of the United States and the Soviet Union. Many of these nations fall into the category of "least developed nations."

None of the three major nations on the subcontinent has experienced noteworthy success with regard to development. India has created a modern industrial sector, but most of the country still lives in poverty. In some respects, Pakistan has had more success than India in stimulating industrial development. On the other hand, Pakistan has been less successful in raising literacy rates, improving health care, and in slowing down its population growth rate. Failure to deal with these problems will likely hurt Pakistan's economic performance in the future. As for Bangladesh, it remains as poor today as it was at independence in 1971. It has made little progress in developing industry, reducing illiteracy, or improving its health care and living conditions.

Creative Endeavors

Creativity on the subcontinent has left lasting marks on religion, philosophy, the arts, and science. Numerous centuries-old writings of the subcontinent are now being translated into English and other languages. Many people have become enthusiastic students of South Asian civilization, and are dazzled by the subcontinent's heritage of beautiful architecture, sculpture, painting, music, and dance. Scholars are intrigued with the region's religions and philosophies, which collectively comprise one of the world's richest storehouses of religion and thought.

In recent times, a number of people from the subcontinent have made important contributions that have influenced people in all parts of the world. Included in the subcontinent's list of notables are Mother Teresa of Calcutta, 1979 recipient of the Nobel Peace Prize; Rabindranath Tagore, winner of the Nobel Prize in Literature in 1913; C.V. Raman, winner of the Nobel Prize in Physics in 1930; and Abdus Salam of Pakistan, winner of the Nobel Prize in Physics in 1979. While Mahatma Gandhi, the great leader in India's struggle for independence, never received the Nobel Peace Prize, his philosophy of protest with its emphasis on civil disobedience and nonviolence has served as an inspiration for people worldwide who are seeking freedom and equality.

1

The Subcontinent of South Asia

Many civilizations have evolved in Asia during the past 7,000 years. Few civilizations, however, have exerted more widespread influence on Asians than the civilizations that developed on the **subcontinent** of South Asia. The ways and ideas of the subcontinent's present-day inhabitants have derived from the patterns of living of several hundred generations of people. The subcontinent's civilizations, moreover, have spread into lands to the north, south, east, and west. At the same time, the people of the subcontinent have adopted and adapted the customs, thought, and inventions of many other peoples. The result has been a depth of heritage and a diversity of cultures that have had a far reaching influence on South Asia's present-day nations—India, Pakistan, and Bangladesh, as well as Nepal, Sri Lanka, and Bhutan.

The subcontinent has attracted almost all the major groups of the Eurasian landmass, either as invaders or as migrants. The mix of peoples has given South Asia a tremendous diversity. The diversity has fostered the growth of more languages and dialects than are found in any other area of comparable size in the entire world. The diversity is also evident in religion. Several major world religions have developed in this region. Today one out of every six people in the world lives in the subcontinent of South Asia.

1. Invasion As a Way of Life

To look at a physical relief map, one would think that the sub-continental region of South Asia was secure from invasion. (See pages 4–5.) The entire northern border is guarded by the highest peaks in the world. In the north and northwest the Kirthar (kir-TAHR), Sulaiman (soo-lay-MAHN), and Hindu Kush (HIN-doo KOOSH) mountain ranges mark a natural border between the subcontinent and the long-settled plateau of Afghanistan and Iran. These mountain ranges fuse with the towering Himalaya (him-uh-LAY-uh) system, which extends in a southeasterly direction for more than 1,500 miles. The jagged and forbidding peaks of the Himalayan ranges separate northern India from Tibet, now a part of the People's Republic of China. Farther east the mountain ranges protect the northeastern part of South Asia from overland invasion. The rest of the subcontinent is separate from other parts of the settled world by vast expanses of ocean and sea. Despite these natural barriers, South Asia has never been free from attack. Its history has been changed time and again by invaders in search of empire, riches, or fame.

Invasion Routes by Land and Sea

Rarely did new peoples come in peace. Most of them came as plunderers or would-be conquerors. Almost without exception the invaders came from the northwest through the easily traveled mountain passes. The most commonly used route was the Khyber (KY-ber) Pass. The northwest came under attack so often because it borders the plateau region of Afghanistan and Iran, one of the oldest inhabited areas in the world. During the past 4,500 years in this region many civilizations, empires, and kingdoms rose and fell. Often great conquerors such as Cyrus the Great, Alexander the Great, and Genghis Khan overran the plateau highlands and advanced through the passes into the northwestern plains of the subcontinent

The lower half of the subcontinent is the world's largest peninsula. The triangular landmass lies between Africa and Asia, intersecting major sea routes between the West and the East. Records from archaeological discoveries indicate that the Romans may have had trading settlements on the western coast before the first century A.D. Other records show that Chinese merchants brought cargoes to the eastern coast. Arabs also came and, along with the Chinese, settled in peninsular India where they acted as go-betweens, transporting goods east and west around the wedge of the subcontinent. During the 1500's

2

(Continued on page 6)

SIDELIGHT TO HISTORY

The Himalayas

The Himalayan system of mountain ranges towers above every other landform on the earth. Composed of three parallel ranges, the Himalayas form the northernmost boundary of the Indian subcontinent, arcing northward for some 1,500 miles. The southernmost range, called the Siwalik (si-WAUL-IK) or Outer Himalayas, rises from the Indo–Gangetic Plain to an elevation of 5,000 feet. This is the plain formed by the Indus and Ganges rivers. The second range, the Lesser Himalayas, has peaks of 7,000 to 10,000 feet. The third range is the Great Himalayas. Forming the southern boundary of China, the crests of this range average 20,000 feet and include the world's highest peak, Mount Everest, now measured at 29,108 feet. To the northwest of the Great Himalayas, and included by some geographers in the Himalayan system, are the Karakoram (kar-uh-KOHR-uhm) Mountains. They are said to be the snowiest and iciest mountains between the world's two polar caps. The second highest mountain in the world, Mount Godwin Austen, also called K_2, rises to a height of 28,250 feet in this range.

The name *Himalaya* is a combination of two words taken from Sanskrit, the ancient language of the subcontinent, that mean "dwelling place of snow." Thus *Himalayas* is an appropriate name for mountain ranges whose higher peaks are always covered with a blanket of snow. So high are the mountains that the climate changes several times from the steamy rain forest of the foothills to the below-freezing temperatures at the top of Mount Everest where the air has so little oxygen that the human body can barely survive for any length of time.

According to recent geologic theories about earth movements and landform building, the Himalayas formed when two of the earth's moving plates collided millions of years ago. Fossils of seashells found on high Himalayan peaks support the theory that a massive collision took place, pushing part of the ocean floor atop the continental landmass. Pressures within the earth resulting from the force of the collision continued the process of mountain building begun by the collision. Even today these forces lift the mountain ranges about two inches a year.

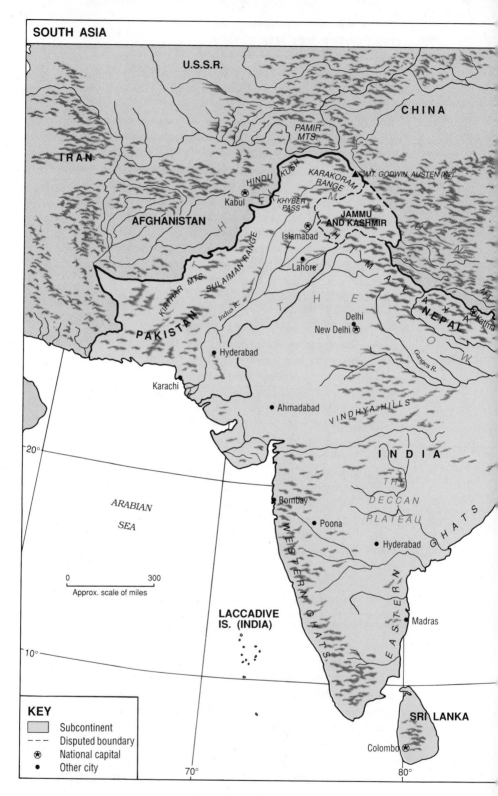

SOUTH ASIA

U.S.S.R.

CHINA

PAMIR
MTS.

IRAN

HINDU KUSH

KARAKORAM
RANGE

▲MT. GODWIN AUSTEN (K2)

Kabul⊛

KHYBER
PASS

JAMMU
AND KASHMIR

AFGHANISTAN

Islamabad

M

KIRTHAR MTS.

SULAIMAN RANGE

Lahore

A

L

A

Y

A

NEPAL

⊛Katmandu

MT.

PAKISTAN

Indus R.

T

H

E

Delhi

New Delhi⊛

Ganges R.

W

O

• Hyderabad

Karachi

• Ahmadabad

VINDHYA HILLS

20°

I N D I A

THE

ARABIAN

DECCAN

SEA

• Bombay

PLATEAU

• Poona

G
H
A
T
S

W
E
S
T
E
R
N
G
H
A
T
S

• Hyderabad

0   300

Approx. scale of miles

E
A
S
T
E
R
N

LACCADIVE
IS. (INDIA)

Madras

10°

SRI LANKA

KEY

Subcontinent

Disputed boundary

⊛ National capital

• Other city

Colombo⊛

70°

80°

4

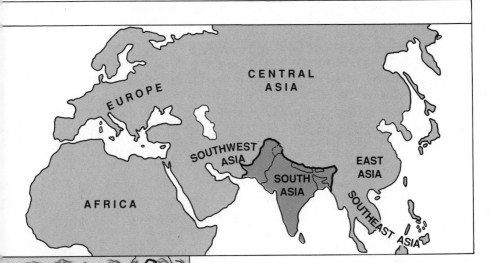

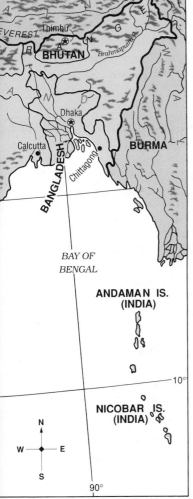

PLACE: SOUTH ASIA. Asia, the world's largest continent, is made up of four other regions besides South Asia: Central Asia, Southwest Asia, East Asia, and Southeast Asia. (See the map above.) Today South Asia contains the nations of India, Pakistan, Nepal, Bangladesh, Bhutan, and Sri Lanka, which lies off the subcontinent's tip. Three prominent geographic features helped form South Asia's main natural regions: the mountain wall, the lowland of the Indo–Gangetic Plain, and the high interior of the Deccan Plateau against which nestle the narrow strips of coastal plain. What are the two highest peaks of the Himalayas?

and 1600's various European countries established trading centers on the eastern and western coasts of the subcontinent. By the late 1700's Great Britain controlled most of the seaward approaches to the subcontinent, and consequently most of the trade. Gradually the British position changed from privileged trader to ruler as the British extended their influence and power over the entire subcontinent. By the mid–1800's Britain had made the subcontinent part of its great empire. Ironically, the last and greatest of the subcontinent's conquerors came not by land, but by the sea.

British Control

Once in control, Great Britain assumed the burden of defending the subcontinent against other potential invaders. British sea power was uncontested, and with Britain controlling the seas, South Asia was in little danger. To guard the landward approaches from the east, the British either took over a country, which they did in Burma, or made **protectorates** of weak states, which they once did in the Himalayan states of Nepal (neh-PAHL) and Bhutan (boo-TAN) and in the former state of Sikkim (SIHK-kuhm), which is now a part of the Republic of India. The only threat to British South Asia came during World War II when the Japanese easily overran Burma and could have crossed the subcontinent's borders. But the Japanese chose not to move into the subcontinent.

Britain's major defensive burden was to control the passes in the northwest. In the decade before World War I this involved making Afghanistan and Persia (present-day Iran) **buffers** against possible Russian advances. During World War II the British erected anti-tank defenses in the passes, and no invader breached the subcontinent's borders. Thus not once during the century of British rule did another power successfully invade the subcontinent.

Present–Day Watchfulness

Today the task of guarding the subcontinent's borders falls to the nations that have been carved out of the region—India, Pakistan, and Bangladesh. As in centuries past, the peoples of the subcontinent uneasily watch the lands and peoples beyond the mountains. Of special concern to India is its border with China. During the 1950's the Chinese Communists took control of Tibet. In 1962, operating from Tibet, Chinese troops advanced into India. A cease-fire agreement was reached and the Chinese withdrew, but the border between the two countries continues to be disputed. Pakistan is wary of Afghanistan, a country that lays claim to certain Pakistani lands that have large Afghan populations. But of greater concern to India and Pakistan has been defense against each other as the two nations fight for control of sections of the border between their two countries.

Check Your Understanding

1. **a.** Describe the boundaries of the Indian subcontinent. **b.** Why might these boundaries be considered a natural defense against invaders?
2. **a.** Who were some of the invaders who broke through the northwestern boundaries? **b.** How did they get through?
3. What role did trade play in the history of the subcontinent?
4. *Thinking Critically:* Why might the subcontinent be said to have a strategic position geographically? How did this strategic position affect the history of the subcontinent?

2. The Geographic Setting

Over the great span of history many divisive factors have been at work in the subcontinent, mostly the result of geographical conditions. Geography has made the subcontinent "a world apart" and has helped splinter the subcontinent into several well-defined natural regions. Besides the region of the Himalayas and other mountain ranges, the subcontinent can be divided into three other main geographic regions—the Indo–Gangetic Plain of the north, the interior plateau called the Deccan, and the strips of coastal plain that rest against the Deccan and extend southward to the subcontinent's tip.

The Indo–Gangetic Plain

For many centuries the most heavily populated and most highly developed part of the subcontinent has been the Indo–Gangetic Plain of the north. Because this region has fertile soil and water for irrigation, it has always had a large agricultural population. It is here that early civilizations on the subcontinent evolved and most of the area's great empires and monarchies were founded.

Hindustan, the land of the Hindus, is an old and popular name for this northern region, which extends from the mountainous frontier in the west to the hills and rain forests of Burma in the east. The region's northern limits are bounded by the crests of the Himalaya ranges. The southern limits of the Indo–Gangetic Plain is marked by the Vindhya (VIN-dyuh) Hills. While these hills of moderate height have always slowed the north-south movements of peoples, cultures, and armies, they may be crossed without difficulty.

The rich soil of the northern region is part of a broad, seemingly endless plain cut by three important river systems: the Indus, the Ganges (GAN-jeez), and the Brahmaputra (brahm-uh-POO-truh). The Indo–Gangetic Plain contains most of present-day Pakistan, part of Bangladesh, and the most heavily populated regions of present-day India. The plain is well described in a classical geographic study:

> Inside the mountain wall, and forming a great curve from the Arabian Sea to the Bay of Bengal, is one of the most important plains in the world. It is more than 2,000 miles from end to end, and usually from 150 to 300 miles broad. There are several outstanding features of this amazing area. One is the dead flatness of the plain—not a hill, scarcely a mound to break the monotony of the level surface. . . . True, there are foothills, such as the Siwaliks, . . . but they occupy . . . a zone which is inconspicuous in its width.
>
> [L. Dudley Stamp. *Asia: A Regional and Economic Geography.*]

Today the Indo–Gangetic Plain is one of the most densely populated regions of the world, probably holding close to 600 million people, most of whom are peasants who reside in the valley's countless villages. Like the rest of the subcontinent, the region contains few really large cities. Of all the settlements in the valley only Lahore in present-day Pakistan; Delhi, Kanpur, and Calcutta in India; and Dhaka (formerly spelled Dacca) in Bangladesh have a population of a million or more.

The Deccan Plateau

Stretching south from the Vindhya Hills and covering most of the southern two thirds of the subcontinent is a large plateau called the Deccan. The Western Ghats (GOTZ), a long range of low but rugged peaks, isolates the Deccan from the narrow plain skirting the western coast. A similar range, the Eastern Ghats, separates the plateau from the long coastal plain.

8

For centuries the mildly rugged borders of the Deccan isolated the region from invaders on all sides. Monarchies in the Deccan were usually able to resist movements of invaders coming from the north and from the Ganges region. But the mountainous terrain and the difficulty of traveling upstream along navigable rivers also kept coastal traders from traveling into the Deccan's interior. As a consequence, few large cities developed in the interior until recent times. Today, the Deccan has Ahmadabad, Poona, Nagpur, and Hyderabad, four of the world's most populous cities.

The Coastal Plains

Running along the sides of the Deccan and joining at the tip of India are narrow fertile strips of heavily settled coastal plain. Rice is grown on the arable land, while the cities of the coastal plains are some of the largest on the subcontinent. Calcutta, the center of trade on the east coast, is the most populous city on the subcontinent. Bombay, the second most populous, is the most important trading center of the west coast. The fourth most populous city, Madras, overcame poor harbor facilities to become the most important port along the eastern coast of the subcontinent's southern tip.

Tillable land in the region is found mainly on the coastal strips. Because most inhabitants in this region live along the coasts and have access to the sea, the region has been a leader in emigration to other countries. Many inhabitants have crossed the 22-mile strait to Sri Lanka or have left the subcontinent for Malayasia, Singapore, other island nations in Southeast Asia, and nations along Africa's east coast.

In modern times Kerala, a province in South India, has become a model for the subcontinent. In a nation where as few as 40 percent of the people are literate, 70 percent of the Keralese can read and write. Because of its skilled work force and the rich mineral deposits of the area, Kerala has a flourishing industrial sector.

The Indus River

Rivers and rainfall have been of vital importance to the subcontinent since the development of civilizations. Three mighty river systems and other smaller rivers drain the subcontinent. The **monsoons,** the winds that usher in and then end the subcontinent's rainy season, are the subject of much of the region's art, music, and literature. Wherever a traveler goes on the subcontinent, water is an overriding concern.

SOUTH ASIAN LANDSCAPES.
Farming takes place in Himalayan valleys (left) and in the paddies of the coastal strips (bottom). In the heartland of the Indo–Gangetic Plain (center, right), the flatness of the floodplain is broken by the effects of erosion. The Thar Desert (center, left) spreads out from the sun-bleached buildings of a town. How do these scenes reflect the subcontinent's geographic diversity?

Since ancient times most of the inhabitants of the northwestern part of the subcontinent have lived in the Indus River Plain, the vast area drained by the Indus River. The river descends in a northwesterly direction from its source in the high Himalayas. The river then turns southwestward near the point where it is fed by five tributaries in an area called the Punjab, a name meaning "five waters." The Indus continues its flow through a desert called the Sind and eventually empties into the Arabian Sea.

The valley of the Indus River was the home of the subcontinent's first civilization, the Harappan (huh-RAHP-uhn). (See pages 26–31.) Several thousand years ago the valley was covered with forests and other vegetation. As civilizations developed, settlers slowly upset the rhythm of nature by cutting down forests, uprooting vegetation, and draining marshes and other wetlands. These human changes gradually affected seasonal wind, rainfall, and temperature patterns. Over the centuries the climate changed from wet and humid to dry. Working together, nature and the inhabitants in the area gradually turned much of the region into dust bowls and deserts. During the British occupation of the area, however, an irrigation system was developed and many thousands of miles of irrigation canals were built. These have helped turn the deserts into valuable wheat- and cotton-producing lands.

The Ganges River

As the Harrapan civilization declined, the center of population in the subcontinent shifted from the Indus River Valley to the Ganges River Valley. For several thousand years the Ganges Valley has been the focal point of life on the subcontinent. Almost all the great empires in the subcontinent's history have risen and fallen in its **floodplain.** As a result the valley is famous for its many historic cities, several of which were the capitals of empires.

Through the centuries the difference between food and famine for people in the Ganges Valley has been the Ganges and its four main tributaries. The tributaries begin in snow-crowned mountains to the north, flow through central Hindustan, and join the Ganges before it empties into the Bay of Bengal. The Ganges and its tributaries irrigate thousands of acres of sugar cane and cotton through a network of free-flowing canals. By contrast, farmers in the Indus Valley depend almost exclusively on irrigation pumps to keep water flowing in their canals. Irrigation in the Ganges Valley enables farmers to produce two crops

S IDELIGHT TO HISTORY

Monsoons and South Asia

Monsoons are seasonal winds that occur in several different parts of the world. But no other part of the world is as influenced by the monsoons as South Asia.

The summer monsoon period generally begins in June and ends in September. The summer monsoons, which form over the ocean, blow toward the land. The winds pick up tremendous amounts of moisture from the ocean. As the winds reach land, they are forced to rise. Water vapor in the air cools and falls to earth as rain. The map on page 13 shows the two paths that the summer monsoons generally take. The summer monsoon rains begin suddenly.

The winter monsoon period reverses the paths of the summer monsoon period, blowing from the land toward the ocean, and has two phases. The first phase is dry and hot. It generally begins in October and ends in March when the second phase takes over. During April and May the temperatures rise higher and higher and the land becomes drier and drier. In parts of the subcontinent temperatures have risen to 115° Fahrenheit, winds have blown with speeds as high as 65 miles an hour, and as much rain as 40 inches has fallen in one day.

Much of South Asia depends on the summer monsoon for its water supply. But the summer monsoon has an unpredictable nature that often causes problems. It may bring too much rain, causing flooding and loss of life and crops. Sometimes the summer monsoon brings insufficient amounts of rainfall to meet South Asian needs. Rivers never fill up and reservoirs stay at dangerously low levels, lowering both agricultural and industrial productivity. About half of the region's hydroelectricity is generated by waterpower from rivers and reservoirs that are fed directly by monsoon rains. The summer monsoon may also come late, delaying the growing season and making life a struggle for the subcontinent's farmers.

Predicting paths, rainmaking capabilities, and the arrival of the monsoons is a gigantic guessing game for people in South Asia. While monsoons can be a great benefit, they can also be a great challenge for South Asians.

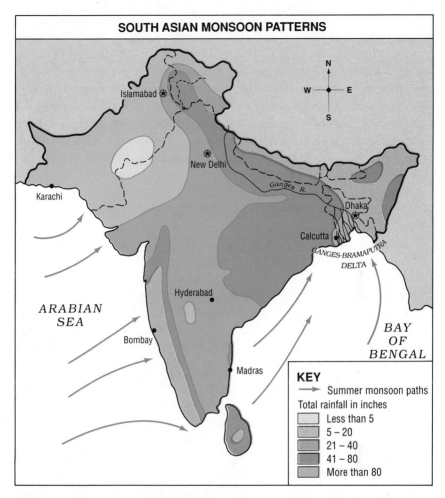

SOUTH ASIAN MONSOON PATTERNS

KEY

→ Summer monsoon paths

Total rainfall in inches

Less than 5
5 – 20
21 – 40
41 – 80
More than 80

ENVIRONMENT: SOUTH ASIAN MONSOON PATTERNS. Rainbearing summer monsoons may drench the land one year but fail the next. Though the average rainfall for much of South Asia is adequate, some parts get less rainfall than others. What area of South Asia gets the least rainfall? What areas get the most?

a year, even when the summer monsoon season is delayed or fails to deliver enough moisture. Irrigation also makes possible the cultivation of land where rainfall is scarce.

The Brahmaputra River

The Brahmaputra joins the Ganges in the area now occupied by present-day Bangladesh. The Brahmaputra begins in the northeastern mountains of the subcontinent and flows through one of the rainiest regions on the earth, making its source of water almost inexhaustible. After the Brahmaputra joins with

13

the Ganges, the many **distributaries** of the two rivers then empty into the Bay of Bengal, forming a delta from the rich layers of soil deposited over the centuries. The delta region is an exceptionally good farming area, but no part of the delta, two thirds of which is in Bangladesh, lies more than 150 feet above sea level. Because it is so low-lying, the delta is subject to frequent flooding, especially during the rainy season. While flooding often takes many lives, ruins crops, and kills livestock and other animals, the receding waters leave behind a rich deposit of new soil.

Check Your Understanding

1. Name and describe the general character of each of the subcontinent's three main regions.
2. **a.** Compare the Indus and Ganges valleys. **b.** How does the Deccan differ from the coastal plains?
3. Why are the monsoons important to the subcontinent?
4. *Thinking Critically:* Why do you think most major centers of population on the subcontinent are located on rivers or along the coastal plain?

3. Village Life and Languages

In studying the history and culture of a people it is all too easy to focus attention on the great and bustling urban centers. After all, monarchs, government leaders, soldiers, philosophers, teachers, and other residents of cities are usually the people whose deeds are recorded in history. But in South Asia, the village has been the heart and pulse of life. Despite the growth of cities on the South Asian subcontinent, four out of five people still live in villages.

Before **partition** into separate nations beginning in 1947, the subcontinent had some 450,000 villages. By the mid–1980's, the Republic of India alone had more than 560,000 villages, and only 3,250 cities and towns had a population of 1,000 or more. Of these only 225 had a population of 100,000 or more. Most of the smaller villages consist of a cluster of huts and cottages. A street, if there is one, consists of a rutted lane no more than a cowpath. Many people on the subcontinent live out their lives in their home villages never traveling more than a few miles away.

Village Houses

The climate and the availability of building materials have influenced the type of houses built by villagers. In the heavily settled regions, trees gave way to cultivated land many centuries ago. With little wood available for building purposes, peasants in tree-scarce regions build houses of sun-dried brick. Often in times of flood and heavy rains, these houses literally "dissolve" away.

In the northeastern and the southern regions of the subcontinent, where trees are abundant, housing differs markedly from the mud huts of the Indo–Gangetic Plain and the northern Deccan. Villagers in the plain areas have houses that are fairly livable during most of the year because they are lightly constructed with wood and various kinds of reeds. They are also well ventilated, an important consideration in the hot, humid climate. But even these wood and reed houses become damp and uncomfortable during the rainy season, and they are also often destroyed by monsoon flooding.

Houses in all villages on the subcontinent do have certain characteristics in common. For the most part, they consist of one room, occasionally two or three. There is little or no furniture. The family takes its meals sitting on the floor, which is usually bare earth. A bed is a mat or blanket. Possessions of a family—household goods, clothing, farm tools—are stored around the room, suspended on pegs, or hung from the rafters.

A Life of Poverty and Struggle

Few people in the world lead as poor an existence as villagers on the subcontinent. Most are farmers who till small plots of land on the village outskirts. The average size is five acres, but many peasants have only an acre or two. Those villagers who do not farm are carpenters, blacksmiths, potters, weavers, or barbers. They earn a living by exchanging their services with farmers for grain, mainly rice, wheat, or jowar—a type of sorghum. Many people on the subcontinent are hopelessly in debt to moneylenders. Often the debts were inherited from parents. Even though children have no obligation to pay their parents' debts, tradition demands that they do. In many cases, a peasant can do no more than pay the interest on the debt.

Recent Improvements

Villages today have more contacts with the outside world than in the past. New roads have been built, primary schools have

VILLAGE CONTRASTS.
These scenes show contrasting scenes of village life in South Asia. In a Punjabi village (above) in the northwestern part of the subcontinent, village life revolves around the well. In Kerala, which receives much more rain than the Punjab, water is everywhere. But Keralese who live along canals (right) often suffer from a shortage of safe drinking water.

been established in many villages, and medical clinics provide health care. Villages also have radios and televisions to keep villagers informed about national and world events. Many villages now have movie theaters. As the subcontinent has become more industrialized, millions of villagers have gotten jobs in nearby cities. Many commute on a daily basis. Others move to the cities where they work. Still other Indians have left their villages and come to India's cities in search of work. Despite all these contacts between village and city, most villagers are hardly a part of the modern world.

Indo-Aryan Languages

People on the subcontinent speak a variety of languages that vary from one another as much as English does from German and Arabic. These languages of the subcontinent represent three of the major language families of the world—the Indo-European, the Dravidian, and the Sino-Tibetan. The greatest number of the people speak regional languages and dialects that belong to the Indo-Aryan language family, a subgroup of the Indo-European family of languages. (See chart, page 18.) People speaking different dialects of the same regional language usually have little difficulty in understanding one another.

Nearly three fourths of the subcontinent's people speak Indo-Aryan languages. In an area beginning with the border region between Turkey and Iran and spreading across Iran, Afghanistan, and the northern portion of the Indian subcontinent, Indo-Aryan languages are spoken by several hundred million people. In the Republic of India alone, almost 600 million people speak Indo-Aryan languages.

The most popular Indo-Aryan language is Hindi. Spoken by more than 325 million people, it is found primarily in the western and central sections of the Indo-Gangetic Plain. It is an outgrowth of Sanskrit, the most enduring of the languages of the subcontinent's invaders. A language closely related to Hindi is Urdu, the tongue of 88 million speakers in India and Pakistan. The oral languages of Hindi and Urdu are almost identical and together are called Hindustani. The main difference between the two languages is in the written script. Pakistanis write Urdu in an Arabic script, while people in India write Hindi using the Devanagari script, an alphabet of syllabic characters.

Ranking high in importance among the various Indo-Aryan languages of the subcontinent is Bengali, which is spoken by approximately 178 million people in the Republic of India and Bangladesh. The most famous user of Bengali was Rabindranath

Language		Speakers
ASSAMESE	(I, B)	▣ ▣
BENGALI	(I)	▲ ▣ ▣ ▣ ▣ ▣ ▣ ▣ ■ ● ● ●
GUJARTI	(I, P)	▣ ▣ ▣ ■ ● ● ●
HINDI	(I)	▲ ▲ ▲ ▣ ▣ ■
KANNADA	(I)	▣ ▣ ▣ ▣
KASHMIRI	(I, P)	● ● ●
MALAYALAM	(I)	▣ ▣ ▣ ● ● ●
MARATHI	(I)	▣ ▣ ▣ ▣ ▣ ▣ ● ●
NEPALI	(I, N, Bh)	▣ ● ●
ORIYA	(I)	▣ ▣ ■ ● ● ● ●
PASHTU	(P)	▣ ▣ ●
PUNJABI	(I, P)	▣ ▣ ▣ ▣ ▣ ▣ ▣ ■ ● ●
SINDHI	(I, P)	▣ ■
SINHALESE	(SL)	▣ ● ●
TAMIL	(I, SL)	▣ ▣ ▣ ▣ ▣ ▣ ● ●
TELUGU	(I)	▣ ▣ ▣ ▣ ▣ ▣ ■
URDU	(I, P)	▣ ▣ ▣ ▣ ▣ ▣ ▣ ▣ ■ ● ● ●

NUMBER OF SPEAKERS		LOCATION			
●	1 million	(I)	India	(N)	Nepal
■	5 million	(P)	Pakistan	(Bh)	Bhutan
▣	10 million	(B)	Bangladesh		
▲	100 million	(SL)	Sri Lanka		

Source: *The World Almanac Book of Facts, 1989*

MAJOR SOUTH ASIAN LANGUAGES.   All of the above languages have 20 million or more speakers. Most of the languages shown on the chart belong to the Indo–Aryan language family. Two languages of the Dravidian language family are Tamil and Telugu. How many people speak each of these languages?

Tagore (1861–1941), who was awarded the Nobel Prize in literature in 1913. Another major language is Gujarati, the language of Mahatma Gandhi (GAHN-dee), India's famous nationalist leader. The language of Gujarati is spoken principally in the Gujarati state in the Republic of India and in parts of southern Pakistan.

Dravidian Languages

About 200 million people speak one of the four regional languages that belong to the Dravidian family of languages. The majority of the people who are Dravidian speakers live in the

FACES OF SOUTH ASIA.
Some people in South Asia, such as this family (top, right), speak a language belonging to the Sino–Tibetan language family. The shepherd (below, right) and the woman (top, left) from Rajasthan speak Hindi. The jeweler (left) and the school children live in areas in which Dravidian languages predominate.

Language Families

Over the last half million years, since people first began to form words out of sounds, thousands of languages have evolved. Although many of these languages have disappeared, linguists—scholars who study the structure and history of languages—estimate that between 2,500 and 5,000 languages are still in use throughout the world. While many of these languages are quite different from one another, all languages have traits in common. All languages use sounds and form sounds into words. All languages organize words into a consistent pattern, and together the words and their patterns communicate a sense or meaning.

Today linguists recognize about 11 different language families. The Indo–European and Sino–Tibetan languages are most important in terms of the number of people who speak them. Languages stemming from the Indo–European family form a broad belt running through Western Europe, the Mediterranean area, the Middle East, and South Asia, as well as North and South America. Most of the people in East Asia speak languages from the Sino–Tibetan group, although several other language families also are found in Southeast Asia and on Pacific islands. A major difference between Indo–European and Sino–Tibetan languages is the word formation. In most Sino–Tibetan languages, words generally consist of a single syllable with a meaning that varies according to the tone and pitch used by the speaker.

The study of language tells us many facts about the development of civilizations through time. Linguistics can provide clues about the migrations of ancient peoples. Information from linguistic studies also tells scientists and historians how people from different cultures were able to mingle and interact.

southern portion of the Indian subcontinent and on offshore islands, including the nation of Sri Lanka. The most famous of the Dravidian languages is Tamil, the principal language of the state of Tamil Nadu (formerly Madras) in the Republic of India.

Signs in English and Bihari at an intersection in Bihar State (right) reflect India's language diversity. English is a useful second language for many Indians. Above, in 1965 angry students demonstrated against a proposed replacement of English by Hindi as the country's official language.

Other Languages

A number of dialects and languages on the subcontinent are unrelated to either the Indo–Aryan or Dravidian families of languages. English, for example, is widely used by the educated classes, since it was the language of government during the period of British control and was taught in South Asian schools. Jawaharlal Nehru (jah-WAH-har-lahl NAY-roo), a founder of India's republic, felt more comfortable using English rather than speaking Hindi. In the Indian states where Dravidian languages are the primary official languages, English is the second language.

In the northeastern border areas of the Indian subcontinent, Sino–Tibetan dialects are spoken. Still other South Asian peoples converse in dialects that linguists also classify in the Sino–Tibetan language family, but these dialects are faintly similar to tongues that are spoken in Southeast Asia and the islands of the Pacific.

Effects of Language Diversity

Historically the linguistic diversity of the subcontinent has raised many serious political problems. For centuries the diversity has been a contributing factor in the fragmentation of South Asia into hundreds of realms. South Asians speaking a particular dialect more readily accepted a ruler who spoke as they did. Although not the only factor hindering political unification, linguistic diversity nevertheless was an important one. Also the diversity contributed much to the division of the subcontinent into traditional "realms" based on strong regional ties. For example, at one time the British divided Bengal into two provinces because it was too large to be governed efficiently. But the people of Bengal were united both linguistically and culturally, and they objected strenuously to the British action. To settle the seething discontent, the British were forced to reunite Bengal.

Since partition, the diversity of languges has been more of a problem for India than for Pakistan or Bangladesh. Language diversity in India has hindered the construction of a truly national state and an effective central government. Officials have difficulty in making their wishes known to members of the National Assembly and to administrators in the provinces. Attempts to standardize the nation's schools have been hindered by the unwillingness of the regions to accept a common language. At present, along with Hindi, the constitution of India recognizes 14 regional languages, of which Sanskrit is one.

Check Your Understanding

1. Why are villages still considered the heart and pulse of South Asia?
2. How do climate and the availability of building materials influence housing construction on the Indian subcontinent?
3. How have recent changes improved village life in South Asia?
4. Compare oral and written Hindi and Urdu.
5. *Thinking Critically:* How do languages reflect the diversity of South Asia? How has language diversity affected South Asia as a whole? Why has language diversity been more of problem for India than for Pakistan and Bangladesh?

CHAPTER REVIEW

■ **Chapter Summary**

Section 1. The subcontinent of South Asia has been a major center of civilization for well over 4,000 years. The region's way of life evolved mainly within the subcontinent, but the region has also been influenced by developments beyond the towering mountain ranges that form its northern borders. Invaders have found passes through the mountain barriers and changed the history of the region many times. The Khyber Pass has been the most frequently used land route, although other people, mainly traders and the British, have entered South Asia from the sea. No matter who controls the subcontinent, which is now partitioned into the nations of India, Pakistan, and Bangladesh, defense of the mountain passes remains a primary concern.

Section 2. Geography has splintered the subcontinent into four well-defined regions. The first region is the mountain wall formed by the various ranges in the Himalayan chain. The second region is the Indo–Gangetic Plain, or lowland. The third region is the Deccan Plateau. The fourth region consists of the coastal plains that nestle against the Western and Eastern Ghats. The Indus, the Ganges, and the Brahmaputra are three major rivers of South Asia. Each has played an important role in the development of the regions' various civilizations because wherever people live in South Asia, water is an overriding concern—because the land receives either too much rain in too short a time during the summer monsoon period or too little.

Section 3. The village is the heart and pulse of life on the subcontinent as four out of five people live in villages, most of them with populations of 1,000 or less. Few villagers ever travel great distances from their homes, which are made of wood in areas where trees are abundant and of sun-dried brick in tree-scarce areas. Most homes have one room with an earthen floor. While radios, televisions, new roads, medical clinics, and primary schools give evidence of improvements in villagers' lives, villagers endure great poverty and hardly seem a part of the modern world.

South Asia is a region with a diversity of languages representing three major language families—the Indo–European, the Dravidian, and the Sino–Tibetan. Nearly three fourths of the people speak Indo–Aryan languages, which are a subgroup of the Indo–European language family. Hindi is the most popular Indo–Aryan language, followed by Urdu and Bengali. Major Dravidian languages are Tamil and Telugu. Language diversity has led to political fragmentation, especailly within the nation of India.

■ **Vocabulary Review**

Define: subcontinent, protectorate, buffer, monsoon, flood-plain, distributary, partition

■ **Places to Locate**

Locate: South Asia, India, Pakistan, Bangladesh, Nepal, Sri Lanka, Khyber Pass, Indus River, Ganges River, Brahmaputra River, Mount Everest, Himalayas, Vindhya Hills, Deccan Plateau, Western Ghats, Eastern Ghats, Calcutta, Bombay, Madras, Punjab

■ **People to Know**

Identify: Cyrus the Great, Alexander the Great, Genghis Khan, Mahatma Gandhi, Rabindranath Tagore

■ **Thinking Critically**

1. How have invasions helped to shape the culture of South Asia?
2. How have the subcontinent's geographical features contributed to South Asia's diversity?
3. What common patterns of living are present in the villages of the region? How has language diversity helped to shape national life in the region?

■ **Extending and Applying Your Knowledge**

1. Dravidians and Aryans were two groups of people who influenced the cultural development of South Asia. Find out more about one of these groups and report your findings to the class, either orally or in writing.
2. Like other regions of the world, South Asia has its own unique foods and distinctive style of cooking. Prepare a pictorial chart with descriptive captions to illustrate some of the region's unique foods or styles of cooking. Display the chart in the classroom or use it as you give an oral report to the class on "Foods of South Asia."

2

The Emergence of Civilization in South Asia

The study of ancient civilizations in South Asia presents a number of vexing problems. Many of these problems stem from the very nature of the region's early civilizations, some of which left only fragmentary inscriptions that have yet to be deciphered.

In the absence of reliable historical records, other sources have had to be used to reconstruct early civilizations in South Asia. These sources are archaeological excavations, sacred writings, and traces of the past in modern-day life. Archeological excavations, for example, have unearthed much evidence about the Harappan civilization—South Asia's earliest known civilization. Priests of the Buddhist and Jainist religions wrote many religious and philosophical works from which historians have been able to glean information about the early Aryans—the people who conquered the Harappans. These writings help fill the gap between the early Aryan period and the time when history in the region began to be recorded.

Finally a study of modern South Asian cultures provides helpful information about the past because people on the subcontinent have rarely been eager to discard their old ideas and practices. An analysis of legends, traditions, and customs of modern-day life in South Asia throws considerable light on the region's remote past. The evidence gleaned from all sources indicates that South Asia is the third oldest center of civilization in the world after the Mesopotamian and Egyptian civilizations.

1. Civilizations of the Indus River Valley

The first center of Indian civilization emerged about 2500 B.C. Based in what is now Pakistan, this Harappan, or Indus, civilization endured for more than 1,000 years. For reasons that are still unclear, the Harappan civilization declined. Meanwhile, Aryan groups from southwest Asia began to move eastward onto the Ganges Plain, where they developed the Hindu way of life. Constantly enriched and modified, Hindu civilization has lasted to the present day.

The Harappan Civilization

Until recent times few people suspected that the roots of civilization in South Asia began in the Indus River Valley in what is now Pakistan. For centuries the center of life on the subcontinent had been the Ganges Valley in present-day India, not the now barren wasteland of the Indus River Valley. In the 1920's, however, archaeological excavations were begun in the Indus Valley. The most important excavations were started in northwestern Punjab and in southwestern Sind, the region encompassing the area near the mouth of the Indus River. To the amazement of nearly everyone, the archaeologists uncovered a number of forgotten cities and towns. Moreover, the excavations proved that the civilization served by the cities extended north and south for at least 1,000 miles, a distance covered by no other ancient civilization.

The two most important cities of the Indus River Valley civilization, which is also called the Harappan civilization, were Harappa and Mohenjo–Daro (moh-HEN-joh DAH-roh). Each city was dominated by a powerful palace-fortress. Obviously designed for defense against rebellion and invasion, each fortress was built on a high elevation formed of baked bricks and earth. Since the fortress rose high above the surrounding plain, lookouts could easily spot approaching invaders.

Archaeologists have found no other ancient cities that were so well planned. Avenues and streets crossed in an orderly pattern. A special district of large, elaborate buildings—probably the palaces of rulers, government offices, and temples—lay on the western outskirts of each city. The eastern part of each city was composed of many smaller buildings—evidently the homes and the working quarters of the common people.

The houses in Harappa and Mohenjo–Daro probably were the finest of their times. Each city had many two-story buildings, something unusual for that day. The buildings had staircases

TIMETABLE

The Subcontinent's Early History

2500–1500 B.C.	Indus River Valley civilization
1500–500 B.C.	Aryan invasions
	Vedic Age
563 B.C.	Birth of Siddartha Guatama
326 B.C.	Invasion of Alexander the Great
323 B.C.	Founding of Mauyra dynasty
269–232 B.C.	Reign of Asoka

and were divided into a number of rooms. The homes of the wealthier people had inner courtyards, facilities for bathing, and drainage systems. Outside the houses, paved drainage channels carried waste along streets and alleys and out of the city. No other ancient people had devised a system of indoor "plumbing" until the Romans did so some 2,000 years later. Not only was the Harappan civilization of the Indus Valley one of the most advanced of its time, it was also the largest.

The Harappans

The origins of the Harappan people, and how they lived, can never be known for certain. Probably the Harappans were descendants of long-time inhabitants of the region. Over a period of many thousands of years, evidence shows that the people had progressed from a Stone Age culture to an advanced civilization. It is likely, too, that the Harappans were closely related to peoples who at an early time had built advanced agricultural communities in the hilly region west of the Indus Valley. Items found in excavations show that the Harappan people had made contacts with centers in Mesopotamia. These recovered artifacts have decorations that closely resemble Mesopotamian art, suggesting that some **cultural diffusion** had occurred. Because the resemblances are few, however, the Harappan civilization must stand as an independently developed way of life.

Clay cylinder seals inscribed with writing have been found in numerous parts of Pakistan. Unfortunately the 400 or so symbols used in the Harappan writing system have defied every effort at translation. The symbols resemble no other early sys-

(Continued on page 30)

27

SIDELIGHT TO HISTORY

The Work of Archaeologists

The idea of uncovering the secrets of a hidden civilization is intriguing to many people. Preceding every momentous discovery of the past, however, are many hours of painstaking work by teams of archaeologists—scholars who reconstruct a cultural picture by excavating and studying prehistoric and historic sites and the remnants, or artifacts, they contain. The archaeologist must draw from a broad range of facts and ideas. An understanding of the social sciences is essential because an archaeologist's purpose is to contribute to the world's knowledge of history and society. The archaeologist also draws from a knowledge of art, architecture, foreign languages, and science—particularly from such fields as biology, chemistry, geology (the study of the earth's structure), paleontology (the study of fossils and geologic remains), and climatology (the study of weather over a long period of time).

An archaeologist always has a reason for picking a particular site for a dig. In this day and age, a site is often chosen because a study of aerial photographs has shown a ridge or mound where nature could not have made one. Such an unnatural condition often indicates the possible presence of a buried village or town. After choosing a site for study the archaeologist examines the surface itself, looking for artifacts that will give a clue about what lies below the surface. Then a detailed contour map of the area to be studied is drawn to determine possible layers of earth at the site. The next step is to determine the geological date of each layer. The simple fact that the bottom layer is always the oldest layer is basic to archaeological studies. Another step is to divide the area into squares. Finally the slow and careful process of digging is begun, one square at a time, one layer at a time. Every bucket of dirt is sifted and carefully examined. Once artifacts, even pieces of artifacts, are found, they are carefully unearthed, their location cataloged, and their type classified. Such information needs to be recorded so that each artifact, or artifact piece, is dated as accurately as possible and any conclusions that can be drawn are made logically.

HARAPPAN LIFE. In 1924, the British government encouraged the beginning of excavations at Harappa and Mohenjo–Daro. Up to that time, archaeologists only suspected the existence of a previously unknown civilization in the Indus River Valley. At left is a part of the unearthed ruins of Mohenjo–Daro.

Pointing to the importance of religion in Harappan life are the statue of a bearded priest (left) and the seals showing a seated god (above, left) and a bull (above, right), the symbol of fertility.

Using two-wheeled carts drawn by oxen, peasants brought cotton, grain, and other goods to the cities in the Indus Valley. At right is an artist's version of the granaries (background) used to store grain and the activity on the busy wharves along the river front (foreground).

tem of writing used in the ancient world. Even if the Harappan script is deciphered, it probably will add little knowledge to present-day understandings of Harappan life. Seals uncovered so far contain no more than a few characters. Archaeologists need fairly lengthy passages, or at least a few connected sentences, to construct any valid judgments about the people behind the writing system.

Historians believe that religion played an important role in the lives of Harappans. It is known that reluctance to change is a characteristic of a conservative, priest-dominated society, and the Harappan practice of rebuilding on all foundations shows a reluctance to change. Besides, many objects of a religious nature have been recovered from the excavations at Harappa and Mohenjo–Daro. Some of these objects represent the awesome powers of life and creation, a favorite theme in early religions. For example, the bull—a symbol of fertility in many early societies—was portrayed in many Harappan figurines. Moreover, statues resembling Shiva (SHEE-vuh), a major Hindu deity of later times, have been found in Harappan ruins. It is quite possible that some of the ideas found in modern Hinduism originated in the Harappan civilization.

A Complex Economy

Much information about the economy of the Harappan civilization has been reconstructed from archaeological evidence. Many occupations were represented in the Harappan way of life. Most of the people, however, were peasants who lived in outlying villages, a pattern that is a major characteristic of the subcontinent to this day. Harappan farmers raised crops of wheat and barley, which were used to provide a livelihood as well as to pay taxes. Harappan peasants were also the first farmers in history to cultivate cotton. In the Indus Valley today, farmers continue to raise wheat, barley, and cotton.

The two well-planned and well-kept cities of Harappa and Mohenjo–Daro, as well as the many articles uncovered from the excavations of these cities and other sites of the Indus Valley, point to the existence of talented artisans. The skilled artisans included carpenters, masons, plasterers, potters, and metalworkers who fashioned jewelry and other articles from copper, bronze, and precious stones. These artisans also fashioned dozens of cleverly modeled toy animals, baby rattles, and miniature wagons and carts in clay and other materials.

Trade was also an important part of Harappan life. Trade took place between the various cities and towns and extended far beyond the borders of South Asia. Knowledge of such trade comes from the small engraved Harappan seals found in Mesopotamia. But judging from artifacts recovered from excavations in both Mesopotamia and the Indus Valley, neither civilization transferred much of its culture to the other through trade.

The Decline of the Indus Valley Civilization

At one time historians and other scholars thought that Harappan civilization was destroyed by invaders from central and western Asia. Although this theory is still feasible, it is more likely that flooding, the cutting down of too many trees, the spreading of the desert, other ecological changes, as well as a change in climate, overwhelmed the Harappan civilization and brought it to an end. It also seems that Harappan rulers tried to keep out change.

As the excavations at Harappa and Mohenjo–Daro proceeded, archaeologists uncovered various layers of city life. The layers represented different time periods in Harappan life. As they dug deeper into the Harappan past, the archaeologists discovered that the topmost (and most recent) layer showed a quality of work that was inferior to the work displayed in the next deeper (and older) layer. Evidently each generation was less careful than the preceding one. Mastery of crafts became a lost art, irrigation and drainage ditches filled with silt, flood damage was left unrepaired, and fortifications were neglected. All of these factors tended to weaken the Indus Valley civilization as newcomers arrived bringing many changes.

The Aryans

The newcomers to the Indus Valley were the Aryans, a people who were the ancestors of most of the Hindus of the subcontinent. While the Harappan civilization was developing, the Aryans were living a nomadic life on the great grasslands that extended from Central Europe into Asia. About the time of the Harappan decline, probably about 1700 B.C., the Aryans, for unknown reasons, began to move out of their traditional pasturelands. Perhaps the climate changed. Food shortages and political rivalries might also have forced some groups to seek new homes. Many Aryan invaders settled in present-day Iran and Afghanistan. Others braved the mountains and found their way through passes into the northwestern part of the South Asian subcontinent. By 1500 B.C. the cities and towns in the Indus Valley were under attack by waves of fierce Aryan warriors who fought from horse-drawn chariots.

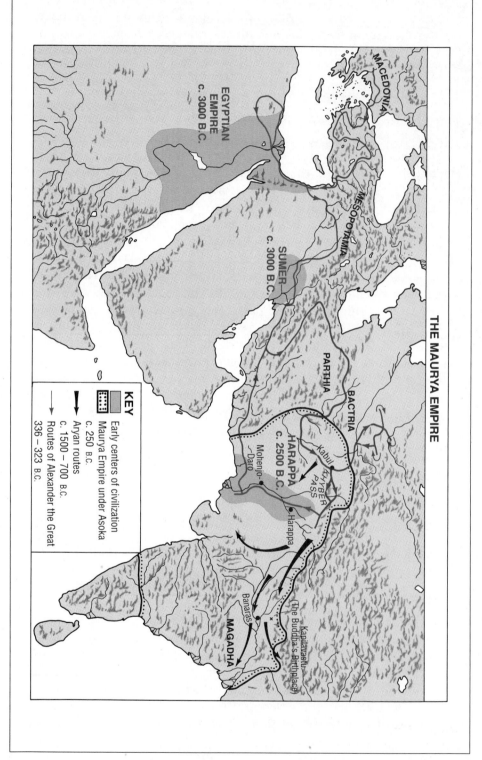

THE MAURYA EMPIRE

KEY

Early centers of civilization

Maurya Empire under Asoka
c. 250 B.C.

Aryan routes
c. 1500 – 700 B.C.

Routes of Alexander the Great
336 – 323 B.C.

MACEDONIA

EGYPTIAN
EMPIRE
c. 3000 B.C.

MESOPOTAMIA

SUMER
c. 3000 B.C.

PARTHIA

BACTRIA

HARAPPA
c. 2500 B.C.

Kabul

KHYBER
PASS

Mohenjo-
Daro

Harappa

Banaras

Kapilavastu
(the Buddha's Birthplace)

MAGADHA

The Vedas

The period of Aryan expansion in the subcontinent, which lasted from 1500 B.C. to 500 B.C., is known as the **Vedic Age.** The term is derived from *Veda* (VAY-duh), the name applied to each of four collections of Aryan legends, myths, battle hymns, and religious beliefs. The oldest of the four collections, the *Rig Veda*, provides glimpses into the life and migrations of the early Aryans. The work is largely religious poetry and has little historical value. In the absence of other sources of information about early Aryan life, however, students of South Asian culture have had to turn to the *Rig Veda* for the information it reveals about the Aryans and their civilization.

The *Rig Veda* shows the Aryans as a fierce nomadic people who depended largely on their cattle for a living. The Aryans lived in small groups that rarely came together except to wage war against a common enemy. After pillaging the communities in the Indus Valley, some of the Aryan groups remained and became part of the existing society. Other Aryan groups moved eastward onto the Ganges River Plain. Centuries of struggle followed as the people living on the Ganges Plain sought to repel the Aryan newcomers.

The Aryans established numerous small monarchies in the Ganges Valley, but they were unable to subdue completely the people who were already living there. From the bewildering number of principalities that are mentioned in the *Rig Veda*, many of them ruled by monarchs with non-Aryan names, historians have concluded that the Indo–Gangetic Plain was divided into a number of constantly warring small states. Historians can be certain of little more than this, however, because the material in the *Rig Veda* was passed down by word of mouth for many centuries before finally being recorded. By the time the material in the *Rig Veda* was set down in writing, the events of earlier generations had been embellished and transformed into myth and legend.

MOVEMENT: THE MAURYA EMPIRE. On the map to the left, three early centers of civilization are shown. The fourth early center was located in China in the valley of the Huang He (Yellow River) and is not shown on this map. The Harappan civilization was destroyed when Aryan invaders forced their way into the northwestern portion of the subcontinent. These Aryans then moved eastward onto the Ganges Plain. By the time Alexander the Great invaded the subcontinent, the Harappan civilization was forgotten. What great empire rose 75 years after Alexander's departure from South Asia?

Check Your Understanding

1. How do the layouts of Harappa and Mohenjo–Daro suggest a high level of civilization?
2. **a.** What do items found in Indus Valley excavations reveal about the Harappan people? **b.** Why do scientists believe that religion played an important role in the lives of Harappans? **c.** Describe the economy of the Harappans.
3. What theories account for the decline of the Indus Valley civilization?
4. *Thinking Critically:* Why is the period of Aryan expansion known as the Vedic Age? Why is the *Rig Veda* important in understanding the life and migrations of the Aryans? What does the *Rig Veda* tell us about the Aryans?

2. The Foundations of Hinduism

During the Vedic Age the foundations were laid for **Hinduism,** a way of life that people on the subcontinent have followed since before the first centuries A.D. Hinduism, which was based on the religion of the invading Aryans, has absorbed many new ideas and customs over the centuries. If some of the Aryans of the Vedic Age could come back to life in the twentieth century, they would be puzzled by many of the practices and beliefs of modern Hindus. But they would also recognize much that was familiar, for many of the basic ideas, customs, and attitudes of the Vedic religion were carried into Hinduism and have persisted into modern times.

The Place of Vedic Literature

The Vedas formed the core of the Aryan religion. Hinduism has no single book such as the Bible or the Koran, the holy book of Islam. Hinduism has several different works, the oldest of which is the Vedic literature: the tales, songs, and ceremonial instructions that the Aryans developed before and during their settlement in the Indian subcontinent. The largest part of this literature is contained in the four Vedas—the *Rig Veda,* the *Sama Veda,* the *Yajur Veda,* and the *Atharva Veda.* The *Rig Veda* is the oldest still-in-use religious book in the world. It was probably put together between 1500 and 900 B.C. The other three

Vedas were compiled later, probably during the closing years of the Vedic Age. The *Sama Veda* is a collection of hymns. The *Yajur Veda* is a manual used by priests in the performance of their religious duties. The *Atharva Veda* is a book of magical spells and incantations. All of the Vedas were passed on by word of mouth from one generation to the next for many centuries before being written down. In the Vedas may be found the roots of basic Hindu beliefs and ideas. Today the Vedas are generally studied only by scholars and priests. Many of the rites and ceremonies of the *Yajur Veda*, however, have been conducted year after year to the present day.

Epics—A Hindu Tradition

Epics are a major part of Hindu tradition. More familiar than the Vedas to most Hindus are two epics, long poems that recount the memorable deeds of famous Aryan heroes. Like the Vedas, the epics were passed on by word of mouth for many generations before being recorded. The longest of the two epics is the *Mahabharata* (muh-hah-BUR-uh-tuh), a poetical work consisting of some 100,000 couplets. *Maha* means "great," and *Bharat* was a legendary monarchy of the Vedic Age. Actually the longest poem in the world, the *Mahabharata* is basically the story of a great civil war in the area of present-day Delhi. The *Mahabharata*'s most famous portion is the *Bhagavad Gita* (BAH-guh-vud GEE-tuh). (See page 37.) The second of the two epics is the *Ramayana* (rah-MAH-yah-nuh), which tells the story of Rama, a heroic Aryan monarch of the Vedic Age. The *Ramayana* relates the adventures of Rama as he undertakes to rescue his wife, who had been kidnaped by a devil-monarch of Ceylon, now Sri Lanka.

As succeeding generations passed on the epics, they took on a religious significance and began to embody many of the basic beliefs of modern Hinduism. The epics are also important to Hindu art and culture, furnishing many artists and writers with endless inspiration for sculpture, paintings, stories, poems, and plays.

Beginnings of the Caste System

The **caste system,** one of the most persistent features of the Hindu way of life, began during the Vedic Age. As Aryan society developed, it became divided into four main social classes. After centuries of challenge between the **Kshatriya** (kuh-SHAT-ree-uh) —the rulers and warriors—and the **Brahmins**—the priests of the Aryan religion, the Brahmins emerged as the topmost class.

Ranking third in the class system were the **Vaishya** (VY-shuh), or peasants. Later this class developed into a class of merchants and townspeople. The **Shudra** (SHOO-drah), or farm laborers, occupied the bottom place in the class system. The Shudras included the conquered peoples who chose to remain in the invaded territory, as well as those Aryans who married into the ranks of the conquered peoples.

As Hindu civilization advanced and new economic activities and skills developed, however, the class system became increasingly complex. The four social classes of Aryan times gradually became the four main **castes** of the Hindu social system. The four main castes were then subdivided many times, mainly along occupational rather than social lines. Today the subcontinent has more than 3,000 castes and subcastes. All Hindus are members of both their occupational caste and the birth class, or **varna,** of their most remote ancestor.

Reformers and government leaders have tried for centuries to lessen caste distinctions, yet caste is still the most important single factor in Hindu life. Forbidden to leave the hereditary caste, Hindus remain members of it during their entire lives. To a large extent caste determines what is permissible and what is forbidden for an individual, especially in rural areas. Whom Hindus can marry, what they can eat, and how they behave toward others are matters ordained by the caste system, its customs and its traditions.

Untouchables

In Hindu society undesirable and "unclean" tasks are assigned to a large group of people called **Untouchables,** *Harijans,* or Scheduled Castes. The origin of the Untouchables is unclear. There is no mention of them in ancient literature. They may have been local people who were willing to do work that Hindus thought to be unclean. Today, on the average, Untouchables are poorer and less educated than other Hindus, and they suffer discrimination in housing, employment, and in other ways.

Since World War II in India where Hindus are in the majority, the lot of the Untouchables, now called the Scheduled Castes, has shown improvement. Mahatma Gandhi, the great Hindu leader of India's pre-independence days, did much to bring about this improvement. Pleading that Untouchables be accepted as human beings, Gandhi violated the caste restriction barring association with them and adopted them as his brothers and sisters. It was Gandhi who gave the Untouchables the name of *Harijan,* which means "Children of God."

The Bhagavad Gita

The long lovely *Bhagavad Gita*, usually referred to as the *Gita*, is part of one of the 18 books in the *Mahabharata*. The *Gita*, however, which itself has 18 chapters, represents less than one percent of the *Mahabharata*. In the *Gita* involving four speakers, Arunja—a hero of the early Aryan age—is faced with the necessity of fighting a civil war to regain the monarchy that belonged to him and his brother. Among his opponents are many of his friends, relatives, and former teachers. Rather than see loved ones on both sides killed, Arunja decides not to fight.

Driving Arunja's war chariot is Krishna, an incarnation of Vishnu the Preserver, one of the principal deities of Hinduism. When Arunja informs Krishna of his decision, a long discussion follows in which Krishna urges Arunja to change his mind:

> Your words are wise, Arunja, but your sorrow is for nothing. The truly wise mourn neither for the living nor for the dead. There never was a time when I did not exist, nor you, nor any of these kings. Nor is there any future in which we shall cease to be. . . . Even if you consider this from the standpoint of your own caste-duty, you ought not to hesitate; for, to a warrior, there is nothing nobler than a righteous war. . . . But if you refuse to fight this righteous war, you will be turning aside your duty. . . . Your enemies will slander your courage. . . . What could be harder to bear than that? . . . Realize that pleasure and pain, gain and loss, victory and defeat, are all one and the same; then go into battle. Do this and you cannot commit any sin. [*The Bhagavad Gita*, adapted from Swami Prabharanada and Christopher Isherwood, translators.]

The *Gita*, which makes no attempt to relate the outcome of the battle or even to indicate such a battle occurred, is a religious and philosophical work. Found in the lines quoted above are the principles of rebirth, the importance of caste, and the rightness of violence in a righteous cause. Other parts of the *Gita* contain additional doctrines that have become a part of Hinduism.

Gandhi's example was an important factor in India's constitution prohibiting discrimination against Untouchables. Laws have also been passed reserving places for the Scheduled Castes in educational institutions, legislatures, and government employment. The improved status of these people is most noticeable in the large cities where outcast families from small rural villages lose their identity as Untouchables. In the cities it is difficult to tell a member of the Scheduled Caste from a Brahmin. Both are likely to wear Western-type clothing or the lightweight garb that is typical on the subcontinent. Caste Hindus and Scheduled Castes work side by side in factories and offices. But in general the plight of the Scheduled Castes, especially in the small towns of rural India, is improving only slowly. In these rural towns, Untouchables cannot blend into the population as they do in large cities. Long-standing traditions and customs are also more likely to be rigidly followed.

Hindu Beliefs and the Caste System

The Vedic and the epic literature contain many principles that have helped to maintain the caste system among practicing Hindus. One of these principles is the idea of **karma,** a belief that the status of all Hindus in any span of life has been determined by their behavior in a previous existence. Linked inseparably to karma is a belief in **reincarnation.** Because of reincarnation, eternity for all living creatures—including deities and even plants—consists of a series of repeated passings of the soul from one life to the next. At the base of both karma and reincarnation, is the belief that life and the world are *Maya*—an illusion of reality. Somewhat like a mirage in the desert, *Maya* is difficult, if not impossible, to understand.

The basic beliefs of Hinduism give a certain sense of futility to Hindu life. Hindus believe that they get what they deserve. Whatever happens, they are simply being repaid for their behavior in past lives. This means that Hindus, whatever the caste, should be guided by *dharma*—duty, law, and obligation—and accept their lot in life. But while it is true that Hindus generally accept life as it is, it must not be assumed that they never protest misery, poverty, and oppression. Hinduism allows rebellion for a righteous cause. The history of the South Asian subcontinent has many chapters full of violence and bloodshed caused by rebels protesting the actions of unwise or incompetent rulers. But while Hindu rebels have brought about political change, they have never sought to change the existing social order created by Hinduism's beliefs.

38

The Development of Hinduism

Hinduism is a broad, inclusive, and hard-to-define faith. The religion of the Aryans cannot rightly be called Hinduism. As it is known today, Hinduism is mainly an outgrowth of Aryan Brahminism with some absorption of ideas from other religions. Much that is accepted in present-day Hinduism has come from descendants of the very people whom the Aryans had overcome. Wandering preachers and hymn singers from cults originating in the Dravidian portion of the subcontinent did as much as anyone to make Hinduism the region's main faith. Before Hinduism emerged as the leading faith in the region, Buddhism—which also grew out of the Aryan Brahminism—enjoyed a long period of dominance. During this period of dominance, Buddhism contributed much to Hinduism as it is known today. (See page 49.)

Perhaps the strength of Hinduism lies in its ability to understand and meet the tremendously different spiritual and philosophical needs of its multitude of followers. Unlike the other major religions of Judaism, Christianity, and Islam, Hinduism has no basic creed to which all its followers subscribe. Its essential beliefs range from simple superstition to the highest philosophical truths. Specific elements of faith for Hindu believers come only from the range of their understanding. Hindus are not expected to believe what they cannot understand. As long as Hindus identify themselves with the Hindu faith, believe the Vedic literature to be sacred, and accept the requirements of the caste system, they are assured of a place in Hindu society.

Check Your Understanding

1. How are the Vedas and the epics related to the religion of Hinduism?
2. **a.** What are the origins of the caste system? **b.** Why are there more castes in present-day Hinduism than in the past? **c.** How is the caste system related to Hinduism?
3. **a.** Who are the Untouchables? **b.** How has life for Untouchables changed in recent years?
4. *Thinking Critically:* Characterize the basic beliefs of Hinduism using such terms as *karma, reincarnation, maya,* and *dharma.* Why is Hinduism generally a hard-to-define faith?

3. The Origins of Buddhism

By the end of the Vedic Age, signs of growing dissatisfaction with Vedic society and religion had appeared. Many people objected to the rigidity of the caste system and the great power wielded by the Brahmins. Moreover, some people were upset because the Brahmins appeared more interested in religious rites and ceremonies than in teaching respect for Aryan tradition.

During the period of mounting unrest, many people on the subcontinent denied themselves material comforts in order to free their minds for religious contemplation. Two such thinkers developed doctrines that greatly affected the emerging Hindu faith. One was Mahavira (muh-hah-VEE-ruh), the founder of Jainism. (See page 43.) The other was Siddhartha Gautama (sid-DAHR-tuh GAW-tuh-muh), otherwise known as the Buddha. **Buddhism,** the faith that eventually evolved from the Buddha's teachings, became one of the world's major religions.

Gautama's Search for Insight

The founder of Buddhism was probably born in 563 B.C., the son and heir of the ruler of the Shakyas, a people who lived at the foothills of the Himalayas in the present-day nation of Nepal. Destined for the throne, Gautama was reared in comfort and luxury. According to tradition, he was shielded from the sight of the ugly and wretched things of life. While a young man, he married and became the father of two children.

Tradition states that one day Gautama left the palace grounds. In quick succession he observed hunger, sickness, and death. Gautama was shocked by what he had seen and wondered why people should have to experience such sorrow and suffering. Gautama decided to go out into the world for help. At the age of 29 he left his wife and children, gave up his inheritance, and began wandering from place to place seeking an answer to his question. For six years neither instruction, study, nor the solitude of a hermit provided him with any answers. But one day Gautama received a sudden flash of insight that gave him the answer to the mystery and meaning of life and its suffering. At that moment, Gautama became the Buddha, the "Enlightened One."

The Four Noble Truths

According to tradition, the Buddha's first students were five monks in the city of Banaras. To them he disclosed the core of his teachings, which he called the **Four Noble Truths.** These truths not only singled out the cause of human suffering but also revealed the way of deliverance.

The first truth was that suffering is a part of existence. The Buddha maintained that mere existence meant pain and sorrow. In his sermon to the five monks, the Buddha is supposed to have revealed this first truth in the following words:

O monks, I will tell you the truth about suffering. Suffering is birth, suffering is old age, suffering is sickness, suffering is death. You are bound to that which you hate: suffering; you are separated from that which you love: suffering; you do not obtain that which you desire: suffering. To cling to bodies, to sensations, to forms, to impressions, to perceptions: suffering, suffering, suffering. [This excerpt and the following four excerpts are from: A. Ferdinand Herold, translated by Paul C. Blum. *The Life of Buddha.*]

The second truth concerned the origin of suffering. The Buddha upheld the essentials of Brahmin philosophy. His explanation for human misery took into account the doctrine of karma and the cycle of rebirth. The Buddha insisted that the basic cause for people's unhappiness is their constant yearning and desire. People become attached to things they must sooner or later lose. They want things they can never have. In explaining this second truth, the Buddha supposedly said:

O monks, I will tell you the truth about the origin of suffering. The thirst for existence leads from rebirth to rebirth; lust and pleasure follow. Power alone can satisfy lust. The thirst for power, the thirst for pleasure, the thirst for existence; there, O monks, is the origin of suffering.

The third truth told what people must do to find peace. To find lasting peace, the Buddha taught that people must snuff out the yearning within themselves. To the five monks, he said:

O monks, I will tell you the truth about the suppression of suffering. Quench your thirst by annihilating desire. Drive away desire. Forego desire. Free yourselves of desire. Be ignorant of desire.

The Buddha's fourth truth revealed the path to permanent peace. In his own life the Buddha had experienced two extremes—a life solely devoted to pleasure and a life deprived of everything. The Buddha warned the five monks also to avoid these two extremes and to follow the middle path that the Buddha had discovered. According to the Buddha, the middle path required eight practices: right faith, right resolve, right speech, right action, right living, right effort, right thought, and right meditation. Now as his fourth point, the Buddha told the monks that people could find permanent peace by walking this **Noble Eightfold Path:**

> O monks, I will tell you the truth about the path that leads to the extinction of suffering. It is the sacred path, the Noble Eightfold Path. . . .

The Buddha believed that attainment of perfect peace was not easy, that people would have to experience numerous rebirths before their inner desires were overcome. Not all people, however, would succeed in achieving victory over self. Those who did not succeed would never able able to remove themselves from the treadmill of repeated rebirths. For those who succeeded in extinguishing their attachment to the things of this world, however, the final reward would be the attainment of **nirvana,** the state of freedom from the cycle of rebirth, the state in which the human soul becomes one with the Universe. Nirvana would be supreme bliss because the individual self and soul would have disappeared completely. In concluding his sermon to the monks, the Buddha told them:

> O monks, now that I have a complete understanding of these four truths, I know that . . . I have attained the supreme rank of Buddha. I am forever set free: for me there will be no new birth.

Brahmin Opposition

Although Gautama did not reject the principal ideas of the emerging faith of Hinduism, his message was not approved by the Brahmins and his teachings at first failed to gain acceptance. Buddha's message differed from the teachings of the Brahmins on two important matters. In the first place the Buddha ignored the rites and ceremonies traditionally performed by the Brahmins. In this simple but effective way, Buddha expressed his view that such religious rites and ceremonies were useless. In addition, the Buddha taught that "enlightenment" could come to anyone at any time. This teaching was an indirect attack on the caste system and contradicted the Brahmins'

S IDELIGHT TO HISTORY

Jainism

It is difficult, and often impossible, to trace a particular idea to a single source. Many basic religious ideas on the subcontinent arose from Vedic tradition and are a part of all the subcontinent's religions. Hinduism, Buddhism, Jainism, and the hundreds of small sects all recognize the probability of a common source. Indeed, Buddhism, Jainism, and the other sects on the subcontinent often were recognized as part of Hinduism, a religion that could mean different things to different people.

Jainist traditions claim that the universe is cyclical, that it passes through an unending number of alternating phases of growth and decline. In each cycle Jainism is revealed through a series of 24 prophets, the last of whom was Mahavira, whose life span is supposed to have been from 540 B.C. to 468 B.C. In many ways the story of Mahavira, the son of a Kshatriya ruler, parallels that of the Buddha, who lived about the same time. Like the Buddha, Mahavira experienced enlightenment. Unlike Buddha who preached an eightfold path to perfection, Mahavira preached that perfection could be reached by following the threefold path of right faith, right knowledge, and right conduct.

As Mahavira systematized it, Jainism has several distinctive features. It neither admits nor denies the existence of deities, claiming that human perfection is the ultimate end of life. Perfection comes through karma and is determined by the individual's present life. *Ahimsa*, the practice of respecting life in every form, is often traced to Jainism. This religion teaches that all forms of creation have souls, even rocks and insects, and are involved in the process of karma. Strict Jainists sweep the path before them to avoid killing living things as they walk.

Most Jainists are merchants because Jainists regard farming as a disturbance of nature. Now few in number, Jainists believe that the universe is in a present cycle of decline. They look forward to the beginning of the next cycle and the subsequent improvement in life.

teaching that people had to climb through the caste system in a succession of lives before being released from rebirth.

When Buddha died about 483 B.C., only a small number of people were followers of his teachings. But the disciples of Buddha kept his teachings alive, founding monasteries throughout the northern part of the subcontinent where his teachings could be studied. It was not until explosive political changes took place in the subcontinent, however, that Buddhism became popular. These changes, which began in the third century B.C., are discussed in the next section.

Check Your Understanding

1. a. How did Buddhism arise? **b.** How does a Buddhist reach nirvana?

2. How does Jainism differ from Buddhism?

3. *Thinking Critically:* Why was Buddhism not widely accepted at first?

4. Buddhism During the Maurya Age

By the time Buddha was born, the numerous governments in the northern part of the subcontinent had evolved into monarchies and republics. Perhaps the most important of these was Magadha (MAH-guh-duh), a monarchy in the lower Ganges Plain. Blessed with rich soil, a busy river trade, iron for metalworking and export, elephants for use in war, and forests where timber could be obtained, Magadha grew in power. About 323 B.C. Chandragupta Maurya (CHUN-druh-GOOP-tuh MAWR-yah) came to the throne. During the next 150 years, he and his successors built a great empire in the northern part of the subcontinent, also called North India. This empire, possibly the subcontinent's first, was the instrument by which Buddhism became the dominant religion in South Asia.

Invasion by the Greeks

The rise of Magadha in the Ganges Plain was facilitated by important developments in the northwest. Shortly before Chandragupta came to power Alexander the Great entered the Indus Plain. After conquering the Persian Empire, he invaded the subcontinent in 326 B.C. Victorious in the Indus Valley, Alexander made plans to conquer the Ganges Plain as well. His troops were weary of war, however, and refused to move on. After making arrangements for the governing of his conquests, Alexander withdrew from the subcontinent and died soon after.

Alexander's empire did not survive his death. In time several of his generals established monarchies of their own. The subcontinent became part of the domain of Seleucus, an empire that included Syria, Babylonia, and Alexander's eastern provinces. Although the glory of their deeds was long remembered in the West, Alexander and his generals were soon forgotten in the subcontinent. Indeed, their names do not even appear in South Asian records of the period.

Establishment of the Maurya Empire

Although Alexander never reached the borders of Magadha, his conquests were inseparably linked with the rise to power of Magadha. For one thing, Alexander had overthrown the small republics and monarchies in the northwest. Chandragupta then took advantage of Alexander's departure and the resulting political vacuum to expand his empire by including these states in his domain. Also it was because of Alexander's conquests that history has a reliable description of the Maurya Empire. Much that is known about this empire is derived from the account of Megasthenes (meh-GAS-theh-neez), an ambassador from the monarchy founded by Seleucus who lived for some years at the court of the Maurya emperor. Megasthenes' account states that the Maurya Empire was efficiently administered by a large staff of officials, and a network of police and spies maintained security within the realm. Megasthenes also wrote glowing accounts of the prosperous economy, the efficient tax system, and the Mauryan way of life.

Asoka, Champion of Buddhism

Buddhism became firmly grounded on the subcontinent because of the support of Asoka (ah-SHOH-kuh), the grandson of Chandragupta Maurya. Although the exact dates of Asoka's reign are not known, he seems to have been in power from 269 to 232 B.C. Asoka, seeking to take over the monarchies in the northern Deccan Plateau, began his reign as a conqueror. Despite great successes, the casualties were staggering. According to Buddhist tradition, Asoka surveyed the battlefield after one of his victories and was appalled by the battle's frightful toll of lives. Thereafter he vowed to abandon war and devote his life to promoting peace.

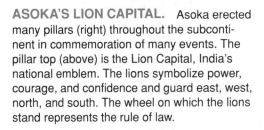

ASOKA'S LION CAPITAL.   Asoka erected many pillars (right) throughout the subcontinent in commemoration of many events. The pillar top (above) is the Lion Capital, India's national emblem. The lions symbolize power, courage, and confidence and guard east, west, north, and south. The wheel on which the lions stand represents the rule of law.

Needing guidance in his pursuit of peace, Asoka turned to Buddhism. Asoka adopted the teachings of Buddhism as the underlying policies of his reign. Showing compassion for all living things, he urged officials and subjects to be just and considerate in their conduct toward one another, made punishment for many types of crime less severe, and discouraged the slaughter of animals, even for food. Asoka had his humane commands inscribed on stately stone pillars that were erected throughout the empire. Many of them are still standing and are the source of much of the information about the empire.

Asoka's conversion to religion benefited both Asoka and Buddhism. The teachings of Buddhism reduced unrest and the threat of rebellion, making it easier for the emperor to build a strong, centralized empire. As a result of Asoka's support, Buddhism became widely known and accepted on the subcontinent. Soon the faith spread beyond the mountain wall into Central and East Asia and across the seas into Southeast Asia.

Asoka's successors, however, lacked his greatness, and barely 50 years after Asoka's death, the last Maurya emperor was overthrown. By that time, the empire had already been decreased in size and had been replaced by the empire of the Shungas (SHOONG-ghus). The Shungas ruled a large monarchy in the Ganges Valley and were accepted as overlords by the lesser monarchies that bordered on their domain. The Shungas Empire, however, was never as successful or powerful as the Maurya Empire. Neither was the Shungas Empire as highly centralized because many of the old Maurya lands became independent monarchies.

Changes in Buddhism

In spite of the destruction of the Maurya Empire, Buddhism continued to grow and spread throughout Asia. As Buddhism spread, it came into contact with many other religious cults and sects. On the subcontinent many of these sects had been absorbed into Hinduism, and Buddhism became more and more like this emerging faith.

By the early centuries of the Christian era, two separate and distinct Buddhist movements had come into being. Those Buddhists who adhered to the earlier teachings of the faith formed the Southern School, which is popularly called Hinayana (HEEN-uh-YAHN-uh) Buddhism, or Theravada (thehr-uh-VAH-duh) Buddhism by its adherents. Hinayana means "Lesser Vehicle." According to the followers of the Southern School, the "vehicle" that transports worthy souls to nirvana has room for some but not for all souls. The second movement became known as the Northern School, or Mahayana (mah-huh-YAHN-uh) Buddhism. The Northern School reflected strong influences from sects in North India and, possibly, even from Christianity. Mahayana means "Greater Vehicle." According to this school, the "vehicle" that conveys deserving souls to nirvana has room for all.

Mahayana Buddhism showed quite a great departure from original Buddhist thinking. For one thing, Mahayana Buddhism transformed the Buddha into an all-powerful, all-knowing, and all-seeing deity. The Buddha was placed at the summit of a number of lesser deities. A second change was in the nature of the state of nirvana. To the Mahayana Buddhists, nirvana was no longer the state of extinction of the soul and of "Oneness with the Universe." Instead, nirvana was believed to be a paradise of the afterworld where eternal bliss was enjoyed by the faithful.

BUDDHIST SCULPTURE.

The most famous of India's stupas, or Buddhist shrines, that at Sanchi (left), has been called the "crowning achievement of North Indian sculpture." The mound is simply constructed, but the gateway in the foreground is a good example of the elaborate decorations that often adorned a stupa's entrance.

In early stupas, for reasons that are not clear, there were no statues or portrayals of Buddha. Rather, he was symbolized by a wheel, a tree, footprints, or an empty throne. Sculptures of the earliest Buddhas show a Roman, or Western-style, influence (above). Later portrayals (left) are much more Asian in pose and appearance.

Buddhism's Influence in South Asia

As Buddhism became widespread, distinctive styles in architecture and art emerged. Temples and other places of worship were built in a similar style. Perhaps the most notable Buddhist structure was the artificial mound, later a building, called a **stupa** (STOO-puh) that was originally designed to hold mementos of the Buddha. When Buddhism spread to China, Korea, and Japan, the stupa inspired the development of the pagoda, a structure that has ever since been characteristic of East Asia.

The transformation of the Buddha into a deity had an effect upon art. Those who placed their faith in the Buddha and wished to be inspired by his symbolic presence cut statues of the Buddha from stone, cast them in metal, or carved them from wood. The posture of these statues, the face and body, and even the clothing indicate some traces of cultural borrowing through contacts with the Greek and Roman empires.

Buddhism won millions of converts in many lands. Without a doubt it has been one of the most potent civilizing and equalizing forces the world has known. Advocating gentleness and mercy, stressing good moral behavior, and offering hope after death to millions of people, Buddhism proved especially attractive to the poor and unfortunate of South Asia. It especially met with wide acceptance among the Shudras and Untouchables. For a variety of reasons, some of which are treated in Chapter 3, Buddhism declined on the subcontinent. Over a period of 1,500 years, Hinduism and other religions captured the loyalties of most people in South Asia. Today less than 1 percent of South Asians are followers of Buddhism.

Check Your Understanding

1. **a.** How did Alexander's conquests prepare the way for the Maurya Empire? **b.** Why was the Maurya Empire successful?
2. **a.** Why is Asoka remembered as a great ruler? **b.** How did Buddhism influence Asoka's success?
3. **a.** How did Buddhism influence the architecture and art of South Asia? **b.** How does Buddhist art reflect the process of cultural borrowing?
4. *Thinking Critically:* How did Buddhism change as it came in contact with other religious groups? Why did Buddhism appeal more to the downtrodden than to other groups?

CHAPTER REVIEW

■ **Chapter Summary**

Section 1. The foundations of South Asian civilization were laid in the Indus River Valley and flourished about 2500 B.C. The most important cities of the civilization were Harappa and Mohenjo–Daro, two of the most skillfully designed cities in the ancient world. Only scant evidence has been unearthed, but the evidence that has been found suggests that the Harappan people had reached an advanced stage of civilization. The Harappan civilization began to crumble about 1500 B.C. under the impact of Aryan invaders from beyond the subcontinent's mountain wall. After advancing eastward onto the Ganges River Plain, the Aryans dominated North India.

Section 2. The Aryans preserved the memories of their conquests, their ideas about humanity and life, and their rituals and ceremonies in the Vedas and epics. This body of sacred literature is the source of Hinduism's basic beliefs, including the division of society into castes and the importance of karma, dharma, and reincarnation. By the end of the Vedic Age about 500 B.C., the Aryans had developed the main characteristics of the Hindu way of life.

Section 3. Buddhism had its origins toward the end of the Vedic Age. The founder of Buddhism was Siddartha Gautama, who abandoned a life of luxury to seek reasons for the suffering he saw around him. After years of searching for answers, Gautama became the "Enlightened One," or the Buddha, finding answers in the Four Noble Truths and the Noble Eightfold Path. Followers of the Buddha founded monasteries where his teachings were kept alive, despite Brahmin opposition, until a change in the region's political climate made Buddhism more popular with South Asians.

Section 4. The Maurya Empire, possibly the subcontinent's first, was the instrument by which Buddhism became the dominant religion in South Asia, at least for a time. Buddhism became popular during the reign of Asoka, who adopted the teachings of Buddhism as the underlying policies of his reign. Because of Asoka's support, Buddhism became widely known throughout the subcontinent, eventually spreading to other parts of Asia. The empire also benefited because Buddhism made it easier for Asoka to build a strong centralized government and to pursue his policies in peace. Buddhism won millions of converts in many lands. With its spread, however, Buddhism underwent a number of changes and split into two distinct movements—the Theravada, or Southern School, and the Mahayana, or Northern School. In all, Buddhism influenced many aspects of Asian life.

■ Vocabulary Review

Define: cultural diffusion, Vedic Age, Hinduism, caste system, Kshatriya, Brahmin, Vaishya, Shudra, caste, varna, Untouchables, karma, reincarnation, Buddhism, Four Noble Truths, Noble Eightfold Path, nirvana, stupa

■ Places to Locate

Locate: Harappa, Mohenjo–Daro, Magadha, Maurya Empire

■ People to Know

Identify: Harappans, Aryans, Rama, Arunja, Krishna, Vishnu, Maravira, Gautama, Chandragupta Maurya, Asoka, Megasthenes

■ Thinking Critically

1. Why do historians think that the people and rulers of Harappa, Mohenjo–Daro, and the other cities of the Indus River Valley civilization were conservative? Why do they think that this conservatism led to their downfall?
2. Why is Vedic literature important to an understanding of the Aryans and their descendants? What relationship exists between Vedic literature and the caste system?
3. Summarize the origins of Buddhism, its acceptance as a popular religion, and its split into two schools.
4. How did the rise of the Maurya Empire contribute to Buddhism's popularity and widespread acceptance?

■ Extending and Applying Your Knowledge

1. Use library references to find out more about Hinduism and Buddhism. Compile a list of beliefs and practices that apply to each religion alone and those that apply to both. Then make a chart that illustrates your findings for a bulletin board display.
2. Many religions set aside certain periods for religious celebrations and other functions. Use reference books and other library resources to compile a description of such periods for either Hinduism or Buddhism. Share your findings with the class in either a written or oral report.

3

Post–Maurya Times to the Rise of Islam

By the end of the Maurya dynasty, the basic characteristics and underlying philosophy of the caste system and Hinduism had taken form in the subcontinent. Buddhism had also arisen, providing inspiration for a rich heritage of religious thought and artistic accomplishment. However, the task of devising efficient methods of administration for the governments of the region remained incomplete, and no ruler, not even the rulers of the Gupta Empire, was able to unify the subcontinent into one great empire. For almost 2,000 years after Maurya times, the subcontinent remained politically fragmented.

The post-Maurya times, however, were a period when the cultural contributions of the past were consolidated with new contributions. For the first 1,000 years after Maurya times, the subcontinent shared the riches of its civilization with peoples beyond its borders. Trade with other parts of the world increased, and as trade contacts increased so did cultural contacts, resulting in the spread of Hinduism and Buddhism to other parts of Asia.

For political organization, the people of the subcontinent relied primarily on the heritage of the past, so much so that religion and tradition determined politics. Although the people of the subcontinent in this period never established a stable, unified political system, they developed social institutions that have given direction to life until the present day.

1. An Era of Invasions

Even at the height of the Mauryan Empire, invaders continued to pour into the subcontinent through the mountain passes in the northwest. By the time the empire came to an end about 183 B.C., one wave of invaders after another was rolling across the mountain wall into the northwestern part of the subcontinent. This era of invasions lasted from about 200 B.C. to A.D. 300. Tracing the history of the subcontinent during this period is difficult because the chief written records, which are the sacred writings of Buddhist and Jainist priests, treat history as incidental to religion. Nonetheless these documents, along with other bits of evidence, reveal several important developments. First, Buddhism spread into many different parts of Asia. Second, the Deccan Plateau and South India, the southern part of the subcontinent, began to assume an important role in subcontinent affairs. Finally, trade opened the door for increased contacts with the West and with Southeast Asia.

The Northwest—A Highway for Invaders

For 500 years the northwest was controlled largely by invaders. The road to the subcontinent was pointed out by Alexander the Great, who settled Greeks in Bactria and Parthia as a means of tightening his control over the area. Although some of the Bactrian and Parthian monarchies that arose in the northwest survived for several hundred years, most were soon overthrown by nomadic groups from Central Asia called Shakas. The Shakas had destroyed the Bactrian states before entering the subcontinent. But in the first century A.D., the Shakas fell before the might of yet another group of nomadic invaders—the Kushanas of Central Asia. For the remainder of the invasion era the Kushanas controlled most of the northwest.

The Kushanas are important in the history of the subcontinent because of their role in spreading Buddhism. Like other non-Hindu invaders, the Kushanas were excluded from the caste system and Hinduism. Some of the invaders adopted Jainism. (See page 43.) Others became Buddhists. The Kushanas carried Buddhism with them as they traveled along the caravan routes into Central Asia and China, spreading their adopted faith to the millions with whom they came in contact. Kanishka, the most famous of the Kushana monarchs, was especially active in promoting Buddhism through missionary efforts in other lands. He also called the meeting that led to the division of Buddhism into Northern and Southern schools. (See page 47.)

North India 200 B.C.—A.D. 1200

B.C.	
200	Beginning of age of invasions
A.D.	
300	End of age of invasions
320–550	Gupta Empire
	Gupta Golden Age
540–606	Period of invasions and fragmentation
606–647	Harsha's empire
647–1200	Division into monarchies and principalities
	Muslim invasions

In time the post-Maurya invaders succumbed to the processes of **cultural assimilation.** They intermarried with the people of the subcontinent and adopted the prevailing customs. Eventually the invaders' identity as a culturally separate group disappeared as they became more and more like the people of the subcontinent.

The Emergence of South India

Little is known about the history of the Deccan Plateau and South India before the invasions. Until the invasion era, that part of the subcontinent south of the Vindhya Hills figured very little in the history of the subcontinent. Hindu culture, however, had penetrated the area. As a result, the region's deities became a part of the Hindu tradition and the people of the area were absorbed into the caste system.

The Deccan came into prominence in the subcontinent during the reign of the Andhra dynasty. The rulers of the Andhra dynasty had established a power base in the northwestern part of the Deccan about 230 B.C. Occasional references to these rulers in various North India sources suggest that they had been important since Maurya times. In the first and second centuries A.D., the Andhra dynasty built an empire that controlled a large part of the Deccan from coast to coast. This empire, which did not last very long, was loosely knit. Through marriage alliances and military campaigns, however, the Andhras established close contacts with the peoples of the north. Thus the Deccan Plateau became the connecting link between Hindustan, or North India, and South India.

South India began to move into the subcontinent's mainstream of history in the last century before the beginning of the Christian era. The shadowy historical records of the time tell of battles among the Cholas, Pandyas, and Keralas—three groups of people who spoke Dravidian languages. These peoples lived in the region comprising the present-day Indian states of Andrha Pradesh, Mysore, Tamil Nadu, and Kerala. (See map page 176.) For many centuries to come this region was called Tamil (TAM-ul) country after the principal Dravidian language in use there. (See page 58.) With the empire of the Andhras serving as a connecting link, the peoples of Tamil country were beginning to absorb Hindu culture. Later they combined the Hindu traditions of the Aryans with their own Dravidian folklore to produce some of India's finest epics, poetry, and music.

The Expansion of Western Trade

The period from 200 B.C. to A.D. 300 was marked by a great expansion of trade to and from the subcontinent. The Greek monarchies in the northwest kept in touch with West Asia and the region bordering the Mediterranean Sea, developing important trade routes that linked the regions together. The Shakas and Kushanas encouraged trade between the subcontinent and their former homes in Central Asia. They also extended trade into China. In the Deccan and South India, commerce increased as traders from the Arabian Peninsula and the regions bordering the eastern end of the Mediterranean opened sea routes from the Roman Empire.

The Arabs were the first to become involved in sea trade with the subcontinent. At a very early period they learned to make use of the summer monsoon winds to drive their ships across the Arabian Sea. Since the monsoon winds reversed in the winter, the Arabs loaded cargo into their sailing ships and waited for the winter monsoon winds to bring them home. During the last century B.C., other sailors from the West came to understand the usefulness of the monsoons. Sea trade flourished, and South India, long overshadowed by the monarchies of North India, began to play a prominent role in the subcontinent.

The goods exported over the sea routes to the West usually ended up in the Roman Empire. For many centuries the pattern of this East–West trade varied little. The people of the Mediterranean region continued to demand the same kinds of goods from

(Continued on page 59)

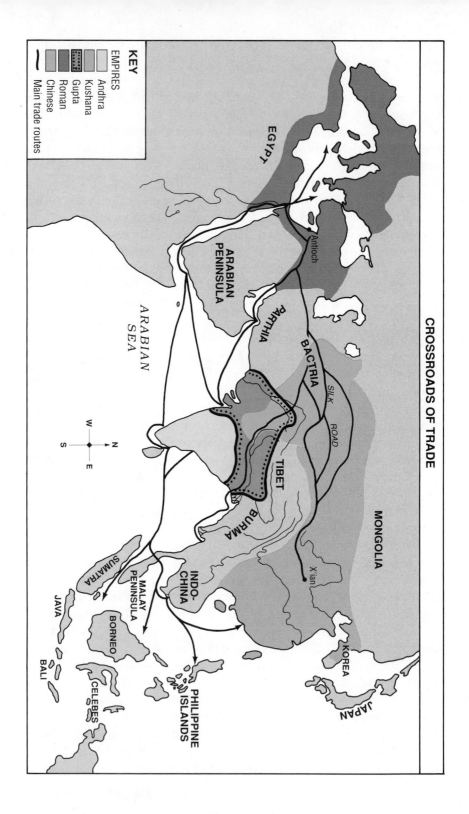

CROSSROADS OF TRADE

KEY

EMPIRES
Andhra
Kushana
Gupta
Roman
Chinese
Main trade routes

EGYPT

ARABIAN
PENINSULA

ARABIAN
SEA

Antioch

PARTHIA

BACTRIA

SILK
ROAD

TIBET

BURMA

INDO-
CHINA

MALAY
PENINSULA

SUMATRA

JAVA

BALI

BORNEO

CELEBES

PHILIPPINE
ISLANDS

X'ian

MONGOLIA

KOREA

JAPAN

N
W   E
S

TEMPLE ARCHITECTURE. The impact of Hinduism and Buddhism is seen in the architecture of South Asia. Angkor Thom (above, left) is pictured as it looked when discovered in 1858. Angkor Wat (above, right) shows the care taken in its restoration. Both of these unique structures were found in present-day Cambodia. The Buddhist temple (left) is in Burma, while the magnificent Hindu–Buddhist temple of Borobudur (below) is located on the Indonesian island of Java.

REGIONS: CROSSROADS OF TRADE. South Asia has always occupied a strategic position in trade between East and West. The main overland routes between the Roman and Chinese empires intersected in the Kushana Empire. Later, the Andhra Empire in South India became a link in the ocean trade between the West and Southeast Asia. How did South Asia benefit from its location as a crossroads of trade?

The Tamil Culture

While the Gupta Empire was rising and falling in the north, the area known as South India was developing its own way of living. Named Tamil after the predominant language in the southern part of the subcontinent, the culture endured from the first century A.D. until the 1300's. Over the centuries, Buddhism, Jainism, and Hinduism were carried into the southland in different ways, and each left its distinctive marks upon the people of South India.

Hinduism had the greatest impact, bringing with it a system of caste divisions. The upper classes eagerly accepted Hinduism, making it a religion of prestige. The common people, however, did not accept the religion as eagerly. They looked on the religion as a newcomer and resented its attempts to change their traditional Dravidian ways. Especially disliked was the form of worship, which emphasized sacrifice. The common people turned to the personal, devotion-centered worship of Vishnu and Shiva. Hinduism in its present form owes much to the common people's manner of worship because modern Hinduism stresses devotion to deities rather than sacrifice.

The Tamil culture left lasting contributions in the fields of literature and art. The later writings of the Tamil people were expressive and lilting. The art of the Tamil culture is best seen in the beautiful Hindu temples of South India. Some temples were built in caves; others were free-standing, constructed like most buildings. (See pages 60–61.) Sometimes an entire temple was carved from a huge rock. The art work within these temples included magnificent murals depicting the Hindu religion and the ways of life carried out in the region.

In the 1300's, Muslims from the north influenced Tamil culture. This Islamic influence, together with the steadily increasing contacts between the northern and southern portions of the subcontinent, brought to an end the distinctive civilization of South India. During its long lifetime, however, the Tamil culture contributed greatly to the cultural life of the subcontinent. By combining the Aryan and Dravidian traditions, it produced a single tradition that is unique to the subcontinent.

the subcontinent. Spices, perfumes, precious stones, fine textiles, carved ivory, and iron ore were brought to the Roman Empire. Peacocks, parrots, monkeys, tigers, elephants, and other rare birds and animals were also sought by the Romans. The people of the subcontinent, however, made few demands for Western goods. As a result, the chief import from the West was gold.

Contacts with Southeast Asia

Contacts between the Indian subcontinent and Southeast Asia developed as a result of trade with the Roman Empire. At the time the lands and islands of Southeast Asia were largely unsettled and undeveloped, but they produced spices, a good that was much in demand in the Roman Empire. Traders sailed to the Malay Peninsula, the area of Indochina, Java, Sumatra, and Borneo, to pick up spices for export to Rome. Many of the traders settled in Southeast Asia's islands and lands. The penetration of Southeast Asia by people from the subcontinent was helped by the Southeast Asian peoples themselves, particularly those in the East Indies. Being seafarers, the Southeast Asians assumed much of the initiative in opening the sea routes between Southeast Asia and the subcontinent of South Asia.

The first monarchies in the history of Southeast Asia developed during the early centuries A.D. Some Southeast Asian rulers invited high-caste Hindus to join their courts as counselors. Many of these counselors spent their lives in the service of these foreign governments and attained high rank. Some of them married women who belonged to the local aristocracy and a few made brides of the daughters of ruling families. Hinduized descendants of these unions were in an excellent position to influence the culture of the upper classes and to modify prevailing patterns of government. Although the upper classes in Southeast Asian lands were Hindus, the common people usually did not adopt Hindu manners, customs, and ideas.

Hindu Influence in Southeast Asia

The influence of Hindu culture gradually waned in the lands to the east of the subcontinent as other faiths and cultures became prominent. Thus the appeal of Hinduism was overshadowed by Buddhism and by Confucianism, the great moral philosophy of China. At a later time, Islam swept through the East Indies, the Malay Peninsula, and the southern Philippine Islands. To this day many peoples of these lands follow the teachings of Mohammed. The last cultural invasion of Southeast Asia occurred in recent centuries with the arrival of Westerners and their way of life. Islam has continued to be the most popular religion, but Christianity has made notable inroads in many areas, particularly in the present-day nations of the Philippines and Indonesia.

Despite the influence of other religions, the early impact of Hinduism was too strong to be erased. Hindu practices and customs have endured in the present-day nations of Southeast Asia. The dances of Thailand, the drama of Indonesia, and the traditional literature of several Southeast Asian nations are testimony to the subcontinent's lasting cultural contributions. As for Hinduism as a faith, it struck permanent roots mainly on the Indonesian island of Bali. Modified by local customs and traditions, Hinduism has strongly influenced the island's present way of life.

Buddhism's Strong Imprint in Southeast Asia

As in the case of Hinduism, traders brought Buddhism to Southeast Asia. During the early centuries A.D. Buddhism became the main religion of China. As trade increased between China and the subcontinent, the sea route between the two regions was used more and more because overland caravan routes simply were too slow and difficult. Buddhist monks settled in ports along the sea route in Southeast Asia. These Buddhist monks erected temples, established monasteries, and won many converts to their faith.

Buddhism began to lose its hold on the peoples of the subcontinent after the era of invasions, but the faith flourished in the lands to which it had been transplanted. In addition to China, the people in the lands of Tibet, Mongolia, Korea, and Japan were brought into the Buddhist circle. In Southeast Asia, Buddhism took root among the people in the region that includes the present-day nations of Burma, Thailand, Cambodia, Laos, and Vietnam.

Cultural Diffusion in Southeast Asia

The remarkable impact of Hinduism and Buddhism in Southeast Asia is seen in many imposing monuments found throughout the region. One of these monuments is the Borobodur (bohr-oh-boo-DOOR) in present-day Indonesia on the island of Java in the East Indies. (See page 57.) Completed in the eighth century A.D., or possibly the ninth century A.D., the Borobodur is a large hill encased by terraces of carved stone. Engraved on the walls of each level are stories and legends from the history and folklore of Buddhism. Perhaps as many as 10 years of work were required to build this noble memorial, which was restored after centuries of neglect by the former Dutch rulers of the post-World War II nation of Indonesia.

Even more imposing than Borobodur are the ruins of magnificent cities and temples built by the Khmer (KMEHR) people. These once-magnificent cities and buildings were erected between the 800's and 1200's A.D., when the empire of the Khmers included much of the Southeast Asian mainland. After the downfall of the Khmer Empire, the cities and buildings fell into ruin and were forgotten for centuries until French explorers discovered them in 1858.

After the initial discovery, many other expeditions penetrated the thick rain forests of present-day Cambodia in Indochina in search of lost cities and temples. The most impressive finds were the ruins of Angkor Thom (ANG-kohr TAHM) and Angkor Wat (WAHT). (See page 57.) The ruined temples and palaces of these ancient cities reflect the impact of South Asian civilization on the Khmers. So too do the countless stone statues, representing both Hindu and Buddhist deities, and the stories chiseled on great stone slabs. Patiently restored by the French, Angkor Thom and Angkor Wat have become known as the "Eighth Wonder of the World." These ancient cities tell an amazing, although incomplete, story of the influence of South Asian culture on life in Southeast Asia.

Check Your Understanding

1. **a.** How did the era of invasions influence developments in South Asia? **b.** Why are Kushanas considered the most important of these invaders?
2. **a.** Describe the trade that took place between South Asia and the Roman Empire. **b.** How did South India begin to play an important role in the subcontinent?
3. **a.** How was Hinduism transplanted to Southeast Asia? **b.** How was Buddhism transplanted to Southeast Asia? **c.** How is the extent of Hindu and Buddhist influence in Southeast Asia known?
4. **Thinking Critically:** Which do you think is a more important agent of cultural diffusion—trade contacts between groups of people or missionary activity? Explain your answer.

2. The Gupta Empire and the Strengthening of Hinduism

Because Hinduism had no founder, no set dogma, and no single deity, the millions of villagers who wanted to retain the deities and religious customs of their ancestors were able to find a place for them in it. Buddhism also won a strong following, but beginning about the 300's A.D., Buddhism's popularity in the subcontinent began to decline. Hinduism then became the dominant religion in the subcontinent.

The Founding of the Gupta Dynasty

At the beginning of the 300's A.D., after centuries of invasions, North India entered a period of peace and unity. The ruler who brought unity to the area was Chandragupta I, founder of the Gupta Empire. Chandragupta's rise to power was sudden and unexpected, but he laid the cornerstone for an empire that endured for more than 200 years. At its peak, all of North India and large parts of the Deccan Plateau were under the empire's control. The frontier regions were fairly secure against invaders. Law and order were enforced within the realm, and imperial officials sought to promote the welfare of the people. The Gupta rulers abolished the oppressive policies of the monarchs they displaced and eased the heavy taxes paid by the people. All of North India benefited from the enlightened rule of the Gupta.

Conditions during and after the Gupta period have been described by Chinese Buddhist pilgrims who visited the subcontinent in search of scriptural materials. One of the most renowned of these travelers was Fa–Hsien (FAH-shee-EN), who described life under the Gupta in these words:

> In the Gupta Empire people were numerous and happy; they have not to register their households, or attend to any magistrates and their rules; only those who cultivate the royal land have to pay [a portion of] the gain from it. If they want to go, they go; if they want to stay on, they stay. The king governs without decapitation or [other] corporal punishment. Criminals are simply fined, lightly or heavily, according to circumstances. Even in case of repeated attempts at wicked rebellion, they only have their right hands cut off. The king's bodyguard and attendants all have salaries. Throughout the whole country the people do not kill any living creature, nor drink intoxicating liquor, nor eat onions or garlic. [Fa–Hsien, *A Record of Buddhistic Kingdoms*, trans. by James Legge.]

As a fervent Buddhist, Fa–Hsien was also pleased by the care given the sick and the poor. He wrote:

> The Heads of the Vaishya families establish in the cities houses for dispensing charity and medicines. All the poor and destitute in the country, orphans, widows, and child-less men, maimed people and cripples, and all who are diseased, go to those houses, and are provided with every kind of help, and doctors examine their diseases. They get the food and medicines which their cases require, and are made to feel at ease; and when they are better, they go away of themselves.

Fa–Hsien undoubtedly exaggerated the facts, but even so it is possible to conclude that the people under the Gupta were socially enlightened.

The Fall of the Gupta

The Gupta Empire began to crumble in the middle of the 400's. Pressures along the frontier became too great for the imperial forces to resist. The last of the Gupta rulers held out for another 50 years, and then the dynasty disappeared. From time to time other substantial monarchies came into being in the subcontinent. In the Ganges Valley the mightiest of these was founded by a prince named Harsha. From 605 to 647, Harsha ruled an empire that equaled the Gupta in brilliance and power. For the most part, however, the 600 years that followed the passing of the Gupta Empire were characterized by chaos and strife.

A significant development during this period of turmoil was the increasing importance of the southern monarchies. For the first time, rulers of states south of the Vindhya Hills felt strong enough to invade the northern region. One monarch even defeated the mighty Harsha in battle. Although various monarchies controlled large sections of the Deccan and South India for many decades, no monarchy was as stable, prosperous, or well governed as the Gupta Empire. Many centuries passed before the Guptas were surpassed as empire builders, and when this happened, conquerors from abroad were responsible. Never again was a Hindu dynasty to exercise the degree of power that the Guptas had exercised.

New Triumphs of Hinduism

Probably the most important development in the post-Gupta age was a strengthening of Hinduism throughout the subcontinent.

In the Deccan and in South India, rulers had openly supported Hinduism since before Gupta times because they did not have to answer to the Buddhist overlords. When the Guptas rose to power, they too espoused Hinduism, integrating certain Buddhist beliefs into Hinduism. In the central and southern regions of the subcontinent, Hinduism had attracted the finest minds. The Dravidian scholars especially had refined and enlarged on the Hindu doctrines. They are credited with giving these doctrines the form in which they exist today. Hindu scholars and holy men traveled throughout the subcontinent, spreading the philosophy of Hinduism wherever they went. Imposing temples were constructed, especially in the Deccan and South India, and throughout the subcontinent Hindu rites and festivals were given official backing.

Devotion to Deities

Hinduism, as it evolved during and after Gupta times, singled out and popularized **Brahma, Vishnu, and Shiva**—three deities whose importance has remained unchallenged since. Brahma, deemed by Hindus as the Creator, had enjoyed a following since ancient times. Although always honored by Hindus, rarely has Brahma deeply stirred their spirit. On the whole, Brahma has been considered too lofty and remote to be approached by human beings.

Vishnu, on the other hand, has been worshipped by countless generations as the Preserver of Life. In Hindu art Vishnu is usually depicted with four arms, symbolizing the deity's all-embracing power. Vishnu's followers teach that the deity has gone through nine major rebirths. According to these teachings, Vishnu's first incarnation was as a fish. In this form Vishnu saved humanity by rescuing the first human from a destructive flood. Rama, the hero of the *Ramayana,* was the seventh incarnation of Vishnu, while the Buddha was the ninth incarnation and the most recent. The tenth rebirth is expected to be in the form of Kalkin, a man carrying a flaming sword and mounted on a white horse who will punish the wicked, reward the good, and establish a new age.

Shiva, the Destroyer, is often portrayed in art and sculpture wearing a necklace of small skulls. Devotees of Shiva, however, do not view the deity with fear. In Hinduism there can be no life without death, no creation without destruction, and no rebirth without the passing of the one's former life. Thus Shiva is looked on by Hindus as a necessary part of the process of birth and life.

64

THE HINDU DEITIES. There
are comparatively few statues of
Brahma (top left), one of Hinduism's
three main deities. In this statue,
each of Brahma's heads point to
one of the four directions, signifying
Brahma's all-seeing nature. Shiva
(top right) is best known in the West
as the Lord of the Dance. As Shiva
danced, light reflected from the
deity's legs, forming the universe.
Both Shiva and Vishnu (right)
appear in a variety of sculpted
forms.

By the 600's A.D. most Hindus belonged to one of two main sects. One sect stressed Vishnu as the high or only deity, while the other preferred Shiva. To the Hindu there was, and is, no contradiction in having two high deities, each of which is regarded by some as the only deity. The Vishnavite believes that Shiva is a lesser form of Vishnu, while the Shivaite holds that Vishnu is a lesser form of Shiva. Historically the followers of Vishnu have always been the more numerous. Shivaites are concentrated mostly in South India and the northern mountain regions of the subcontinent.

The Waning of Buddhism

The roots of Hinduism were established long before the Buddha was born. Hinduism was growing into an enduring faith during the centuries that Buddhism was sweeping across Asia. Because the practice of Hinduism was broad and tolerant, South Asian Hindus accepted many of the teachings of the Buddha—even finding a place for the Buddha in Hindu theology. For their part, Buddhists on the subcontinent were quite willing to compromise with the beliefs and customs of Hinduism, even making use of Brahmin priests on occasion. Buddhism on the subcontinent eventually became so much like Hinduism that it was regarded as a sect of Hinduism. Like many other "offshoots" of a major faith, Buddhism then entered into a state of steady decline.

The final blow to Buddhism on the subcontinent was delivered by the Muslims. Pushing into the northwestern part of the subcontinent from the 700's on, the Muslims destroyed the great Buddhist monasteries, burned the libraries, and killed the monks. Most of the monks who survived the Muslim onslaught fled the subcontinent. Already in a state of decline, Buddhism as a separate faith disappeared from South Asia.

Check Your Understanding

1. Why is the Gupta remembered as one of the great dynasties of South Asia?
2. Why did Hinduism make great gains following the fall of the Gupta?
3. **a.** What are the three major deities of Hinduism?
   b. How does a Hindu view each of these deities?
4. *Thinking Critically:* Why did the strengthening of Hinduism parallel the decline of Buddhism?

3. Cultural Achievements

The Gupta Age (320–550) marked a great flowering of cultural achievement on the subcontinent. Thus is it considered a golden age. Its cultural achievements, however, were based on the work of earlier generations of which little is known. Few historical records were kept and few artistic accomplishments have survived through the ages. Yet there is sufficient evidence to show that South Asians had distinguished themselves in the search for knowledge and in the expression of their artistic talents long before the Gupta came to power. During the subcontinent's Golden Age, South Asians carried on where their forgotten predecessors had left off. The subcontinent became a center of learning for much of Asia. Of the famous universities that flourished during these years, the university at Nalanda was the most famous of all. This university attracted students from all over South Asia and from China, Tibet, and Japan. Teachers at Nalanda taught not only philosophy and religion but also art, architecture, medicine, and agriculture.

Advances in Mathematics and Science

By Gupta times, practical mathematical concepts were more highly developed in South Asia than in any other ancient land. Transmitted to other parts of Asia as well as to the Western world, these concepts revolutionized arithmetic computation and advanced mathematical studies. One practical arithmetical tool credited to South Asian scholars is Arabic numerals. The idea of zero, one of the most important concepts in mathematics, is another South Asian contribution. So is the idea of infinity. South Asian philosophers had long been intrigued by infinity, and at some time in the distant past applied the idea of infinity to mathematics.

Learned scholars on the subcontinent were greatly interested in the physical and natural world. Certain references in the Vedic literature indicate that the ancestors of the Hindus studied the movements of the heavenly bodies. Centuries before scholars in the West, these ancestors knew that the earth revolved around the sun and that it rotated on its axis. Ultimately, scholars on the subcontinent accumulated enough astronomical knowledge to make possible the preparation of a fairly accurate calendar. But because the Hindus, like other people of the premodern era, lacked the telescope, their understanding of astronomy remained limited. South Asians also explored physics and chemistry. So-called "atomic theories" were developed by early

Hindu thinkers, but these ideas had greater implications for religious thinkers than for scientists and were more the product of philosophical speculation than of scientific inquiry.

By the end of the Gupta period, South Asians had acquired considerable medical knowledge. They had learned to diagnose and treat many ailments. During the Gupta Age, surgeons set broken bones and used plastic surgery to repair mutilations. For such work the surgeons developed more than 100 specialized instruments. Also South Asian doctors were aware that cleanliness prevented infection—an important fact not understood by Western doctors until modern times.

Doctors in South Asia developed a wide range of medicines and drugs. As a result of constant experimentation with the properties of plants and herbs, South Asians discovered numerous drugs for use in the treatment of disease. One of the most important findings was that the oil of the chaulmoogra tree is effective in treating leprosy, a disease that can destroy parts of the body. Only in the present-day has this medicine been replaced by antibiotics.

The Works of Kalidasa

If South Asians had produced only the Vedas, they would have assured themselves a respected place in world literature. But in later centuries writers on the subcontinent turned out many masterpieces. Unfortunately many of these works are looked on by most Westerners as overly ornate and seemingly lacking in true feeling.

One author of medieval times who has been widely acclaimed in both the East and the West is Kalidasa (kah-lih-DAH-suh), who lived during the reign of Chandragupta II (375–415). At the court of the Gupta, Kalidasa was considered one of the "Nine Gems"—outstanding writers who enjoyed the patronage of the imperial rulers. Kalidasa's works, which reflect the culture of the times, center around the theme of love—believed by Kalidasa to be the highest and finest of human emotions. The pearl of Kalidasa's writings is *The Recognition of Sakuntala,* a tender play telling of the meeting, separation, and reunion of a monarch and his beloved wife.

A popular poem written by Kalidasa is the "Cloud Messenger," a short account of the longing and anguish experienced by an earth-spirit when he has been banished from the divine city for a year. Separated from his wife, the spirit uses lovely word-pictures to describe his loneliness.

I see your body in the sinuous creeper,
    your gaze in the startled eyes of deer,
your cheek in the moon, your hair in the plumage
    of peacocks,
and in the tiny ripples of the river I see
    your sidelong glances,
but alas, my dearest, nowhere do I find
    your whole likeness.

[Quoted in Basham, *The Wonder That Was India.*]

Other Outstanding Writers

Many of India's best known writers lived during or shortly after
the Gupta Age. Dandin (DUN-din), Subandhu (sub-UN-doo) and
Bana (BAH-nuh), all of whom lived during the late 500's and
early 600's, were masters of the art of writing prose narrative.
Dandin's *Tale of the Ten Princes,* an account of the adventures
of 10 heroes, is valuable for its keen portrayal of life among the
common people of the subcontinent. Subandhu's fame is based
on his ornate descriptions rather than excellence of narrative.
His one great work, the *Vasavadatta,* has almost no story to
tell. Bana gives us much valuable historical material in his
Deeds of Harsha, an account of the events leading up to Harsha's rise to power.

Outside of Kalidasa, the finest poet of South Asia was Bhartrihari (BUR-trih-HUH-rih), a writer of the 600's who wrote many
short poems on the subjects of worldly wisdom, love, and the
call of the religious life. One of his untitled masterpieces is both
amusing and discerning:

You may boldly take a gem from the jaws of a crocodile,
    you may swim the ocean with its tossing wreath of waves,
you may wear an angry serpent like a flower in your hair,
    but you'll never satisfy a fool who's set in his opinions!

You *may,* if you squeeze hard enough, even get oil from sand,
    thirsty, you *may* succeed in drinking waters of the mirage,
perhaps, if you go far enough, you'll find a rabbit's horn,
    but you'll never satisfy a fool who's set in his opinions.

[Quoted in Basham, *The Wonder That Was India.*]

A type of South Asian literature that has influenced Western
literature is the folklore of the subcontinent. It is impossible to
trace authorship of folk tales, for the stories arose over many
centuries. Many of the stories in *Arabian Nights,* including some

of the exploits of Sinbad the Sailor, are based on South Asian folklore. The *Panchatantra* (pun-chuh-TUN-truh), a collection of stories of talking animals, reached the West in the 500's. The story of Reynard the Fox, popular in the folklore of many European countries, for example, had its origins in one of the fables of the Panchatantra.

Religion's Impact on Art and Architecture

Nearly all the art and architecture in ancient India was of a religious nature. By the first centuries A.D., South Asians—both Hindus and Buddhists—had begun to acquire skill in working with stone. For centuries they carved temples out of solid stone in caves and on hillsides. As they became skillful in stonework, they created elaborate designs for the temples. These temples were decorated both inside and out with hundreds of beautifully carved stone columns, intricate highly detailed statues of deities, and delicately chiseled carvings. Bas-reliefs, carvings that project slightly from a flat stone surface, instructed the faithful in well known legends and stories from both Vedic and Buddhist tradition.

The high point of religious art and architecture was reached in the Deccan Plateau. The cave temples of Ajanta (uh-JUN-tuh) and Ellora (eh-LORE-uh), begun during the second century B.C., were nearly 1,000 years in building. A majority of the 61 caves at these two locations were built by Hindus, but some were the work of Buddhists and Jainists. All were hewn out of the solid rock of hillsides. The outside walls are adorned with sculptured figures, columns, and pictorial panels. The interiors are subdivided into many chambers, galleries, corridors, alcoves, and stairways. For sheer grandeur, the temples rival structures built anywhere in the world.

Free-Standing Temples

Beginning about the 600's, monarchs and wealthy merchants throughout the subcontinent began to donate large sums of money for the building of magnificent temples. Since these were built from the ground up, rather than carved out of solid rock, they are called free-standing temples.

Despite the vastness of the subcontinent, Hindu temples were remarkably uniform in their basic plan. The core of the temple was the shrine where the statue of the chief deity was kept. A closed passage joined this shrine to the hall used by the worshipers. The hall was entered from an open porch. Above the shrine rose a great tower, and lesser towers were placed on

AJANTA. Ajanta, located in a desolate section of the northern Deccan Plateau, is the site of 29 of the subcontinent's most famous cave temples. The temples shown on this page were built in the 600's. Typical massive pillars (at right) guard the entrance of many temples. The building fronts, or facade, (top, left), of the temples are decorated with statues of Hindu and Buddhist deities, heroes, and bas-relief panels that represent scenes from their lives. The wall painting, or fresco, of the Buddha (top, right) was found in a cave temple.

other parts of the building. A courtyard surrounded the temple, and within the courtyard were a number of shrines for lesser deities. A great wall enclosed the entire courtyard. Styles varied from one part of the subcontinent to another, and architectural refinements were added over the years, but the basic plan remained unchanged.

Temple building continued until it was forbidden by Muslim invaders. Unfortunately many of the great free-standing temples that existed have disappeared. They housed gold and silver statues of deities, and precious metals also were used in the temple construction itself. As much for plunder as for religious reasons, Muslims, beginning in the eleventh century, destroyed the temples and carried away the gold and silver. Few of the great temples of North India survived the Muslim invasion. Today the finest examples of temple architecture are found in the Deccan Plateau and South India, areas spared the brunt of the Muslim attacks.

Check Your Understanding

1. What contributions were made by South Asians:
   a. to arithmetic? **b.** to mathematics? **c.** to science and medicine?
2. Describe some of the characteristics of South Asian literature, using examples from great writers and their works.
3. *Thinking Critically:* Summarize the influence of religion on South Asian art and architecture. How are advances in culture reflected in the subcontinent's temple building? Why are few free-standing temples remaining?

4. Post–Gupta India

From the early days of the Harappan state until the rise to power of the British Empire in South Asia, which is treated in Chapter 5, no government succeeded in establishing its rule over all of the subcontinent. Except for the Maurya, no dynasty was able to establish even a strongly centralized government over a large area. The Guptas had direct political control over the Ganges Valley, but many monarchies in the empire simply paid **tribute** to their overlord. After the fall of the Guptas, this fragmentation became even greater. Lacking strong central authority, the subcontinent became divided among thousands of small monarchies and principalities.

Impact of the Land Revenue System

According to tradition, the ruler owned all the land in the monarchy or principality. The ruler, however, was free to surrender the right to collect the revenue from these lands. From the 600's on, the land revenue system came into being. Through it, many rulers compensated court officials and military officers with revenue grants instead of salaries. Technically the land remained the property of the ruler, but in practice the overlord was the real owner. In exchange for the revenue grant, the overlord was expected to give the ruler a share of the revenue collected from the land as well as undivided loyalty. The overlord was also expected to supply the ruler with soldiers in time of war, to use the ruler's currency, and to glorify the ruler in monuments, inscriptions, and writings.

Over the centuries this land revenue system became quite complicated. As overlords grew wealthy, they assumed titles of royalty, calling themselves **rajas.** They also granted revenue rights to members of their courts, thus creating overlords loyal to them. Regardless of the size of the holdings, an overlord eventually came to be regarded as a raja. Over time, as many overlords inherited grants made by several rulers, loyalties became hopelessly divided. With rulers constantly at war with each other, victories and defeats led to frequent ownership changes of revenue-bearing lands. By the year 1000, a bewildering number of small monarchies existed on the subcontinent. The system of land revenue had become so hopelessly tangled that it was never clear who owned what lands, which ruler owed tribute to whom, or who should be loyal to which ruler.

The Life of a Ruler

Despite the confused situation in the post-Gupta age, certain generalizations can be made about rulers on the subcontinent. One generalization concerns the traditional role of the ruler. First and foremost, the ruler was supposed to be a protector. It was the ruler's responsibility to keep out aggressors, to protect life and property, and to preserve traditional customs. Also the ruler was expected to promote learning and culture. Rulers vied with one another to attract the leading writers, artists, musicians, and philosophers.

In return for the ruler's services as patron and protector, the ruler expected to live a life of luxury. The ruler's palace was as splendid as the monarchy could afford. The palace was run by a chamberlain, or manager, who directed a large staff of servants. The court of a wealthy monarch included several wives, called a harem, and dozens of doctors, poets, musicians, advisers, and artists. All persons in the court were supported primarily to satisfy the whims of the ruler.

Despite the splendor of a court, the ruler did not have unlimited power. More often than not, the ruler had to pay tribute to an overlord. The advisers to a ruler traditionally exercised great influence. It was not unusual for a raja to be overthrown by the court's advisers. One of the chief checks on the authority of a raja was public opinion. South Asians were normally peaceful, but they became rebellious when their rights or religious traditions were violated. Many a thoughtless raja was overthrown by revolt.

Village Life

Eight out of ten South Asians lived in villages, making the villages the core of a monarchy. Yet a South Asian ruler seldom had political agents in the villages. Instead a ruler would place governors in key cities and towns. Nearly all the villages' contacts with the ruler's government were through these officials. Often governorships became hereditary. In effect the officeholders became uncrowned rulers. It was not at all unusual for a governor to revolt and establish a monarchy. Many of the South Asian monarchies of long ago were formed in this way.

Villagers generally looked after all matters of purely local interest. They seldom saw an agent of the ruler. Said the villagers: "The rains have come! The rice-blades spring! The farmer cares not who is king!" But there were times when even the smallest hamlet attracted the attention of government officials. One occasion was tax-collecting time—a visit that hardly called for rejoicing. The villagers, generally a poor and wretched lot, could expect no compassion from the ruler's agents. "Five eggs," the villagers would say, "was all the raja taxed the village; his soldiers took a thousand fowls in pillage."

Another dreaded occasion was the "royal tour." Many rulers made periodic tours of their monarchies to hear local grievances and to punish anyone who failed in the obligations to the ruler. On such journeys the raja would take many servants, messengers, and members of the court. Even well-to-do landlords, who usually managed to avoid the payment of taxes, were reluctant to entertain the royal-tour group. "A raid of elephants," an unlucky host would sigh, "is better than a visit of a raja with a clan."

Village Government

The affairs of each village were conducted by a council of elders. The size of this council often varied, but by modern times the **panchayat** had become commonplace. The five elders of the panchayat were elected, generally for five-year terms. Although the panchayat was composed of elected officials, it was hardly democratic. Councils were usually dominated by the more prosperous villagers and the representatives of the higher castes. In many monarchies, council members had to meet the approval of the raja.

The panchayat set individual tax assessments, negotiated the amount to be paid into the raja's treasury, and often acted as tax collector. The council also concerned itself with construction and maintenance of public works, such as the irrigation system, the village reservoir and wells, and roads. The council was seldom called on to make laws because villages were governed by customs, tradition, and religious regulations. The council acted, however, as judge and jury, ironing out squabbles among villagers. The council also imposed fines and punishments whenever necessary. It also decided such ticklish issues as which son would get the best farming plot when the holdings of a feeble or deceased father were divided. Enforcing a decision was seldom a problem. Despite considerable grumbling, villagers generally accepted the judgment of the elders. If the elders could not settle a problem, a higher official of the territory was called in to give a final decision.

The village panchayats continue to be the most important agency on the local level. Present-day India has more than 400,000 panchayats, which collectively govern the rural population. In general, the panchayats are responsible for agricultural production, local industry, medical care, management of common grazing grounds, and maintenance of village streets, reservoirs, wells, and sanitation. In some places the panchayats also supervise elementary school education, keep the village records, and levy and collect taxes.

Caste Councils

Village elders did not interfere in questions concerning religious obligations. If a Hindu violated the traditions of caste, the case was tried before a council consisting of members of that caste.

Punishment for religious violations ranged from penance to excommunication, or expulsion from the caste. A Hindu who was excommunicated had to leave home, occupation, and oftentimes family. The excommunicated Hindu had to join the ranks of the Untouchables. The excommunicated's only hope for redemption was rebirth into a caste in the next life.

Developing a Nationalist Spirit

South Asian villagers had little interest in affairs outside the village. They did have certain regional ties, for a people having common language, customs, and history felt a closer kinship to each other than to neighboring peoples having different traditions. Regional ties were especially strong in South India. But nowhere on the subcontinent was there a nationalist spirit. It was not until the mid–1800's that South Asians began to think in terms of **nationalism.** Many South Asia monarchs had visions of building a large empire. Some managed to put together fairly extensive monarchies, but none was able to build an empire such as the Maurya or the Gupta, and no South Asian ruler was able to unite the entire subcontinent.

Many books on South Asia stress the failure of the people to achieve political unification. But South Asians should not be blamed for not welding together a **nation** embracing the entire subcontinent. Few peoples in history have succeeded in organizing a **central government** for a territory the size of the South Asian subcontinent. The peoples of South Asia experienced the same lack of success in achieving political unity as did their contemporaries in Western Europe. Even today Europe, which is no more diverse geographically or ethnically than South Asia, is split into 33 nations, including the Soviet Union.

Check Your Understanding

1. How did the land revenue system encourage political fragmentation in South Asia?
2. **a.** How was a ruler in South Asia expected to serve the people? **b.** How could a ruler expect to be rewarded for service to the people? **c.** How was a ruler's power limited?
3. **a.** How were villages governed? **b.** Why did village councils seldom make laws?
4. *Thinking Critically:* Why did the concept of nationalism take hold slowly on the subcontinent?

CHAPTER REVIEW

■ **Chapter Summary**

Section 1. Soon after the death of Asoka, the Maurya Empire of North India disintegrated. For the next 600 years, invaders swept over the region. These invaders either were driven out or were absorbed by the numerically stronger and culturally superior Hindus. Meanwhile the Deccan Plateau region and the region known as South India entered the mainstream of South Asian history. Peoples of these regions made important contributions to Hinduism, and traders from the Deccan and South India brought the West and the subcontinent closer together through commerce. In the subcontinent as a whole, Buddhism grew weaker and Hinduism became stronger. Contacts with other lands and peoples increased. Southeast Asia especially was influenced by developments within the subcontinent. Through trade, both Buddhism and Hinduism spread into this region and became a part of Southeast Asian culture.

Section 2. The period of invasions in North India came to an end when the Gupta dynasty came to power during the fourth century. This period of comparative peace was short-lived, however, because the later Gupta rulers could not contend with the ever-present military pressures on the northwest frontiers. By the mid–600's the Guptas were no longer an effective political force, and the region entered a period of chaos and political fragmentation. Politically the Deccan and South India were also fragmented, but culturally the regions showed some progress. South India especially made notable contributions to Hinduism. It also developed the Tamil culture. Throughout the subcontinent, Buddhism continued to lose ground, and by the 700's it had nearly disappeared. Hinduism had assumed the dominant position on the subcontinent that it holds to this day.

Section 3. The Gupta Age (320–550) has become famous as the subcontinent's Golden Age of culture. Scholars, writers, and artists of this period distinguished themselves by advancing knowledge and by producing masterpieces of literature, art, and architecture. Kalidasa, a writer supported by the Gupta dynasty, was the greatest of the poets and playwrights of the period. The most famous art and architecture, however, have survived in the Deccan Plateau region and in South India. In the Deccan are found the magnificent cave temples at Ajanta and Ellora, while South India has the subcontinent's finest free-standing temples.

Section 4. An indirect result of the political confusion of the subcontinent from 200 B.C. on was an increasing reliance on local self-government. With rajas constantly at war with one another or with invaders, the villages were free to conduct their own affairs. Village councils, always an important part of the subcontinent's life, provided leadership for the peasants. Problems that village councils were unable or unwilling to handle were solved by caste councils. The reliance on local governments continued in succeeding centuries because the South Asian people were unable to fully develop a spirit of nationalism and unite into a nation.

■ **Vocabulary Review**

Define: cultural assimilation, Brahma, Vishnu, Shiva, tribute, raja, panchayat, nationalism, nation, central government

■ **Places to Locate**

Locate: Deccan Plateau, South India, Bactria, Parthia, Roman Empire, Chinese Empire, Southeast Asia, Java, Angkor Thom, Angkor Wat, Ajanta, Ellora

■ **People to Know**

Identify: Alexander the Great, Shakas, Kushanas, Arabs, Khmers, Guptas, Chandragupta I, Maurya, Harsha, Kalidasa, Dandin, Subandhu, Bana

■ **Thinking Critically**

1. How did invasions and trade affect Hinduism and Buddhism on the subcontinent and in the rest of Asia?
2. Why did Hinduism grow stronger on the subcontinent while Buddhism declined?
3. Why has the Gupta Age been considered a Golden Age of cultural achievement on the subcontinent?
4. How did the land revenue system contribute to the political fragmentation of the subcontinent? Why was South India less fragmented than other parts of the subcontinent? How did fragmentation delay the development of nationalism on the subcontinent?

■ Extending and Applying Your Knowledge

1. Research the fable of Reynard the Fox as it is told in Western literature and as it was told in South Asian literature. Compare the stories as told in West and East and share your findings with the class in an oral report.

2. Like peoples of many other lands, the people of South Asia explained many occurrences in nature and history through the telling of legends. Research some of the legends that are important to South Asians. Choose one to narrate to the class or to illustrate through a series of drawings.

4

Islam in India

From the early 700's on, the South Asian subcontinent reeled under the shock of successive invasions by Muslims, upholders of the teachings of Mohammed the Prophet, the founder of the Islamic religion. The invaders from the Middle East founded new monarchies in the northern and central part of the subcontinent. Unlike many of the subcontinent's invaders of the past, the Muslims did not accept the culture of the Hindus. Instead, the Muslims persuaded many Hindus to change from the faith of their ancestors to Islam.

Civilization on the subcontinent was permanently enriched by the transplanted faith and culture of Islam. Hindu scholars were intrigued by the highly developed Muslim philosophy and literature. Seldom did Hindu scholars abandon their Hindu faith in favor of Islam, but their exploration into Islam's many new ideas sometimes resulted in new philosophical and religious movements. In addition, Muslim art, architecture, and literature inspired many Hindu artists to blend Islamic artistic views and techniques with those of traditional Hinduism.

The mixing of the two cultures produced a complex civilization with many cultural and political strains and tensions. These strains were increased during the 1500's when the Muslim empire of the Moguls dominated much of the South Asian subcontinent. Although several Mogul rulers attempted to foster cordial relations between followers of the two faiths, the gulf between them widened and has continued to the present.

1. The Era of Muslim Invasions

Not long after the Gupta Empire disintegrated, the entire Near East—an early name for the entire eastern end of the Mediterranean, including Egypt and the Arabian Peninsula—was conquered by the militant disciples of Islam. Bursting out of the Arabian Peninsula, these Arab Muslims overran many neighboring lands. Their initial expeditions against the subcontinent were unsuccessful, but by 712 the Muslims had taken over the monarchy of Sind. (See map, page 85.) Soon after the Arab invasions, other converts to Islam joined the struggle for power and riches in the subcontinent. These Afghans and Turks opened what rightly can be called the subcontinent's period of Muslim domination.

Mahmud of Ghazni

Between the years 1000 and 1026 invaders on horseback swept across the plains of North India with disturbing frequency. In battle after battle Afghan and Turkish invaders overwhelmed the armies of the Hindu rajas. These new invaders were the soldiers of Mahmud (mah-MOOD), a Turkish chieftain from the monarchy of Ghazni (GAHZ-nee) in Afghanistan. They were following traditional Islamic principles that stressed conquest of other lands and societies as a means of glorifying Allah, the Islamic name for God.

With the official blessing of the Caliph of Baghdad, the spiritual leader of the Muslim world, Mahmud headed 17 devastating expeditions into North India. The Turkish and Afghan soldiers under Mahmud's command terrorized Hindu and Buddhist priests, killed many of them, and tore down hundreds of shrines and statues of Buddhist and Hindu deities. They also plundered countless palaces, sacked and destroyed virtually all the Hindu temples in their path, and scattered those Hindu armies that dared oppose them. Mahmud expanded the tiny monarchy of Ghazni into a great empire. More important, Mahmud's conquests made the Islamic faith the mainstay of the subcontinent. Mahmud died in 1030, and soon after the empire fell apart. His descendants, however, controlled the region of the Punjab until the late 1100's.

Muhammad of Ghor

In the late 1100's another Turkish chieftain named Muhammad of Ghor took over lands originally conquered by Mahmud of Ghazni. Like Mahmud, Muhammad came from a line of Afghan

81

South Asia During the Muslim Era

712	Arab conquest of Sind
1000–1026	Invasions of Mahmud of Ghazni
1175–1192	Invasions of Muhammad of Ghor
1206–1526	Delhi Sultanate in North India
1221	Invasions of Genghis Khan
1336–1565	Vijayanagar Empire in South India
1398	Invasions of Tamerlane
1498	Arrival of the Portuguese
1519–1526	Invasions of Babur
1526–1837	Mogul Empire
1526–1658	Mogul Golden Age

rulers. Between 1175 and 1186 Muhammad conquered all the territory in North India that the Ghazni dynasty had ruled. Then in 1191, Muhammad began an assault on the North Indian monarchies that even Mahmud had not been able to subdue. In the first campaign the Muslim armies were defeated. In the following year, Muhammad returned to North India with a much larger force, and after bitter fighting, his armies were victorious. Muhammad, however, had no more intention of remaining in North India than had Mahmud. Returning to his capital in Afghanistan, Muhammad gave his generals the task of securing his conquest on the subcontinent. Within a few years the generals had extended Muslim rule over most of North India.

The Delhi Sultanate

Aybek, the most trusted of Muhammad's generals, made Delhi his headquarters. When Muhammad was assassinated in 1206, Aybek became the ruler of North India. Aybek's rise to power marked the beginning of the Delhi Sultanate, a foreign dynasty that ruled North India for 320 years (1206–1526). During that period 34 monarchs sat on the throne at Delhi. The average reign was a brief one because the 320-year reign of the Delhi Sultanate was one long bloody scramble for power. Sultans frequently were deposed by their own officers, and even a ruler's children or other family members helped plot palace revolts. Often, the result was the death of the sultan.

S IDELIGHT TO HISTORY

Mohammed and the Spread of Islam

Mohammed (570–632), the founder of Islam, was born in Mecca. He did not adopt the belief in a single God until he was an adult. As a youth he accepted the many deities that were a part of traditional Arab life. In his travels as a merchant and camel driver, however, Mohammed came into contact with many Christians and Jews. Gradually he became convinced that the Christian belief in a single God was true. According to Mohammed, he became completely persuaded when the Angel Gabriel appeared to him, about the year 610. In his vision Mohammed was told to preach the idea of one God throughout the world.

Mohammed began preaching there was only one God, whom he called Allah. He told all who would listen about his experience with the angel and of other revelations that he said had been given to him. Mohammed's teachings, however, were not accepted in Mecca, his Arabian birthplace and home. He left Mecca for the nearby town of Medina. This emigration, called the Hegira, took place in the year 622. The people of Medina accepted Mohammed's teachings. Thereafter the new religion, now called **Islam,** or "submission to God," spread with amazing speed.

Because the Hegira marked a turning point in the history of Islam, it is regarded as the beginning of the Muslim era. Muslims believe that God conveyed his message to the world by way of a number of great prophets. The first prophet was Abraham and the last great prophet before Mohammed was Jesus. Muslims believe that Mohammed was the last and greatest of the prophets. For this reason, Muslims sometimes refer to Mohammed simply as the Prophet.

At the time of Mohammed's death in 632, Islam was limited to the Arabian Peninsula. During the next 35 years, however, the fiercely devoted followers of Mohammed spread the new religion into North Africa, Persia, and Central Asia. Within another 35 years, Islam had encircled the lower half of the Mediterranean Sea and had penetrated into the subcontinent of South Asia. Throughout the centuries, Islam has continued to attract followers worldwide. Today it ranks second only to Christianity in the total number of believers.

Despite the insecurity of the Delhi throne, some sultans were able rulers. They supported the construction of public works, promoted trade, and patronized learning and art. Many of the sultans were cruel, however, and were feared and despised by Hindus and Muslims alike. The reigns of such rulers were nightmares for the people.

During the 1200's and 1300's, armies of the Delhi sultans fought their way into the Deccan Plateau region. A few generals even penetrated the southernmost part of the subcontinent, an area never before reached by conquerors from North India. For a time the Delhi Sultans reigned over the most extensive empire ever put together in South Asia. A few rulers of unusual ability were able to maintain a firm grip over this vast empire. But as the empire swelled in size, the sultans found direct government of their domains impossible and assigned **viceroys** to administer distant areas, giving them troops to enforce the laws. In some remote areas the sultans left intact the existing governments. After receiving tribute and promises of loyalty and taxes from a ruler in such an area, the sultan would allow the conquered ruler to continue governing.

Resistance to Islamic Penetration

When a Hindu state in the Indo–Gangetic Plain fell to the Muslims, its ruler was often replaced by the Muslim conquerors. Sometimes a North Indian ruler was executed. When conquered rulers were permitted to retain their thrones, they were careful not to antagonize the Muslim sultan. Islam, the religion of Mohammed thus became a major force in North India. But the Deccan and South India were distant from Delhi, and the sultans found it difficult to keep a close check on conquered rulers from there. Moreover, the Hindu rulers in the Deccan and South India offered stubborn resistance to Delhi efforts at expansion. Eventually the Deccan fell to the Delhi Sultanate, but the Deccan's Hindu way of life was not substantially changed by the Muslim invaders.

South India was quite successful in resisting the sultans. In 1336 a Hindu monarchy was founded at Vijayanagar (VIJ-uh-yuh-NUG-er). Strong, wealthy, and vigorous, the new Hindu state refused to bow to Muslim power. It built an empire of its own, which included that part of the subcontinent south of the Khrishna River. The monarchy of Vijayanagar actually outlasted the Delhi Sultanate. In 1565, Islamic rulers in the Deccan joined forces to sack the city of Vijayanagar. This attack brought to an end the last important Hindu empire.

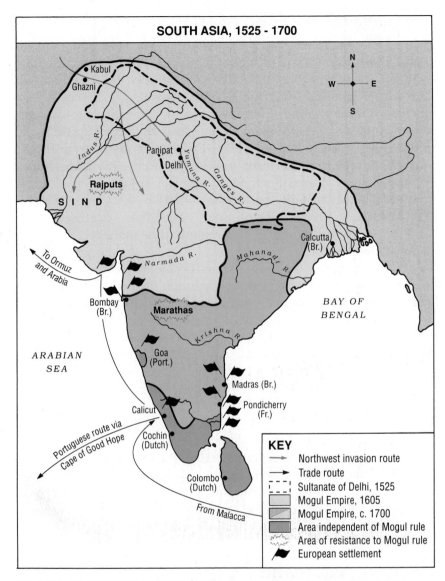

SOUTH ASIA, 1525 - 1700

KEY

→ Northwest invasion route
→ Trade route
- - - Sultanate of Delhi, 1525
    Mogul Empire, 1605
    Mogul Empire, c. 1700
    Area independent of Mogul rule
    Area of resistance to Mogul rule
⚑ European settlement

PLACE: SOUTH ASIA, 1525–1700. An important aspect of the Muslim era was the formation of the Delhi Sultanate. The Sultanate was replaced by the Mogul Empire, which by the time of Akbar's death in 1605 included all of North India and much of the Deccan Plateau. Under Aurangzeb, (1658–1707), the Empire had expanded to include most of the subcontinent. Conquest was never complete, however, because some Hindu peoples, namely the Rajputs and Marathas, were never subdued by the Moguls. How long did it take for the Mogul Empire to take over most of the continent?

Defending the Northwest Frontier

Every sultan had to guard against invasion across the northwestern frontier. Rulers in Afghanistan constantly were attacking settlements across the subcontinent's frontiers. Sultans also had to counter attacks from the **Golden Horde,** the fierce Mongol armies of Genghis Khan that swept out of Central Asia. Genghis Khan, founder of the Mongol Empire, led the first Mongol expedition into North India in 1221. From that moment until the day the Sultanate fell, North India experienced periodic attacks by the Golden Horde. Fortunately for the sultans, the Mongols did not choose to add the subcontinent to their huge empire. The Mongols came only for plunder. South Asia, Southeast Asia, and Japan were the only major regions that managed to escape Mongol domination.

Destruction in the subcontinent reached a peak in 1398 when Tamerlane swept into North India. Tamerlane, a descendant of Mongols who had settled in Central Asia, was cunning, ruthless, merciless, and without equal in the conduct of mounted warfare. Rarely was he bested in battle. When Tamerlane invaded North India, he ignored his own Muslim background of tolerance and plundered Hindu temples, as well as cities and towns on the Indo–Gangetic Plain, setting them on fire.

During the final century of the Delhi Sultanate's existence, the empire steadily distintegrated. Its domain was reduced as one ruler after another asserted independence. The rulers of the restored Hindu monarchies continued their relentless wars with each other. Continuous strife was also the normal pattern in the shrunken domain of the sultans in northwest India. Once again political disunity on the subcontinent of South Asia encouraged invaders.

The Portuguese Maritime Empire

In 1498, during the twilight of the Delhi Sultanate, Portuguese ships commanded by Vasco da Gama dropped anchor off Calicut in southwestern India. (See map, page 85.) The arrival of the vessels came after many years of effort by Portuguese explorers to find an eastern sea route to Asia. Before long, the Portuguese traders followed the new route to the East. For centuries Islamic peoples—Arabs, Egyptians, and Turks—had a **monopoly** on Eastern trade with the West. But by sailing around Africa, the Portuguese had broken the Islamic monopoly on the lucrative trade with the West. The luxury goods of South Asia, Southeast Asia, and East Asia could now reach Western Europe without going through the Arab-controlled lands in the Near East. In time, the Spanish, the Dutch, the English, and the French appeared in the ports of Asia seeking trade and empire.

The Portuguese, with their superior sea power, soon made it clear that they intended to establish a monopoly of their own. Between 1509 and 1511 they seized the island of Ormuz and the ports of Malacca and Goa. (See map, page 85.) Not long afterward Portuguese ships reached the East Indies and ports in mainland Southeast Asia and South China. In 1542 the Portuguese entered Japan. Goa became the headquarters of the far-flung Portuguese empire.

At first, the Portuguese were welcomed in South Asia by the local rulers. At the time of the Muslim invasions, travel to foreign lands had become an "impure" practice for high-caste Hindus. Therefore, trade between the subcontinent and other lands was conducted largely by the Arabs and the Chinese whose sailing vessels regularly visited important ports in South Asia. The Hindu rulers welcomed the Portuguese because their arrival meant an expansion of trade. Opposition to the Portuguese came from Muslim merchants who resided in the port cities of the subcontinent and whose ancestors had emigrated from the Near East centuries earlier. The Muslim merchants opposed the Portuguese because they were Christians and because they were commercial competitors. The Muslims, however, were no match for the ruthless and enterprising Portuguese, who gradually extended their commercial activities northward through the subcontinent. By the end of the 1500's, the trade with South Asia had made many Portuguese very wealthy.

Check Your Understanding

1. **a.** How did the period of Muslim domination of South Asia begin? **b.** What was the outcome of Mahmud's conquests in South Asia?
2. **a.** How was the Delhi Sultanate established?
   b. Why were the Delhi sultans insecure as rulers?
   c. How did sultanate rule in South India and North India differ?
3. **a.** Who were the Mongols? **b.** How did they contribute to the disintegration of the Delhi Sultanate?
4. **Thinking Critically:** How did the establishment of the Portuguese maritime empire in South Asia reduce the power of the Muslims on the subcontinent?

2. Golden Age of the Moguls

The English word *mogul* (MO-guhl) means an "important or powerful person." Derived from the Hindi word *mughal*, it was introduced into the English language during the 1600's by English visitors to India. These travelers were awestruck by the splendor of the Mogul Empire and impressed by the capability of its Muslim rulers. Although the rulers differed greatly from one another, five of the six Mogul rulers of the 1500's and 1600's left lasting marks on the subcontinent. Besides bringing another golden age to South Asia, they built an empire that included nearly all of the subcontinent.

The Mogul Empire

While the Portuguese were building a commercial empire in South India, a Turko–Mongol prince was destroying the political empire of the Delhi sultans. The prince was Babur (BAH-bur), a descendant of both Genghis Khan and Tamerlane. Babur felt that Tamerlane's conquests had given the family a valid claim to the subcontinent. Babur raided North India in 1517 and again in 1519. He began a full-scale invasion in 1524, but had to recall his troops because he needed them elsewhere. Late in 1525 Babur again invaded North India. In the battle at Panipat in spring 1526, the sultan was killed and Babur continued unopposed into Delhi. With the capture of Delhi, the Sultanate came to an end, and a new and more powerful empire began.

Babur died in 1530 only a few years after his momentous victories. His son and successor experienced severe military and political defeats and spent most of his adult life in exile in Persia. It was Babur's 14-year-old grandson Akbar who took over where Babur had left off. In 1556 at Panipat the forces of the newly crowned Akbar overcame an Afghan ruler who had occupied much of North India. During the rest of Akbar's reign, the forces of the Mogul Empire seldom lost a battle. When Akbar died in 1605, the Mogul Empire embraced the larger part of the Indo–Gangetic Plain.

Akbar the Great left a lasting imprint on the history of the subcontinent. He was a first-rate organizer, an exceptional administrator, and an empire builder of unusual political vision. More so than all other Muslim rulers before him, Akbar realized the necessity of enlisting the support of the Hindu population in the government of his realm. He included talented Hindus in the administration of his constantly growing empire. By providing Hindus with an opportunity for careers in government,

Akbar won their loyal cooperation. His reliance on the Hindus for support was a major reason for Akbar's success in controlling his many conquests.

Akbar ensured the loyalty of the Hindus by acting boldly to eliminate their grievances. Before Akbar's reign, Muslim rulers in South Asia, as well as throughout the Islamic empire, had customarily imposed special individual taxes on non-Muslims. These taxes were called head, or poll, taxes. Imposing them on non-Muslims only underscored the privileged position of the followers of Mohammed. Akbar abolished all special taxes on non-Muslims in 1579. This action was bitterly opposed by Akbar's Muslim advisers, but Akbar believed that Hindu support was worth a decline in popularity among Muslims. Nonetheless, Akbar's popularity continued until his death in 1605.

Akbar's Successors

The first two rulers to follow Akbar were Jahangir (jah-HAHN-JEER), who reigned from 1605 to 1628, and Shah Jahan (jah-HAHN), who reigned from 1628 to 1655. Both rulers imitated their illustrious predecessor in many ways. With each of them enjoying a long reign, Akbar's policies were followed on the subcontinent for another 50 years. In keeping with Akbar's example, the two rulers extended Mogul power without placing undue strain on Mogul resources. First, they were careful to consolidate their conquests and to provide an efficient administration for conquered lands. They also enlisted the support and cooperation of Hindu leaders by granting them favored positions in the Mogul court. Finally, the two emperors promoted friendly relations between Muslims and Hindus.

Jahangir and Shah Jahan were especially careful to preserve the Mogul system of alliances. Babur and Akbar had put together the Mogul Empire by winning allies among the princes of the subcontinent. In return for the privilege of managing their own affairs, these allies aided the Mogul dynasty in time of war. Both Jahangir and Shah Jahan grasped this hard fact of subcontinent politics and warfare and took care to respect the rights of their Hindu allies.

Mogul Emperors and the Arts

Because they possessed great wealth, the Mogul monarchs were able to surround themselves with every luxury that could be produced by the region's artisans or imported from other lands. Moreover all the emperors from Babur to Shah Jahan had a love of beauty and elegance. Each cherished the Persian in-

MOGUL ART. The Mogul school of art was especially famous for portraiture. The painting (left), which was used to illustrate a manuscript, shows four sultans, clockwise from top left: Humayan—the son of Babur, Babur, Akbar, and Jahangir. The small picture (bottom, left) reproduces a miniature portrait of Shah Jahan. Such miniatures, six or seven inches in height, were also used to illustrate books. A painting (below) entitled "Jahangir in the Garden" is one of the finest examples of the art of the Mogul Empire's golden age. What is meant by the term *golden age?*

fluences of their ancestral homeland. Most emperors retained Persian artists and architects at their courts. In addition, the Mogul rulers supported Hindu artists and architects. Hindu and Persian elements eventually blended into a new Indo–Persian, or Mogul, tradition. Generously supported by the Mogul emperors, this Indo–Persian tradition ushered in a new golden age for the subcontinent.

The finest Mogul art was produced during the reign of Jahangir. Akbar had introduced into the subcontinent the techniques and themes of Persian painting, and these had been combined with traditional Hindu styles. The new Mogul school of art became particularly renowned for its portraits, pictures of animals, and use of color. Unlike Hindu art, which was almost completely religious in nature, Mogul art was secular, or non-religious. The artists of the Mogul school portrayed the material aspects of Mogul court life—the ceremonies and functions of political life, as well as the pomp and the pageantry that went with it.

Of more lasting interest than Mogul art are products of its architecture. The Mogul emperors were especially interested in the construction of beautiful buildings. Neatly and painstakingly symmetrical, the structures were usually topped by a graceful dome. Slender towers rose at each corner. Walls were cut with beautiful ornamental tracery, or openwork, and dome-shaped gateways broke the long expanses of outside walls. Shimmering white marble and red sandstone were lavishly used in the construction of the buildings. Hundreds of magnificent tombs, mosques, palaces, and forts were erected by the great Mogul emperors.

The most famous period of Mogul architecture occurred during the reign of Shah Jahan. Comparatively uninterested in painting, Shah Jahan became the greatest of the Mogul builders. The Taj Mahal, designed as a tomb for his beloved wife, is one of the most famous buildings in the world.

Use of the Urdu Language

The appreciation of the Mogul emperors for Persian culture extended to the field of language. The Mogul emperors encouraged the adoption of Persian for both writing and speaking. Gradually Persian was fused with the Hindi tongue of North India, resulting in the creation of a new language called Urdu (OOR-doo). The grammar and basic vocabulary of Urdu are drawn from Hindi, but the language has been enriched by words and expressions that are of Persian origin. Urdu has been spoken by the

The Taj Mahal, perhaps the most famous structure in all of present-day India, is built of white marble on a red sandstone base and is surrounded by beautiful gardens. Why did Shah Jahan build the Taj Mahal?

educated classes of North India for several centuries and has been embodied in a first-class literature. Today Urdu is the official language of present-day Pakistan.

The New Policies of Aurangzeb

The last of the mighty Mogul emperors was Aurangzeb (AWR-ung-zeb), who ruled from 1658 to 1707. While Aurangzeb chose not to follow many of the policies of his predecessors, he shared their ambition to enlarge the Mogul Empire. Called the World Shaker, Aurangzeb was determined to bring the entire subcontinent under his dominance. To attain his goal, he spent the last half of his reign in the Deccan, leading military operations. By 1690 he was the ruler, in name at least, of all of the subcontinent except the extreme south.

Unfortunately Aurangzeb planted the seeds of his empire's downfall at the same time he was extending its dominance. One of Aurangzeb's greatest mistakes was enforcement of Islamic practices and laws. He reintroduced the discriminatory poll tax on non-Muslims. He curbed Hindu customs and practices that conflicted with Islamic law. He also ended many privileges that Hindu nobles had enjoyed under earlier Mogul rulers. As a strict Muslim who scorned luxury, Aurangzeb was very modest in his habits and outlook. Condemning cultural pursuits, he dismissed artists and architects from the royal court. Aurangzeb's strictness created ill will among Hundus, and helped to end the golden age of Mogul culture.

Another mistake made by Aurangzeb was quarreling with traditional allies of the Mogul Empire. He aroused the unending hatred of the powerful Sikhs (SEEKS) by executing their **guru** when that leader refused to accept the Islamic faith. Aurangzeb also became involved in wars with the Rajputs (RAHJ-pootz), the most important allies of the Mogul dynasty. Still another blunder was attempting to overcome the Marathas (muh-RAH-tuhz), a powerful Hindu people of the Deccan. Although most of Aurangzeb's campaigns in the Deccan were directed against the Marathas, he never conquered them.

The Disintegration of the Mogul Empire

Aurangzeb had built a huge empire through his military conquests, but it began to fall apart while he was still alive. Because of his campaigns in the Deccan, Aurangzeb was away from his capital from 1681 until his death in 1707. His long absence from Delhi caused the Mogul administative machinery to break down and become corrupt and inefficient. Many states became virtually independent. Certain rulers, especially among the Sikhs and Marathas, became more powerful than the emperor. But even if Aurangzeb had been served by an honest and capable government, he could not have stopped the empire's decline. Aurangzeb had drained the treasury to finance his costly wars and had lost the support of most of his allies.

The Mogul Empire continued after Aurangzeb's death, with his descendants occupying the throne at Delhi until 1857. But the Mogul domain shrank until it included only the region around the capital city. Finally, the empire disappeared.

Check Your Understanding

1. How did the Delhi Sultanate end?
2. **a.** How did Akbar bring a solid foundation to the Mogul Empire? **b.** How did Akbar win Hindu support?
3. **a.** Why is the period of the Mogul Empire up to the end of Shah Jahan's reign considered a golden age of culture? **b.** How did Jahangir promote culture? **c.** How did Shah Jahan promote culture?
4. How did the Mogul Empire influence the development of Urdu?
5. **Thinking Critically:** How did Aurangzeb contribute to the decline of the Mogul Empire?

3. Resistance to Mogul Rule

The Moguls never were masters of all the subcontinent. Even at the height of Mogul power many monarchies on the subcontinent defied every Mogul effort to control them. As the Mogul Empire began to fall apart, independence movements became increasingly evident. You will read in Chapter 5 how Europeans filled the power vacuum that was left by the decline of the Mogul Empire. However, as the Europeans began to gain power, semi-independent Muslim monarchies and Rajput, Sikh, and Maratha rulers—not the Mogul emperors—blocked European plans for expansion.

The Rajputs

If any one people can be given credit for preventing complete domination of the subcontinent by the Moguls, that people would be the Rajputs. Their homeland, which by the late 1700's consisted of 36 monarchies, was Rajputana. (See map, page 120.) Claiming descent from the Kshatriya of Aryan times, the Rajputs were proud of their fighting ability. One of their proverbs was "A wall may give way: a Rajput stands fast." Invaders of the subcontinent who had to force their way through Rajputana found its defenders invincible. Not even Akbar, the mightiest of the Mogul emperors, was able to conquer the Rajputs. Instead the great Akbar gained the loyalty of the Rajputs by granting them special privileges. Eventually the Rajputs became the center of his sytem of alliances.

To a great degree, the Rajputs were responsible for preserving Hinduism in North India. In the face of Muslim onslaughts, they preserved their Aryan traditions and culture, and their Brahmins tightened caste restrictions to exclude Muslims. By the time Aurangzeb came to power, two communities—Hindu and Muslim—were well established in North India, and neither community had much use for the other. Aurangzeb's attempts to impose Muslim law on the Rajputs transformed these allies of the Mogul Empire into dangerous enemies.

The Sikhs

The Sikhs were another people of North India that caused trouble for the Moguls. Unlike the Rajputs, the Sikhs had no heritage to unite them. They emerged as a people only at the beginning of the Mogul era. While Babur was destroying the Delhi Sultanate, a new religion, **Sikhism,** was rising in the region. The Sikhs were those who adopted this faith.

The founder of Sikhism was Nanak (1469–1539) who was born a Hindu. As he grew older, however, Nanak began to search for a religion that would better meet his spiritual needs. He turned to Islam and studied the teachings of Mohammed. Unable to find spiritual satisfaction in either Hinduism or Islam, Nanak devised a faith that would rise above the differences in the two religions. From his studies of Islam he acquired an unshakeable faith in the concept of one God, a distaste for the caste system, and a dislike for religious images. From the Hinduism of his birth Nanak borrowed the idea of toleration for widely differing points of view. At the center of the faith devised by Nanak was the worship of the principle of "Truth." Eventually the doctrines of Sikhism were set forth in a holy book known as the *Adi Granth*. Recitation of and reflection on the verses of this book are still the core of Sikhism.

The Sikhs aroused the antagonism of both Hindus and Muslims because they adopted beliefs and customs unlike any in either Hinduism or Islam. For example, the Sikhs condemned both Hinduism and Islam for a preoccupation with observances and ceremonies. Nanak provided the basis for the condemnation in the *Adi Granth:*

> Religion consisteth not in mere words;
> He who looketh on all men as equal is religious.
> Religion consisteth not in wandering to tombs or places of cremation, or sitting in attitudes of contemplation.
> Religion consisteth not in wandering in foreign countries, or in bathing at places of pilgrimage.
> Abide pure amidst the impurities of the world;
> Thus shalt thou find the way to religion.
>
> [Quoted in: R. C. Majumdar, et al. *An Advanced History of India.*]

The beliefs and customs adopted by the Sikhs set them apart from other people on the subcontinent. To begin with, all Sikhs adopted the common name of *Singh,* meaning "lion." Men who practiced Sikhism did not cut their hair or shave their faces. Instead they wore turbans and long beards. Other distinguishing marks of a male Sikh were the wearing of an iron bracelet on the wrist and a dagger at the belt. The Sikhs became a powerful, militant, and industrious group, and they have played an important role in South Asian life. By the end of the 1600's, they had withdrawn into a section of the Indus River Valley where they established their own self-sufficient villages. These Sikh communities in the Punjab formed the last region to fall under British rule. (See page 119.)

Inside the Golden Temple at Amritsar, the most sacred shrine of the Sikhs, a preacher addresses believers. How does the speaker exemplify the distinguishing marks of a male Sikh?

The Marathas

A third people who actively resisted the Moguls were the Marathas. Living in the region of the Western Ghats, the Marathas were looked down on by their fellow Hindus for many centuries. In the Hindu caste system they were Shudras, members of the lowest caste. Hard-working peasants, they lived in comparative peace within the Mogul Empire until Aurangzeb came to the throne. Then the Marathas were persecuted by Muslim zealots. The persecution caused the Hindu people to think in terms of establishing a nation of their own. From that time on, the Marathas were a constant source of harassment and irritation for the Mogul emperors.

The person most responsible for arousing the nationalism of the Marathas was Shivaji (SHIH-VUH-jee), who lived from 1627 to 1680. A descendant of Maratha monarchs and soldiers, he was inspired by his mother to free his people from the tyranny of the Moguls. Before Shivaji was 20 years old, he began the career that made him the most dangerous of the Mogul Empire's foes. Called the "Mountain Rat of the Deccan" by Aurangzeb, Shivaji succeeded in carving an empire out of Muslim lands. His cavalry swept across the central part of the subcontinent, even subduing the Rajputs and threatening for a time the Mogul capital at Delhi. Today the Marathas still tell stories of Shivaji's boldness in war, his humane treatment of prisoners, his kindness to women and children, and his tolerance in matters of religion.

After Shivaji's death, his empire fell apart. A **confederacy** of Maratha chieftains remained, however, and these rulers dominated much of the subcontinent until the early 1800's. Unfortunately for the Marathas, their confederacy was a loosely knit political alliance. The rulers had an unwillingness to cooperate with one another. They also showed an inability to govern effectively, a practice that eventually led to their downfall. Taking advantage of the confederacy's weaknesses, the British finally subdued the Marathas. (See page 121.)

Important Muslim States

A number of Muslim-controlled states survived the fall of the Mogul Empire and made their influence felt on the subcontinent. The greatest of these Muslim states, in terms of size and wealth, was Hyderabad (HY-duh-ruh-BAHD), which began as a Mogul province in the Deccan. In 1724 an officer of the imperial government forced the Mogul emperor to appoint him the first Nizam, or ruler, of Hyderabad. Known as Asaf Jah, this officer exercised strong leadership and made Hyderabad a virtually independent part of the empire. He prevented the complete decline of Islam in the south by checking the tide of Maratha power. Although Hyderabad's population was predominantly Hindu, the Muslim Nizams ruled this important monarchy until the government of present-day India assumed control of it in 1948.

In South India, probably the most important post-Mogul monarchy was Mysore (MY-sohr). Founded on the ruins of the empire of Vijayanagar, Mysore is famous as the birthplace of Chandragupta I, founder of the Maurya dynasty. Like Hyderabad, Mysore during the Mogul age was ruled by Muslims, although most of the people were Hindus. During the decline of the Mogul Empire, Hyder Ali and his successor, Tipu Sahib (TEE-poo SAH-heeb), made the monarchy of Mysore the chief power in South India. These two Mysore sultans resisted the efforts of British leaders to extend British influence in the region. The death of Tipu in a battle with the British effectively ended Muslim influence in Mysore. After Tipu's death, the British were in control of Mysore, although officially a Hindu ruler occupied the throne.

Check Your Understanding

1. **a.** How did the Rajputs prevent the Mogul Empire's complete domination of the subcontinent? **b.** How did the Rajputs help to preserve Hinduism in North India?
2. **a.** How did Sikhism develop? **b.** How did the Sikhs cause trouble for the Mogul Emperors? **c.** How did the customs of the Sikhs set them apart from other people on the subcontinent?
3. What caused the Marathas to think of independence from the Mogul Empire?
4. What roles did Hyderabad and Mysore play in the political life of the subcontinent?
5. *Thinking Critically:* Why could no one state on the subcontinent become powerful enough to take the place of the disintegrating Mogul Empire?

4. Islam's Far-Reaching Influence

The Islamic civilization had a far-reaching influence in South Asia. The beliefs, manners, and customs of Islam were transplanted to the subcontinent over the course of several centuries. As in Africa, Europe, and other parts of Asia, the transmitters of the Islamic way of life were soldiers and merchants. They won converts by persuasion or by the sword, and the converts in turn sought to recruit new followers. Before the close of the Delhi Sultanate, Islam had become the subcontinent's second major religion. By the end of the Mogul Empire, Islam was a permanent and important institution on the subcontinent.

Islam's Resistance to Assimilation

Until the soldiers of Mohammed the Prophet arrived in the subcontinent, most newcomers—whether invaders or immigrants—brought with them ways of life that were less advanced than the way of life on the subcontinent. Most newcomers could add little or nothing to South Asia's culture. Often as not, the newcomers eventually abondoned their own ways and faith and became "Hinduized" in a process called assimilation. Such was not true of the followers of Islam. By A.D. 1000 when Muslims began to penetrate the subcontinent in earnest, Islam had a culture that was equally as advanced as the Hindu culture, a result of absorption and **cultural borrowing** from the many peoples they had conquered. Because Islam forbade **compromise** of any sort with other faiths, the Muslims who entered the subcontinent rejected Hinduism and kept themselves apart from its culture.

The Islamic resistance to assimilation resulted in a permanent division of the subcontinent along religious lines. The northwestern part of the subcontinent, which had borne the brunt of every Muslim attack, became a center of Islamic power. Followers of the Prophet came to this area as soldiers only to remain as permanent settlers. Ultimately their descendants outnumbered the Hindus. Islam also became the religion of most people in the northeastern part of the subcontinent. Islam's insistence that all followers of Mohammed were equal in the sight of Allah attracted thousands of Untouchables and low-caste Hindus. The northeastern part of the subcontinent had an especially high number of converts. In North India many Buddhists became Muslims after Islamic warriors had all but destroyed Buddhism as a major force on the subcontinent.

The concentration of Muslims in certain regions was of great importance in 1947 when the British gave the subcontinent its independence. Two nations, not one, were created by a partition of the subcontinent along religious lines. The northwestern part of the subcontinent became West Pakistan. The northeastern part—1,000 miles away—became East Pakistan. The rest of the subcontinent became the present-day Republic of India. Later, in 1971, East Pakistan declared itself a separate nation, calling itself Bangladesh.

Muslim Oppression of Hindus

The Hindus of the subcontinent were accustomed to absorbing newcomers to their land and were not prepared to cope with the Muslim zealots who rejected them. For their part, the Muslims set out to establish their faith by force. The wars they waged against the Hindus were religious crusades, called **jihads.** From the viewpoint of the Muslims, Hindus were **infidels**—nonbelievers in the "true" faith of Islam. Infidels in other parts of the world had accepted Islam rather than be killed, but the Hindus refused to "submit to the will of Allah."

The Muslim wars against the Hindus were extraordinarily bitter and furious. The Muslims showed no mercy. They believed that by killing the infidel Hindus they could gain favor with Allah. They also believed that death in battle while fighting for Islam would give them a special place in Paradise. This belief

Other Religions in South Asia

Several other religions that developed outside the region were represented in South Asia by the time the Mogul Empire came to an end. These were Christianity, Judaism and Zoroastrianism (zor-oh-AS-tree-ahn-ih-zum)—a major religion of ancient Persia. Each of these religions was founded on the worship of one god. Zoroastrianism became established in the subcontinent during the 1200's. At that time, groups of Persians came to the subcontinent to escape the Mongols. The newcomers joined smaller communities of Persians who had fled their country in earlier centuries to escape persecution at the hands of Arab Muslims. Known as Parsis, the Hindu word for Persians, most of the Zoroastrians settled in Bombay, where they have distinguished themselves as business people and community leaders.

Zoroastrianism has changed over the centuries. Its founder, Zoroaster, lived in Persia in the 500's or 400's B.C. He rejected the polytheism of his contemporaries and worshiped one god. Zoroaster believed that people had a choice between doing good and doing evil. He taught that the forces of good would triumph in the end and that good people would be rewarded while evil people would be punished. In time Zoroastrianism's emphasis upon achieving moral purity gave way to a focus on ceremony.

Communities of Christians have existed in the subcontinent for nearly 2,000 years. When the Portuguese settled on the subcontinent in the 1500's, the missionaries who accompanied them discovered that Christianity had preceded them. Saint Thomas, one of the original Twelve Apostles chosen by Jesus as his first disciples, is credited with introducing Christianity into the subcontinent soon after Jesus's death. Today about 3 percent of India's population are Christians.

Judaism has been practiced on the subcontinent since the first Jews came to South Asia over 1,900 years ago. The first community of Jews settled in Cochin on the Malabar coast. (See map, page 85.) Jewish communities in present-day India are small. In 1961 there were about 18,500 Jews. Since 1961, the number has decreased substantially because of emigration, mostly to Israel.

MAJOR RELIGIONS OF SOUTH ASIA

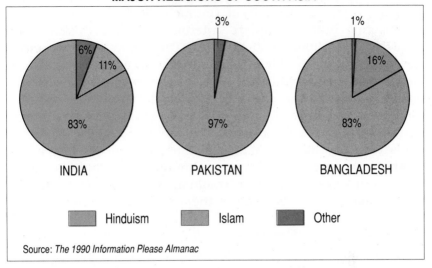

Hinduism	Islam	Other

Source: *The 1990 Information Please Almanac*

MAJOR RELIGIONS. The two major religions of South Asia are Hinduism and Islam. In which country is Hinduism predominant? Where is Islam the predominant religion?

made Muslims fearless in battle. Muslims tore down Hindu holy places and smashed the statues and carvings representing Hindu deities. The religious zeal of Islam's followers laid the groundwork for centuries of fighting, bitterness, and hatred between Hindus and Muslims.

The Clash of Cultures

Even after many centuries of living alongside one another, Hindus and Muslims never achieved mutual understanding. The Hindu way of life was determined by the traditions of the caste system. The guidelines for Muslims were set forth in the Koran, the holy book of Islam. The two culture systems were often in conflict. One serious difference had to do with dietary laws. The Hindu tradition encouraged vegetarianism and the veneration of cows. The Koran allowed Muslims to eat any kind of meat except pork. Every time a Muslim butchered a cow, Hindus were provoked to fury. Yet the Muslims felt that the Hindu ban on the butchering of cows deprived them of food. Over the centuries many riots and much bloodshed have stemmed from Muslim and Hindu differences over dietary restrictions.

Islam and Hinduism also differed in their beliefs about life. Muslims believed in equality in the sight of God. In the eyes of early Muslims the caste system, with its emphasis on arbitrary and unequal class distinctions, was an affront to Allah.

Because Muslims were outside the Hindu caste system, Hindus assigned them to the rank of Untouchables.

Differing attitudes toward intermarriage was another sore point between Hindus and Muslims. The Hindu father arranged the marriages of his children, and almost always found marriage partners for them within his caste. He never approved a child's marriage to a person outside the Hindu faith. Muslim men, on the other hand, were often free to choose their own wives. It was fairly common for warriors of the Prophet who settled conquered lands to marry infidels. Many Muslims continued this practice on the subcontinent by marrying Hindus. Most Hindus took offense at this violation of their tradition. Yet Muslims also looked with dismay on the marriage of their daughters to Hindus.

Segregation of Wives

In one custom, Hindus and Muslims were in agreement. Wives, whether Hindu or Muslim, were kept isolated from the outside world. According to Hindu tradition, a wife's place was in the home. Her job was to look after the household and tend to the children. The wife was free to leave the house only for such necessary chores as drawing water at the well or washing laundry at a nearby stream. At such times, the wife chatted with other wives from neighboring households. But the wife always avoided conversation with men.

Muslim wives were also expected to confine their activities to home and family. The Muslim religion imposed on them even stricter regulations than were binding on Hindu women. Married Muslim women were obliged to observe **purdah** and to veil themselves in the presence of all but their closest relatives. Whenever a Muslim woman left her home, she wore a veil called a **burqa** that extended from the crown of her head to the ground.

Although purdah is still upheld by Muslims in India, Pakistan, and Bangladesh, it is gradually dying. Many modern Muslim women have given up the practice of purdah. In South Asia, however, women draped in burqas are still a common sight. The custom is a constant reminder of the differences in the status of women that exist between Western cultures, most of which are based on Christianity, and non-Christian cultures of the Middle East and Asia. Many non-Christian cultures limit women's years of education, restrict them to homemaking and childrearing, and fail to treat women as the equals of men in the workplace. Because of the restrictions imposed by their cultural traditions and upbringing, few Muslim women have attained the status enjoyed by Western women.

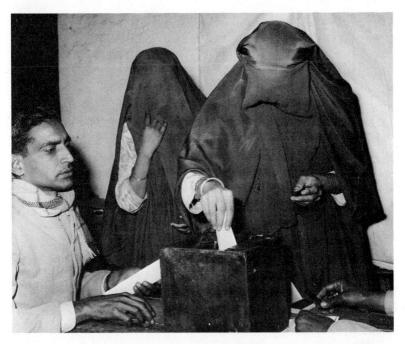

Muslim women in burqas cast their ballots in an election in present-day India. Although still bound by tradition to wear the head-to-toe veil, many women have learned about civic responsibilities and are exercising their right to vote under the Indian constitution.

Islam's Spread to Southeast Asia

Not long after the Delhi Sultanate was founded in the subcontinent, Islam gained a foothold in the East Indian island of Sumatra, now a part of Indonesia. No one knows whether the Muslims who carried the message of Islam were Arabs or people from the subcontinent. Probably they were merchants from ports in South India. From Sumatra, Islam was carried to the Malay Peninsula and to other islands of the East Indies. Eventually Islam became the faith of most people on the peninsula and in the East Indies.

The arrival of the Spanish in the region finally halted the expansion of Islam in Southeast Asia. Muslim converts had brought Islam into the Sulu Archipelago and the southern Philippine Islands during the 1400's. When the Spanish arrived in the 1500's, Islam was already established. The Spanish, however, were successful in converting most of the inhabitants of the central and northern islands to Christianity. But even today the Moros of the Sulu Archipelago and of Mindanao, the southernmost of the Philippine Islands, count themselves followers of Mohammed.

103

Check Your Understanding

1. Why did the Muslims use force in establishing their faith on the subcontinent?
2. **a.** On what points did Hindu and Muslim cultures clash? **b.** On what point were they in agreement?
3. How did Islam spread to Southeast Asia?
4. *Thinking Critically:* Why were the Muslims able to resist assimilation into the Hindu culture? What was the result of the Muslims' resistance to cultural assimilation for the subcontinent?

CHAPTER REVIEW

■ Chapter Summary

Section 1. Not long after the Gupta Empire disintegrated, Muslims invaded the subcontinent. After about A.D. 1000, Islam became a major influence in South Asia, competing with the civilization of the Hindus. Mahmud of Ghazni and Muhammad of Ghor, the earliest of the well-known Muslim invaders, came principally for plunder. The successors of Muhammad of Ghor, however, built the Delhi Sultanate, which dominated most of the northern and central parts of the subcontinent. But other invaders from the north continued to breach the subcontinent's frontiers, making it difficult for the Delhi sultans to maintain stability in the empire. The most troublesome attackers were the Mongols under Genghis Khan, Tamerlane, and Babur. The Portuguese also "invaded" by sea, establishing a trading empire that was welcomed by the sultans.

Section 2. Under Babur's grandson Akbar the Great, the foundations of the mighty Mogul Empire were firmly established in India. The Mogul rulers were held in high esteem by contemporary peoples of Asia and Europe. The Moguls ruled the largest and most powerful empire the subcontinent had ever known. The Mogul rulers were patrons of the arts, and their support ushered in a golden age of culture for the subcontinent. The finest Mogul art was produced during the reign of Jahangir, while the most famous period of Mogul architecture came during the rule of Shah Jahan. The ambitious Aurangzeb, however, placed too great a strain on the empire, and even before his death, the Mogul Empire had entered into decline.

Section 3. During the final years of the Mogul Empire, various Hindu groups began to resist Mogul power. The most important of these groups were the Rajputs and the Marathas. The Rajputs were responsible for preserving Hinduism in the northwestern part of the subcontinent. The Mogul attempts to impose Muslim law on the Rajputs transformed them into dangerous enemies. The Marathas resisted Muslim control in the Deccan. A third force that resisted the Mogul's domination was Sikhism, a faith that took on a militant stance and became a powerful force in the Punjab. After the Mogul emperors lost their power, the Muslim states of Hyderabad and Mysore preserved Muslim power on the subcontinent.

Section 4. The coming of Islam stimulated many changes. The teachings of Mohammed the Prophet found especially fertile ground in the northwest and the northeast, and became the second major religion of South Asia. In the 1300's and 1400's, zealots used the subcontinent as a base for extending Islam into Southeast Asia. Numerous converts were won in the Malay Peninsula, the East Indies, and the southern section of the Philippine Islands.

■ Vocabulary Review

Define: Islam, viceroy, Golden Horde, monopoly, guru, Sikhism, confederacy, cultural borrowing, compromise, jihad, infidel, purdah, burqa

■ Places to Locate

Locate: Near East, Arabian Peninsula, Sind, Ghazni, Vijayanagar, Calicut, Goa, Panipat, Sumatra, Malay Peninsula, Philippine Islands

■ People to Know

Identify: Mahmud of Ghazni, Muhammad of Ghor, Aybek, Mohammed the Prophet, Genghis Khan, Tamerlane, Vasco da Gama, Babur, Akbar, Jahangir, Shah Jahan, Aurangzeb, Rajputs, Marathas, Sikhs, Nanak, Shivaji, Zoroaster

■ Thinking Critically

1. Why did the Delhi Sultanate find it difficult to maintain a stable empire on the subcontinent?
2. How did Akbar provide a firm foundation for the Mogul Empire? How did Jahangir and Shah Jahan build on this foundation? Why did the empire decline under Aurangzeb?
3. Why were the Moguls never able to master the whole subcontinent?
4. How did the customs and social systems of Hinduism and Islam clash? What effect has the clash of cultures had on present-day life on the subcontinent?

■ Extending and Applying Your Knowledge

1. Prepare a chart of the people who had a major influence on the political or cultural life of South Asia from 712, the date of the Arab conquest of Sind, to 1707. List names in one column, life span in a second column, the date or dates each affected the subcontinent in a third column, and in the fourth and last column, lasting influence(s) (either good or bad) on South Asia. Use the chart in giving a report to the class on people who were important in South Asian history.
2. Give an oral or written report on a facet of South Asian art or architecture and the influences that shaped it. For example, find out more about the Taj Mahal or research major characteristics of painting during the Mogul golden age, using one or more reference books or books on art and architecture.

5

The Rise of the British Raj

"The British Empire," it has been said, "was created in a fit of absentmindedness." Insofar as the subcontinent—the part that became known as the British Indian Empire—is concerned, this statement is true. The British East India Company laid the foundation for the greatest of all empires on the subcontinent. Yet its original interest in South Asia was strictly commercial. Once its commercial interests were threatened, however, the East India Company realized that it could not stand apart from the subcontinent's politics. The company took steps to assure its primacy in the region.

The very successes of the East India Company caused the British Parliament to curb the powers of this great commercial corporation. Over a period of many years, the **British raj,** or rule, in the subcontinent was gradually shifted from the British East India Company to the British Parliament. The final step in the shift came after a bloody rebellion that occurred in 1857–1858. Then the East India Company was abolished and the British Crown became sovereign on the subcontinent. Twenty years later the subcontinent called India was annexed to the British Empire.

During the closing years of the 1800's, the British undertook to develop their great Indian empire. Through various reforms and developmental programs, the British transformed the subcontinent of India into the "Jewel of the British Empire." Nonetheless the peoples of the subcontinent, like any other people denied their political freedom, resented the presence of a dominant foreign power on their soil.

107

1. The British East India Company

On December 31, 1600, Queen Elizabeth I of England granted a charter to the East India Company. The charter gave the company a monopoly on English trade with the East. In 1613 the Mogul emperor Jahangir gave the East India Company his official approval for a trading post at Surat, a town just south of the Vindhya Hills. From these small beginnings the East India Company built a commercial empire that eventually controlled a large part of the Indian subcontinent. Exercising powers normally reserved for a national government, the company provided a firm footing in the region that eventually became the British Indian Empire.

Competition for Trade

While Jahangir, Shah Jahan, and Aurangzeb were extending the Mogul Empire, merchants from European countries were beginning to compete for trade rights in the subcontinent. In the late 1500's, Indian commerce was almost exclusively in the hands of the Portuguese. But in the 1600's the Dutch, English, and French steadily chipped away at the Portuguese commercial monopoly—not only in the Indian subcontinent, but in many other parts of Asia. Within a generation or two, Portuguese commercial interests were surpassed by these newcomers.

The Dutch, English, and French were better organized than the Portuguese to carry on trade in Asia. As a royal monopoly, the Portuguese enterprise suffered from excessive governmental interference, lack of initiative, and the inefficiencies of a large-scale operation. The competitors of the Portuguese were private trading companies whose activities were carefully watched by investors in the home countries. These businesspeople were interested in profits, not in rewarding political favorites and building an empire.

By 1700 the British and the French East India companies had made their respective nations the leading European powers on the subcontinent. The Dutch, who still maintained ports on the subcontinent, were concentrating on trade with the East Indies. The British had established centers of trade and power at Bombay in the west, Madras in the south, and Calcutta in the northeast. (See map, page 120.) The French East India Company had built bases near the British settlements at Madras and Calcutta. Since British and French merchants were in direct competition with each other, a conflict between these two trading companies seemed unavoidable.

Rivals in business, the British and French companies soon became opponents in war. South India had never been completely subdued by the Mogul emperors, and rulers of states in this region were striving constantly for supremacy. Some of them soon saw the Europeans as potential allies in this struggle. For many years the trading companies tried to avoid direct involvement in subcontinental rivalries. The companies much preferred to concentrate on their business interests. In time, however, company officials came to realize that the policy of nonintervention in political matters could not be maintained. Native rulers often requested military help from Europeans in return for commercial privileges. Moreover, trading posts were sometimes attacked in the wars between native states. Consequently French and British officials in subcontinental India obtained from their directors the right to intervene in local affairs as circumstances dictated.

Over a period of years, the British trading company received especially broad powers to protect its interests. By the late 1600's the company had the right to acquire territory, negotiate treaties, and engage in war. Despite greater restrictions, the French company, too, became a powerful force. It is not surprising, therefore, that the British and the French East India companies became involved in political and military affairs on the subcontinent and began to supply troops to rulers of native states.

The Larger British-French Rivalry

The rivalry between British and French trading companies in subcontinental India was part of a larger clash of interests. During the 1700's the parent countries were also confronting each other in Europe and in the Americas. To gain military or economic advantage, the British and French governments were willing to encourage fighting in subcontinental India. This played into the hands of ambitious leaders of the French and British trading companies who were intent on founding empires. Meanwhile native rulers on the subcontinent were eagerly seeking help from one or the other of the companies to further their own expansionist schemes. One writer has summarized the importance rulers on the subcontinent attached to foreign aid:

> In the Indian politics of the time all was . . . power politics, and personal ambition; there was no emotional bar, such as patriotism might have provided, against invoking the help of the foreigner. . . . the technical advantages enjoyed by the European would bring victory to whichever side they were given. In the absence of conviction, of national and religious feeling, politics was a matter for lords and their followers, the longest-ranged guns, the quickest-firing musket, the steadiest soldiers would decide the issue. The [European] makeweight had become the balance, the client could become the master.   [Vincent A. Smith, *The Oxford History of India.*]

The war of Austrian Succession (1740-1748), which found France and Great Britain (formerly England) on opposite sides in Europe, led to the clash of British and French forces on the subcontinent. The opening move in the clash was the capture by the British navy of French ships off the coast of Madras. It was not long, however, before the French came back to win many military and diplomatic victories.

Joseph Dupleix (dyoo-PLAYKS), governor of the French trading post at Pondicherry, deserves credit for the French successes. A brilliant man, Dupleix had a sixth sense in politics and diplomacy. No British person on the subcontinent could match him in steering a course through the complexities of subcontinental intrigue or in using local rulers to further his country's ends. By aiding native rulers in dynastic struggles he received major concessions, including control of all lands south of the Krishna River.

With Dupleix as leader, the French won many battles against the British and their allies on the subcontinent. Unfortunately

110

This engraving of eighteenth-century Bombay shows the private army of the British East India Company at drill. Company officials lived in luxury, leaving the hard work to laborers from the subcontinent.

for the French, however, there was only one Dupleix. When incompetent French generals were defeated, Dupleix was blamed for the generals' shortcomings and called back to France. Dupleix's successor signed a treaty with the British that gave up everything Dupleix had gained.

Robert Clive

During the fighting in South India, Robert Clive, a young British employee of the East India Company, left the life of an office clerk to become a military officer in the company's army. He served with distinction, directing many British victories over the French. After his victories in the south, Clive was called to the north, for the company's position in Bengal was being threatened. The Muslim ruler of Bengal and its dependencies died in 1756, and his successor set out to re-establish control over European-held territories in his realm. The new ruler's first target was the British post at Calcutta. The new ruler won a quick victory, which was made famous by the "Black Hole of Calcutta" incident. Captured British soldiers were imprisoned on a hot June night in a small room without food or water. By the next morning many of the prisoners, by British accounts as many as two thirds, had died. For years thereafter, British imperialists described the room where the prisoners died as a "black hole."

Ships from four different countries are pictured in Calicut's harbor, one of the first Indian ports visited by European traders.

In exploiting the incident, the British pointed to the soldiers' imprisonment and death as an example of uncivilized Indian behavior. The British descriptions of what happened, however, are thought to be greatly exaggerated.

Calcutta was recaptured by Clive in January 1757. By this time news of the Seven Years' War (1756–1763) between Great Britain and France had reached the subcontinent. Despite the protests of Bengal's ruler, Clive attacked and captured the most important French post in Bengal. A few months later Clive met and defeated the forces of the native ruler at the Battle of Plassey. Clive's victory brought Bengal under company control. Later Bengal became the base from which the British launched their drive for an empire on the Indian subcontinent.

Methods of Tax Collection

Before the coming of the East India Company to the subcontinent, the rulers of the region's states gained revenue by taxing land and crops. The East India Company in its administration of the territories it controlled followed the lead of these rulers. In Bengal the company adopted the procedures of the Mogul Empire. Akbar had divided his empire into 12 provinces, a number that had risen to 21 by the time of Aurangzeb. Each province had a **diwan.** In many parts of the empire the diwan gave the responsibility for tax collecting to the landowners of large estates in the villages. These tax-collecting landowners were called **zamindars.** No zamindar, regardless of how little he collected, could fail to forward the required amount to the diwan.

SIDELIGHT TO HISTORY

Robert Clive, Architect of Empire

Robert Clive (1725–1774) is remembered as the person who made the first effective moves that led to the creation of Britain's Indian Empire. At the age of 19, Clive left his home in England, sailed halfway round the world, landed in India, and became a clerk for the East India Company. A year later, Clive asked for and received a transfer to the company's army. The clerk-turned-soldier had found an occupation that was well suited to his restless and adventuresome nature. Within a short time, he demonstrated his military genius and was soon winning important battles in South India and Bengal. These victories laid the foundations of the British Empire in India.

After his military triumph at Plassey in 1757, Clive became the first governor of Bengal. Under Clive's able direction, Bengal became the most profitable of the British trading areas. By the time he returned to Great Britain in 1760, Clive's achievements on the subcontinent had become legendary. For his great services he received from the British monarch an Irish peerage and the title of Baron Clive of Plassey. Clive returned to the subcontinent, where he was appointed governor of Bengal a second time, serving from 1765 to 1767. Clive administered Bengal efficiently and at first reduced corruption. When Clive took on revenue collection in the territories under the company's control, Clive sowed the seeds that later led to the company's loss of its political power and its eventual end.

East India Company officials had many opportunities to enrich themselves illegally, and not all officials could resist the temptation. As a result of a number of problems, including the large size of the territory to be controlled, the East India Company's administration became inefficient and corrupt. Returning to Great Britain after the end of his second governorship, Clive met with personal trouble. Charges of misconduct were brought against him by officials in Parliament. After a long investigation Clive was acquitted in 1773 of all charges of personal wrongdoing. But the stress of the long trial took a toll on his physical and mental health. Depressed by the ordeal, Clive took his own life in 1774.

As hereditary tax collectors, the zamindars could collect taxes only in the lands they owned. It was their job to collect enough taxes to forward the required amount to the diwan and to compensate themselves for their work. Usually the zamindars collected a tax from each peasant that was about 10 percent higher than the amount due. But, to enrich themselves, some zamindars taxed the peasants at much higher rates.

In 1765 Robert Clive signed a treaty with the Mogul emperor that gave the East India Company the right to collect taxes in Bengal and the neighboring provinces of Bihar and Orissa. For almost 30 years the zamindari system was continued, with the diwans acting as intermediaries between the company officials and the zamindars. Although abuses of tax collection had been common under the Mogul emperors, the tax-collecting abuses increased sharply after 1765. British officials demanded huge bribes from the diwans, the diwans demanded even larger sums from the zamindars, and the zamindars, in turn, extorted still larger sums from the peasants.

A Changing Company Role

Years of trading, fighting, and plotting had wrought great changes in the East India Company. From a small trading concern, the company had evolved into a major political and military force with centers of power in the west, the southeast, and the northeast of the Indian subcontinent. Bengal, with Robert Clive as governor, had become especially powerful and independent. Almost from the beginning, however, the East India Company had experienced difficulty in administering its realm. One very important reason for the trouble was that the principal holdings were widely separated. The main sites of the company's power—Bengal, Bombay, and Madras—formed a huge triangle that covered nearly the entire subcontinent. Within the three points of the triangle were numerous Hindu and Muslim monarchies, few of which were consistently friendly to the British. Given these conditions, it was difficult for one person to administer efficiently all three regions. Each center had a governor who ruled as he pleased. With so much independence and so little supervision, governors and other officials both enriched themselves illegally and made agreements with Hindu and Muslim rulers that conflicted with British interests.

In 1773 the British government took action to limit the growing power of the company and to halt the illegal and unwise activities of company officials. In that year Parliament passed the Regulating Act, a bill that established a Governor–General and Council to supervise the company's territories on the subcontinent. The governor of Nepal was to be Governor–General, with authority both to administer his own province and to supervise the actions of the governors at Madras and Bombay. Both Governor–General and the Council were to be appointed by and accountable to Parliament.

The Policies of Hastings

Warren Hastings, a career employee of the East India Company, was the first Governor–General appointed under the Regulating Act. Hastings was told not to expand British control in subcontinental India. His basic task was to hold the territory already occupied by the company. Hastings was also to attempt to win the respect for British leadership among the hundreds of native rulers on the subcontinent.

If Hastings was to achieve these goals, he had to overcome many obstacles. In Bombay the British found themselves on the losing side in a struggle for power among the Marathas, and Hastings had to send troops to that region to maintain the company's position. In the south he had to deal with powerful and ambitious rulers who had combined their forces to attack the British. Also in the south were the French, who were attempting to regain territories that they had lost to the British. The French were also aiding Great Britain's rebellious American colonies in their war for independence. In the northeast the company was at war with several native rulers. In the words of Hastings, there was "a war actual or impending in every quarter [area] and with every power in Hindustan."

It is a tribute to Hastings' genius that he maintained the company's position in the face of overwhelming odds. He could count on little help from the British government, for its resources were strained in fighting the American colonies and their European allies. The governors at Madras and Bombay continued to make imprudent agreements with Hindu and Muslim rulers, and these governors were too far away for Hastings to take any action before the damage was done. Indeed, many of Hastings' difficulties with the native rulers were brought about by such agreements. But despite the odds, Hastings preserved the company's dominant position—an accomplishment that was of great importance for the future of the subcontinent.

A Profitable Trade

Having the Indian subcontinent as a colony helped Great Britain make its trade with China more profitable. British merchants

Warren Hastings, left, was Governor–General of India from 1774 to 1785. He extended British rule in India and is credited for improving the tax system and the courts. He also encouraged the study of Indian culture.

doing business with China were hard-pressed to pay for cargoes of tea, silk, and porcelain because few Western goods appealed to the Chinese. The British merchants had to pay their bills in silver bullion, which caused a drain on Britain's silver supply. But the drain on silver bullion ended when the Chinese accepted opium as payment in trade or paid cash for it. Opium is a drug made from a plant native to the subcontinent that came to be in great demand in China. The opium trade became a major source of income, with the company selling the drug to merchants who disposed of it in China. Later the opium trade led to war between Britain and China. In 1839 the Chinese government attempted to wipe out commerce in the dangerous drug. After the Chinese confiscated and destroyed British stocks of opium at a Chinese port, Britain dispatched warships and troops to China. This Opium War raged on and off for three years before the Chinese were forced to surrender after a British show of force.

Economic Importance to Great Britain

By Hastings' time, the subcontinent had become a key factor in the British economy. Britain was heavily in debt because of the Seven Years' War and the American Revolution, and it was entering a crucial phase of the **Industrial Revolution.** British civil servants who made fortunes in the service of the company returned to the homeland to spend their wealth. Many stimulated the economy by investing in new enterprises. The profits from Britain's trade with the subcontinent, as well as the profits obtained by trading the subcontinent's products with other areas, helped to pay Britain's debts and to buy the machines and build the factories needed for **industrialization.**

Check Your Understanding

1. **a.** Why did the British, French, and Dutch governments charter companies to trade with the subcontinent of India and other parts of Asia? **b.** Why were these trading companies able to surpass the Portuguese? **c.** Where were the chief British trading ports located?

2. **a.** Why was there keen rivalry between the British and the French companies? **b.** Why did these companies become involved in the rivalries between Hindu and Muslim rulers of native states? **c.** What was the outcome of the Anglo–French rivalry?

3. Why is Robert Clive important to the subcontinent's history?

4. Why did Parliament limit the role of the East India Company during the 1700's?

5. What goals were achieved by Hastings?

6. *Thinking Critically:* Why did the subcontinent become increasingly important to Great Britain?

2. Great Changes in the Indian Subcontinent

Because of the growing importance of the subcontinent, Parliament in 1784 took further steps to safeguard its interests by passing the **India Act.** This bill limited the East India Company to commercial activities. All civil, military, and financial matters related to British India were to be taken care of by Parliament. The East India Company, which had shown signs of becoming a "state within a state," thus was stripped of virtually all its powers.

The India Act increased the powers of the new Governor–General, who was Lord Cornwallis, the British general whose surrender at Yorktown brought an end to fighting in the American Revolution. During his seven years in office as Governor–General of India, Cornwallis introduced a number of important reforms. Although his successors had some interest in furthering reform, they were more concerned about strengthening the British hold on subcontinental India. By 1850 the subcontinent was largely a British possession. From 1784 to 1850, everything British and much that was traditional to the subcontinent underwent considerable change.

Reforms Under Cornwallis

Cornwallis introduced a **civil service** system. The lack of such a system had made it easier for corrupt or incompetent officials to mismanage company affairs. All company employees had been recruited in Great Britain. Sent to India with little or no training, most of the employees had known nothing about Hindu or Muslim ways and had little desire to learn about them. Because the company's directors all lived in Great Britain, they provided little supervision. As a result greedy and dishonest employees at all levels had been able to carry on illegal trade and to pocket bribes. Many of these employees grew very wealthy and were able to retire to their homeland after only a few years of service in the company's employ.

The corrupt practices of the company's employees in India underscored the need for reform. Although Clive and Hastings had brought about considerable improvement in Bengal, the first systematic and widespread reforms were introduced by Cornwallis. Shortly after he came to the subcontinent, Cornwallis drastically reorganized the administration. Company officials engaged in commercial functions were relieved of political, judicial, and military responsibilities. This action greatly restricted opportunities for bribery and kickbacks. To further reduce temptation, Cornwallis made sure that government officials received substantial salaries. These reforms marked the beginnings of the Indian Civil Service system.

The Governors–General who succeeded Cornwallis steadily improved the Indian Civil Service. Prospective officials were carefully screened. The officials occupying key posts in government were a new breed of employees who greatly improved administration throughout British India.

Reforms in the Zamindari System

When Lord Cornwallis became the Governor–General, he introduced a drastic change in Bengal's tax system. His **Permanent Settlement** (Assessment) of 1793 recognized the zamindars as the owners of the lands from which they previously had collected taxes. The traditional rights of the cultivators were ignored. They now became tenants paying rent instead of taxes to the zamindars. Moreover, the diwans were stripped of their power, and all revenue collected was paid directly into the company's treasury at Calcutta.

The Permanent Settlement eliminated many old abuses, but it created a new evil—absentee landownership. Because many zamindars were unable to make the required tax payments, their lands were confiscated and sold to the highest bidder. Purchasers often were speculators living in the cities. Life, which already had been hard for the peasants, became harder. Zamindars might have been unscrupulous tax collectors, but at least they understood the problems confronting the peasants. The new absentee landowners had no interest in the welfare of their tenants. Although the Permanent Settlement reduced corruption, it also upset a system that had worked effectively for hundreds of years.

Britain's New Attitude

The turn of the century saw a reversal in Britain's attitude toward the subcontinent. The earliest Governors–General had been under orders to preserve but not extend company territories. But in 1798 the Earl of Mornington, a confirmed imperialist, became Governor–General. Convinced that the company should be supreme in the subcontinent, he abandoned the policy of nonintervention in favor of a policy of **imperialism.** In 1799 his armies decisively defeated those of Tipu Sultan, killed the famous leader, and made Mysore into a virtual puppet state of the company. A few years later the Earl of Mornington took from the Marathas important territories that had separated the British possessions in Madras and Bengal. The Earl's policy of imperialism enraged the British public, forcing Parliament to ask for his return.

The years 1808–1813 saw little military action on the part of the British. The Governors–General during this period were careful to avoid any action that might indicate the British were trying to take over the subcontinent. But in 1813, with the appointment of the Earl of Moira as Governor–General, a policy of imperialism again took hold. By 1826 the Marathas had been completely subdued and Assam and Lower Burma had been annexed. In addition, a number of smaller states on the subcontinent had been forced to surrender many of their sovereign rights to the company. While formally retaining control of internal affairs, in practice these states were subject to frequent company interference.

By 1845 the last obstacle to company supremacy on the subcontinent was the area called the Punjab. Here the Sikhs, under the guidance of Ranjit Singh, had brought most of the Indus Valley under their control. After Singh's death in 1839, however, the Sikhs were left without capable leadership. In a series of hard-fought wars between 1845 and 1849, the company defeated the Sikhs and annexed the Punjab to its domain. With

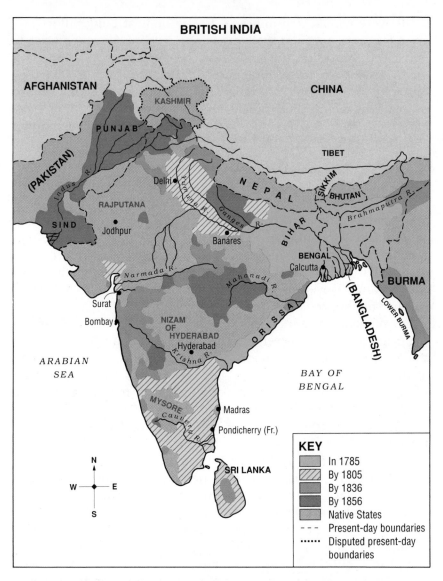

BRITISH INDIA

AFGHANISTAN

CHINA

KASHMIR

PUNJAB

(PAKISTAN)

TIBET

Indus R.

Delhi

N E P A L

SIKKIM

BHUTAN

RAJPUTANA

Punjab R.

Ganges R.

B I H A R

Brahmaputra R.

SIND

Jodhpur

Banares

BENGAL

Calcutta

BURMA

Narmada R.

Mahanadi R.

(BANGLADESH)

LOWER BURMA

Surat

Bombay

NIZAM OF HYDERABAD

O R I S S A

ARABIAN SEA

Hyderabad

Krishna R.

BAY OF BENGAL

MYSORE

Cauvery R.

Madras

Pondicherry (Fr.)

N
W — E
S

SRI LANKA

KEY
- In 1785
- By 1805
- By 1836
- By 1856
- Native States
- - - - Present-day boundaries
- ...... Disputed present-day boundaries

REGION: THE BRITISH RAJ. When the East India Company established its first trading post at Surat, no one dreamed that by 1856 the British would directly govern three fifths of the subcontinent. Many of the native states owed their continued existence to British support. Hence they were independent in name only. Other states—notably Hyderabad, Kashmir, and various Rajput monarchies—stubbornly resisted the British raj and were still outside the British fold in 1856.

these victories, the company destroyed the last serious threat to its supremacy in the subcontinent.

Several factors enabled the British East India Company to score one political or military victory after another. Chief among them was the lack of unity among the rulers of the native states. Jealous of one another, these rulers were unable to form an effective **coalition** against the British. A few princes might unite, but then an equal number would join the British side. Both the Marathas and the Sikhs might have held off British domination, for both groups were large and had extensive military experience. But seldom could the 12 confederacies of Sikhs or the numerous Maratha rulers stop quarreling among themselves long enough to present a united front. Therefore the company's military might coupled with India's lack of unity made possible British control.

Additional Land Reforms

Until the Earl of Mornington arrived as Governor–General, Bengal and the surrounding area was the only region on the subcontinent in which the company collected taxes. In other parts of the subcontinent, revenue came almost entirely from trade. With the development of an imperialistic policy, the company became the virtual ruler of dozens of small native states. Seemingly the changed situation provided an opportunity to introduce a uniform method of tax collection. Because customs varied widely from region to region, this was not done.

In South India the company began to deal directly with the **ryots,** the peasants and cultivators of the land. After a careful survey of a plot and its productivity, the company and the ryot agreed on the amount to be paid as an annual tax. These "settlements" usually remained in effect for 30 years. When a term expired, a new settlement was made.

The new method of tax collection, called the **ryotwari,** was also adopted in Bombay and some parts of the Deccan. In the northwest and in scattered parts of South India, however, company officials concluded agreements with the village community as a whole. The villagers themselves undertook to determine the tax contribution to be made by each of the local cultivators. These agreements were also of a temporary nature, usually for a period of 30 years.

British changes in the traditional methods of landownership and tax assessment have been both praised and criticized. On the good side, land reforms resulted in lower taxes for many peasants. Moreover, peasants became free to move. An unfortunate result of these reforms was an increase in the number of landless peasants. This trend cannot be ascribed entirely to British policy, however, because for centuries peasants had been subdividing land inherited from parents. By the time the British came to the subcontinent, many plots simply were too small to support a family.

Locals in the Civil Service

Conquest intensified another problem—employment of local people in the Indian Civil Service system. Cornwallis, a man of strong prejudices, had introduced the policy of excluding people native to the subcontinent from important positions in government because he thought them lazy and unreliable. Consequently even Hindus of outstanding ability were compelled to accept lower-level jobs if they wished a career in Britain's civil service. Naturally the discriminatory policy aroused deep resentment among people of the subcontinent.

In 1853 competition for civil service positions finally was opened to all. But even then candidates from the subcontinent were at a great disadvantage. The examinations tested the candidate's knowledge of Western history and culture and called for a command of the English language. Not until 1864 did a local candidate score well enough to qualify for a major post in the civil service.

Changes in Education

British expansion brought changes in education to the subcontinent. Traditionally education was limited to classical languages such as Sanskrit, Arabic, and Persian. History, science, and mathematics were not taught. On the elementary level the curriculum consisted of the three R's and studies of traditional religious myths and legends. Students, whether in elementary or higher levels of education, learned almost nothing about the world outside the subcontinent.

The first changes in education had been introduced by Christian missionaries during the 1700's and early 1800's. These missionaries established schools that taught English as well as other subjects not traditionally taught on the subcontinent. At first the British government itself did little to change local education. But in 1835 Parliament passed a bill limiting the payment of public funds to schools teaching English. Then in 1854 the government created a nationwide system of education that ranged from primary schools to colleges. Dialects of the subcontinent were to be the languages of instruction. In-

By 1875, when this photo was taken, a few local people had managed to land top positions in the Indian Civil Service system.

cluded in the curriculum, however, were the subjects commonly taught in Western schools.

The education bills of 1835 and 1854 had far-reaching effects. Not the least of these was that English became widely understood among the educated **minority.** The new schools became centers for the spread of Western ideas and customs. In them many subcontinentals acquired their first systematic understanding of English history, government, laws, and culture. Because Civil Service examinations were based on Western knowledge, these schools naturally attracted youth aspiring to careers as government officials. In time, many of these students came to assume positions of leadership—under the British.

Social Reform

In the field of social reform, Governors–General usually avoided interfering with customs that were part of the subcontinent's **traditions.** The caste system and child marriage, therefore, were allowed to continue. Even today many thousands of child marriages take place each year. Even when the British thought the customs should be abolished, Governors–General were slow to act. Thus it remained for Lord William Bentinck, who came to office in 1828, to declare suttee illegal.

Borrowed Words from the Subcontinent

The English language has often been enriched by borrowing and incorporating words from other languages into its vocabulary. The various languages of the subcontinent have been an interesting source for some of these borrowed words. The following are a few examples.

Brahmin On the subcontinent, a Brahmin was a member of the highest caste, usually of the priesthood class. In English a Brahmin is a person of high social standing.

bungalow From the Hindi term *Bangla,* meaning "house." In English it generally refers to a one-story house with a low-pitched roof.

calico A type of cotton cloth that was manufactured in Calicut. Other types of cloth originating in the subcontinent are chintz, khaki, and madras.

curry From the Tamil/Malayan word *kari,* a powder made from spices grown in South India. A dish of chicken seasoned with the powder is called curried chicken.

loot From a Sanskrit phrase for "one who robs." In English the term means plunder, booty, or stolen goods.

mogul Adapted from the name of the Mogul dynasty of rulers. In English it means a great person, or magnate.

pariah From a Tamil term meaning "drummer." Also a member of a low caste in South India. In English the term has come to mean an outcast, or someone to be avoided.

punch From *panch,* the Hindi term for "five." Originally a beverage made from five ingredients, in English the word refers to any drink made by mixing several different beverages.

pundit From the Hindi for a learned person. In English it also means a learned person or someone who gives opinions in an authoritative manner.

thug From the Hindi for thief. In English it means a ruffian, a cutthroat, or a gangster.

The practice of suttee was closely associated with the Hindu practice of cremating the dead. In part of North India high-caste widows showed their respect for a departed husband by giving up their own lives on the burning funeral pyre. Some went willingly; others did not. A widow who was reluctant to follow the custom of suttee was usually compelled to do so, often by community and family pressures. Bentinck successfully fought to have suttee declared illegal in Bengal. During the next generation, the practice of suttee was outlawed in other regions as well.

Actually Bentinck was not the first official to try to suppress suttee. Akbar and other rulers had tried to stop this practice long before Bentinck. Although a resurgence of suttee took place in the 1800's, the practice of suttee was less common at that time than many Western historians suggest.

In 1843, as part of Britain's policy of ending human bondage in its colonies, slavery was made illegal in the subcontinent. Slavery had existed on the subcontinent since ancient times. Although never extensive, slavery was a practice of prosperous households, where slaves performed domestic tasks. Slave labor was also used in mines and in the craft guilds. The end of slavery encountered little opposition. Nontheless, slavery still exists in frontier areas of Pakistan.

Check Your Understanding

1. **a.** How did the India Act affect the East India Company? **b.** How did the India Act affect the subcontinent?
2. Compare the company's administration of its holdings before and after Cornwallis became Governor–General.
3. How was the zamindari system modified by Lord Cornwallis?
4. How did the company gradually assume control of most of the subcontinent?
5. What advantages and disadvantages stemmed from British changes in traditional methods of landownership and tax assessment?
6. **Thinking Critically:** How did British rule on the subcontinent affect education? child marriages? the practice of suttee? slavery?

3. The Sepoy Rebellion and Its Aftermath

The growth of British power in the subcontinent aroused opposition in many places. Many rulers of small states, noting the displacement of ruling families in both Hindu and Muslim states, feared that sooner or later they themselves would fall victim to British ambitions. Landowners, badly hurt by programs of reform, faced economic ruin. Many people were embittered by the superior attitude of the British, their discrimination toward subcontinentals, and their interference with age-old religious and social practices. In 1857 these grievances came to a head in the **Sepoy Rebellion,** a revolt that shook the very foundations of British rule on the Indian subcontinent.

The Use of Sepoys

During the early 1800's the armies of the East India Company underwent a slow but significant change. In the 1700's Britain's military strength in subcontinental India was based mainly on Europeans. The company's comparatively small military units were made up of European **mercenaries.** In times of crisis, as during the wars with the French, company troops were reinforced with soldiers from the British army. But as military requirements increased, the company began to recruit soldiers from the subcontinent. Such troops were known as **sepoys** (SEE-poys). By 1850 British forces in the subcontinent numbered almost 250,000. Only one sixth of these forces were Europeans.

The sepoys played a major part in many important military campaigns. Led by British officers and trained in the techniques of European warfare, the sepoys fought well when their morale was high. British officers, however, sometimes treated sepoys unfairly. Not only did the British withhold pay or food for petty reasons, they also showed less consideration for sepoys than for European soldiers. Such treatment lowered sepoy morale and reduced their fighting ability.

The Sepoy Rebellion

In 1857 carelessness led to a revolt among the sepoys. Hindu and Muslim troops stationed near Delhi were issued rifle cartridges greased with animal fat. To use these cartridges, the sepoys had to bite off the tips. The Hindu troops believed that the ammunition had been coated with cow fat. The Muslims believed that the cartridges were coated with pig fat. To troops already discontented, a seemingly deliberate disregard for their religious beliefs was sufficient reason for **mutiny.**

THE SEPOY REBELLION. The mutiny by Indian troops brought destruction to all parts of the subcontinent. One of the hardest-hit towns was Lucknow (above). The British did considerable damage, but the mutineers also destroyed property to keep it out of British hands. Mutinous sepoys (below) divide their spoils. Loyal sepoys, such as the soldier at the right, remained in the army.

When British officers realized their mistake, they withdrew the greased cartridges—an action that came too late. Many officers were killed by the sepoys. The mutineers then marched to Delhi, the old Mogul capital. There the sepoys persuaded the local garrison to join them. After gaining control of the city, the sepoys proclaimed the aged and powerless Mogul emperor leader of a movement to overthrow the British raj. Some supporters of the emperor even dreamed of restoring the Mogul Empire to its former glory.

News of the Sepoy uprising triggered other rebellions. The rulers of some Hindu states in the northern and central parts of the subcontinent joined in the struggle. Many British civilians and soldiers were slain. In some cities, besieged British communities repulsed repeated attacks while awaiting relief. Horrible atrocities committed by the rebels provoked terrible reprisals on the part of the British. The memory of the brutality and viciousness exhibited in these initial stages of the rebellion endured long after the Sepoy Rebellion had been suppressed by the British government.

British authorities should not have been caught off guard. Dozens of lesser revolts had occurred during the preceding 30 years. Despite early setbacks, however, the British soon were able to contain the revolt. Regular army regiments in the subcontinent were reinforced with troops from other parts of the British Empire. Furthermore, some units of sepoys, particularly the Sikhs, remained loyal to the British. Both sides suffered heavy losses, but at the end of 14 months the Sepoy Rebellion had been crushed.

Abolition of the East India Company

The great mutiny of 1857–1858 convinced Parliament that the East India Company no longer served a useful purpose. Having steadily reduced the authority of the company since 1773, the British government now took the final step. In 1858 Parliament abolished the company and formally annexed its territories on the subcontinent.

Under the act of 1858 control of Britain's territories was entrusted to a new Secretary of State for India, a member of the British cabinet. This Secretary, although nominally responsible to the Prime Minister and Parliament, in practice had unlimited authority over the government of the subcontinent. The Governor–General was now given the title of Viceroy, signifying that he was the personal representative of the British monarch. Actually, he was nothing more than the on-the-spot agent of the

Secretary of State for India. The days of the strong Governor–General were over.

Government in Non–British Territory

At the end of the Sepoy Rebellion, 562 states on the subcontinent were still controlled by native rulers. These states ranged in size from Kashmir and Hyderabad, which were as large as France or Germany, to holdings the size of a small town. The states controlled by these rulers occupied about two fifths of the subcontinent. The rest of the subcontinent was under direct British rule. (See map, page 120.)

The East India Company, again and again, had enlarged its holdings at the expense of native states. But the British government had no intention of following such a policy. Queen Victoria proclaimed that "We desire no extension of our present territorial possessions." The British, however, reserved the right to intervene in the administration of any state with a ruler found guilty of mismanagement. Furthermore the British Crown would control foreign, military, and financial affairs in all the native states.

Despite these restrictions, the native rulers fared well. In the final settlement, the native rulers retained their local authority and received a generous share of the income from their states. As long as the rulers governed in a competent fashion, they were assured that they would never have to surrender their domains to the British government. Britain also promised to protect small states from larger neighbors.

Improved British–to–India Communications

The Sepoy Rebellion came at a time when the British government was desperately trying to improve the communications between London and the subcontinent. A letter from London to Bombay or Calcutta had to be carried by steamship to Alexandria, then overland to the Red Sea, and then again by steamship to its destination. Such a journey took three months. A clever Governor–General might take advantage of the poor communications to carry out steps not approved by the British government. Many of the incidents that infuriated the people of the subcontinent might have been avoided had there been speedier communications between London and the subcontinent.

The opening of the Suez Canal in 1869 was an important step in improving transportation and communication between the subcontinent and Great Britain. The Suez Canal enabled British steamships to make the journey to the subcontinent without stopping to unload and reload at Suez. The opening of

On the Indian subcontinent the British developed the most extensive railroad system in Asia. In the photograph above, workers are laying track in East Bengal.

the Suez Canal shortened the voyage between Bombay and London to about 25 days. Thus the Canal not only increased the speed of communication and travel, but it also increased trade between Britain and the subcontinent.

A tremendous improvement in communications also resulted from the completion of a telegraph line between London and the subcontinent in 1870. British officials in the subcontinent no longer had a good excuse to make decisions on vital matters without consulting British officials in London. Nor did British officials on the subcontinent have to wait weeks for instructions from home. Direct telegraphic communications enabled the British government to exercise much closer control over subcontinental affairs.

Internal Communication Improvements

During the early days of Company rule in the Indian subcontinent, communications within South Asia were very poor. When the British government tightened its political hold on the subcontinent, it had to cope with the problem of improving internal communications.

Even before the Sepoy Rebellion, the British government had made some improvements in the subcontinent's internal communications. In 1851 the British government authorized the construction of a telegraph system. In 1854 it introduced an efficient postal service. Work was begun on a railway system, and by 1871 railroads linked all the provinces together and connected outlying regions with the subcontinent's principal ports. Road building was also given a high priority. Some of the dirt roads of Mogul times were paved and new highways were built to connect the subcontinent's major cities.

By 1914 the subcontinent could boast of the best system of roads in Asia. The telegraph and postal systems were in full operation. Railroad trackage had risen to 35,000 miles. By World War II this total had reached 43,000 miles. Today even though thousands of miles of the old British Railway System are in present-day Pakistan, present-day India ranks fourth among the world's nations in total railway mileage.

Irrigation Expansion

In an agricultural region such as the subcontinent, irrigation is of vital importance. From the days of the Harappan civilization the construction of canals, dikes, and irrigation ditches had been an important function of the government. Remarkable irrigation systems had been built. The British followed the example of earlier rulers in actively promoting irrigation projects.

The East India Company had undertaken the task of repairing and restoring neglected irrigation systems. In 1866 the British government began the construction of a number of large canals and several thousand miles of feeder canals. The northwest especially benefited from this British program. In Punjab, much of which is in present-day Pakistan, more than two million acres of land were reclaimed by irrigation. By the beginning of the 1900's the northwest was supporting a population of 800,000 people.

The extension of irrigation has been a major responsibility of the subcontinent's governments, both during British rule and after division of the subcontinent into the separate nations of India, Pakistan, and Bangladesh. More than 140 million acres in present-day India are under irrigation. From the 1950's onward, more than half of all government spending on agriculture has been directed toward irrigation projects. Expanding irrigation has been an important priority in Pakistan and Bangladesh as well.

Annexation into the British Empire

In 1876 the British Parliament passed legislation that made Queen Victoria Empress of India. This act marked an important change in Britain's relationship with the subcontinent. From 1858 until 1876, the British government had considered the native states of the subcontinent to be independent sovereign

At left is Britain's Queen Victoria as she looked in 1876 when she was proclaimed Empress of India.

governments. By making Queen Victoria Empress of India, Parliament annexed the native states, making them part of the British Empire. The inhabitants of the entire subcontinent became subjects of the British Crown, and the reigning monarch in Great Britain became the ruler of the subcontinent. The act of 1876 officially made the British government the dominant power in the subcontinent, the status Great Britain had enjoyed unofficially since the Sepoy Rebellion in 1857–1858.

Check Your Understanding

1. Why did many people on the subcontinent fear the growth of British power in South Asia?
2. **a.** How did the East India Company come to employ sepoys? **b.** Why were the sepoys generally discontented? **c.** How did the Sepoy Rebellion begin? **d.** How did it end?
3. How did the government of the subcontinent change after the Sepoy Rebellion?
4. How did Britain's relationship with the subcontinent change in 1876?
5. *Thinking Critically:* What were the major effects of improved transportation and communication between London and the subcontinent? How did improvements in these and other areas affect life within the subcontinent?

4. The Subcontinent's Value to Great Britain

The importance of the subcontinent in the worldwide British Empire increased steadily in the years after the Sepoy Rebellion and Great Britain was determined to hold this imperial prize. Having won effective control over the entire subcontinent, the British were in a far better position than the East India Company had been to exploit the subcontinent's resources.

Increased British Presence

For almost a century after the Sepoy Rebellion, many people from Great Britain enjoyed profitable careers in subcontinental India. Qualified candidates from the subcontinent were employed in the clerical and administrative ranks of the Civil Service, but the higher offices were reserved for the British. Developmental programs and technical services also were staffed with specialists from Great Britain. Few people of the subcontinent had the engineering, medical, and scientific skills required to staff such programs.

After the Sepoy Rebellion, more British soldiers came to the subcontinent. Before the mutiny most of the sepoys were high-caste Hindus and Bengali Muslims. The disloyalty of soldiers recruited from these groups caused British officials to rely more on Sikhs of the Punjab, the tough Gurkhas from Nepal, and Pathans from the northwest frontier. Simultaneously the British government sharply increased the proportion of British regulars in the forces maintained in the subcontinent. Thousands of British soldiers saw service on the subcontinent between 1858 and 1947.

Trade as a Key Link

British trade with the subcontinent increased steadily after 1850. The products of British factories found a ready market in the subcontinent. In time the prosperity of British textile mills was heavily dependent on the subcontinent, for the region was a prime market for inexpensive cotton cloth. Moreover, the transport of these goods in British ships meant more profits for Britain's merchant marine.

Foreign countries as well as lands that were part of the British Empire also increased their trade with the subcontinent. Great Britain, however, maintained its position as India's foremost trading partner. Between 1870 and 1910 the subcontinent accounted for nearly 20 percent of Britain's total overseas commerce.

Other Source of Profits

Trade was not the only benefit Britain derived from the subcontinent. Costly developmental programs required large amounts of **capital.** To finance such projects, bonds were sold in both Great Britain and the subcontinent. The purchasers of these bonds received handsome interest payments on their investments. The British also invested money in establishing factories, mines, railroads, and plantations on the subcontinent. Moreover, British **capitalists** often loaned money to both the imperial and the native governments in the subcontinent. Even the Indian Civil Service contributed to the British economy. Each year the number of retiring Civil Service employees increased. The money these retirees received in pensions helped to strengthen the British economy when these retirees returned to Great Britain.

Benefits to Farmers

The lot of the subcontinental farmer, for centuries a difficult one, improved at least a little under British rule. This improvement was largely due to technological advances and to increased trade. Sir Reginald Copeland, a specialist on British India, made this statement:

> Now suddenly, owing to the railways and the complementary development of ports, sea transport, commercial law and practice, the machinery of modern business, the products of the [subcontinent's] peasant's labour in his fields or at his craft became saleable and profitable far outside his own locality, not only anywhere in India [the subcontinent] but in the world at large. Indian wheat, in particular, was soon selling in the world market, and prices soared from their poor local level to those fixed at Liverpool or Chicago. Other agricultural products shared in the growth of the export trade—rice, oilseeds, cotton, jute, tea. Their higher value meant a little rise in the peasant's standard of living. . . .
> [Sir Reginald Copeland, *Britain and India.*]

Industrial Benefits and Advances

Peasants might have seen a slight improvement in their way of life, but it was the local industrialist who gained most from the relationship with Great Britain. The growth of foreign trade, the founding of new and modern industries, and the expansion of the domestic market provided greater opportunities for business people in the subcontinent. Notable advances were made in the organization of a modern textile industry. The cheap products of British mills had gradually undercut the subcontinent's most important **cottage industry**—home spinning. For centuries clothmaking has been a supplementary source of income for thousands of peasants. Now subcontinental industrialists opened modern textile plants that could compete with British factories. By the early 1900's the subcontinent was a major producer of cotton cloth for the world.

The **heavy industries** also provided investment opportunities for local industrialists. The building of railroads meant a need for iron and steel. This need made necessary the tapping of the subcontinent's rich iron resources. The Tata family of Bombay was a pioneer in the development of the subcontinent's iron and steel industry. The family's mills at Jamshedpur became the greatest in the region, making the subcontinent one of Asia's leading producers of iron and steel.

Stirrings of Protest

Many fortunes were built by people who capitalized on the opportunities of the expanding economy on the subcontinent. Although business people grumbled about rising taxes and the lack of **tariff protection,** they had no serious quarrel with the British raj. Approving its policies and generally optimistic about the future, these business people were ready to cooperate with the imperial government. They saw this cooperation as a means to even more opportunities and profits.

Many subcontinentals, however, pointed to the disadvantages of British rule. They singled out the breakdown of time-honored traditions, the discriminatory policies of the British, and the continuing "draining away" of the subcontinent's wealth. Such views came together in a movement called nationalism that would have great significance for the future. This nationalist movement is the subject of Chapter 6.

Check Your Understanding

1. How did Britain's relationship with the subcontinent aid the British economy?
2. How did Great Britain finance many of the projects that it developed in the subcontinent?
3. How did the subcontinental farmer benefit from the British presence?
4. *Thinking Critically:* How did British rule stir unrest in the subcontinent?

CHAPTER REVIEW

■ Chapter Summary

Section 1. During the period of Mogul rule, France and Great Britain chartered trading companies that became increasingly involved in subcontinental India. The involvement of the trading companies led to wars against each other in the subcontinent, wars that were both an outgrowth of the competition on the subcontinent and an extension of their countries' political rivalries in Europe and in North America. From these clashes Great Britain emerged victorious. Its trading company, the East India Company, under the leadership of Robert Clive then proceeded to lay the foundations for the last and greatest of the empires in the subcontinent. But as the company's power grew, so did abuses of its power. Parliament in 1773 passed the Regulating Act, which provided for some supervision of company activities. Nonetheless, under Warren Hastings, the company's dominant position on the subcontinent and its importance to Britain's economy were preserved.

Section 2. In the late 1700's the British Parliament decided that the East India Company was rapidly outliving its usefulness. Thus Parliament began to restrict the company's powers while increasing those of the British government. The India Act passed in 1784 brought civil, military, and financial matters under the control of Parliament and limited the East India Company to commercial activities. Britain's military might coupled with the subcontinent's lack of unity made possible British control. As the British government took an increasingly imperialistic role in the subcontinent, social, land, and tax systems underwent changes. Some of these reforms brought benefits to people in the subcontinent. Others aroused resentment and contributed much toward a growing dissatisfaction with the British presence in the subcontinent.

Section 3. Dissatisfaction with company rule came to a head in the Sepoy Rebellion. The rebels were crushed, but their action brought about a drastic reorganization of the administration of the subcontinent. The East India Company was abolished, settlements were made to encourage the loyalty of native rulers, and the British Crown assumed full responsibility for the British presence in the subcontinent. In 1876 Parliament formally annexed the subcontinent of India to the British Empire. By this time improvements had been made in communication and transportation between London and the subcontinent, especially by the opening of the Suez Canal. Other improvements were also made within the subcontinent. Irrigation systems were expanded, railroads and roads were increased and improved, and telegraph and postal systems were in full operation.

Section 4. By the time the subcontinent was annexed to the British Empire, its value to Great Britain was enormous. The Indian Civil Service supplied employment for thousands of British citizens, provided a market for goods manufactured in British factories, and provided numerous Britains with opportunities for profitable business investments. Subcontinentals also benefited from direct British rule, but capitalists who helped develop cotton mills and the iron and steel industries benefited far more than the peasants. Some local people believed that the disadvantages of British rule were far greater than any advantages, and they began to organize a nationalist movement.

■ **Vocabulary Review**

Define: British raj, diwan, zamindar, Industrial Revolution, industrialization, India Act, civil service, Permanent Settlement, imperialism, coalition, ryot, ryotwari, minority, tradition, Sepoy Rebellion, mercenary, sepoy, mutiny, capital, capitalist, cottage industry, heavy industry, tariff protection

■ **Places to Locate**

Locate: Surat, Bombay, Madras, Calcutta, Plassey, Mysore, Punjab, Hyderabad, Kashmir, Suez Canal

■ **People to Know**

Identify: Jahangir, Joseph Dupleix, Robert Clive, Warren Hastings, Lord Cornwallis, Earl of Mornington, Ranjit Singh, William Bentinck, Queen Victoria

■ **Thinking Critically**

1. How did the British East India Company evolve into a major political and military force with centers of power in the west, the southeast, and the northeast of the Indian subcontinent? What roles did Robert Clive and Warren Hastings play in the company's rise to dominance?
2. How did the Indian subcontinent change after the passage of the India Act in 1784? Which reforms initiated by Lord

Cornwallis and his successors were of benefit to Great Britain? Which were beneficial to the subcontinent?

3. How did British attitudes bring about the Sepoy Rebellion? How did the subcontinent benefit from the abolition of the East India Company's charter?

4. Why was the British government determined to keep control of the Indian subcontinent?

■ **Extending and Applying Your Knowledge**

1. Using the Index of the *National Geographic* at your local library, make a list of two or three articles about the Indian subcontinent, its people, or its customs. Choose one article to read and report on to the class.

2. Rudyard Kipling was an English writer born in India. Among his works are *Plain Tales from the Hills*, a collection of short stories about Anglo–Indian life, and such poetry as *Gunga Din*. Choose one of his stories to read and report on. Pay close attention to his attitude toward his non-English characters. Based on what you have read in this chapter, comment on whether it is what you expected and give your reasons.

6

The Road to Independence

By welding the many states of the Indian subcontinent into an empire, Great Britain brought a political unity to the region. One of the outcomes of this unification, however, was the arousal of nationalist feeling and agitation for a large voice in government on the part of the people of the subcontinent.

The demand for a responsible voice in government, which began in the 1900's, came largely from people who were educated in the Western tradition. They knew about Western ideals of self-government, and they could not understand Britain's position in resisting self-government for the subcontinent. The outstanding critic of the British position was Mohandas K. Gandhi (GAHN-dee). Combining Western ideals, traditions from the Hindu heritage, and the tactics of both ancient and modern politics, Gandhi built nationalism on the subcontinent into an explosive force. Ranking next to Gandhi in influence was Jawaharlal Nehru, an early convert to the nationalist cause.

Together the two leaders changed the goal of Indian nationalism from mere participation in government through **home rule** to complete independence. Great Britain moved ever so slowly and hesitantly, however, toward changing the governmental structure of the subcontinent. Any concessions Britain made to appease the nationalists' demands generally were too little and too late. Moreover, every British concession seemed to bring new nationalist demands. Eventually the British resigned themselves to complete withdrawal from the subcontinent.

1. Emergence of the Nationalist Movement

In the years following the Sepoy Rebellion (1857–1858), a new group of leaders arose among the people of the subcontinent. These new leaders came from the enlarged middle class—the owners and managers of new industries, the members of the professions, and the intellectuals pursuing careers in education, literature, journalism, and religion. These men had little in common with the older generation of leaders, the rulers of the subcontinent's native states. The new leaders were better educated, more Western in their outlook, and more concerned about the subcontinent as a whole. As this educated middle class became more active in political affairs, the British government had to make more concessions in the direction of self-government and home rule for the Indian subcontinent.

Attitudes Toward the West

In the late 1800's a growing number of young people from the subcontinent attended Western-style schools. In these schools they were introduced to ideas and bodies of information that were largely unknown to their ancestors. Many of these young people went to Great Britain for further study. After securing university and professional training, they returned home to begin successful careers.

These people who had been trained in Western-style schools straddled two widely differing worlds—the traditional world of the subcontinent and the Western world. Not all, however, received the same impression of Western culture. Some were enthusiastic about it and adopted Western ways wholeheartedly. These admirers of everything British condemned anything in subcontinental life that conflicted with British standards. Their cherished goal was to use the West as a model for changing their society. Others were appalled by Western ways. To these people, the West seemed to place too much emphasis on the acquisition of wealth and on ruthless competition. What this second group of Western-educated people thought they saw in the culture of the Western world caused them to idealize their own heritage and to value it even more.

Regardless of their attitude toward the West, educated subcontinentals resented the behavior of British officials. The European **sahibs** made a mockery of British ideals of liberty and respect for the individual. Legislation and the administration of justice invariably favored the European minority in the subcontinent. The non-British minorities were discriminated against and

140

The Independence Movement

1885	Formation of the Indian National Congress
1905	Partition of Bengal
1906	Formation of the Muslim League
1909	Morley–Minto Reforms
1914–1918	World War I
1917	Montagu's promise of self-rule for the subcontinent
1918–1919	The Rowlatt Acts
1919	Amritsar Massacre
	Montagu–Chelmsford Reforms
1927	Simon Commission
1930	Gandhi's March to the Sea
1930–1932	Round–Table Conferences
1935	Government of India Act
1937	First provincial elections
1939–1945	World War II
1940	"Two India" proposal by Muslim League
1942	"Quit India" movement
1947	British withdrawal from the subcontinent
	Creation of India and Pakistan

were denied the liberties that the British constitution afforded Britain's citizens. Especially aggravating was discrimination practiced in the Indian Civil Service, which virtually closed high positions to local candidates well into the 1800's. Discrimination such as this led to the formation of several nationalist organizations on the subcontinent.

The Indian National Congress

A retired official of the Indian Civil Service was instrumental in forming the subcontinent's most important nationalist organization. At the urging of Allan O. Hume, a citizen of Great Britain, the **Indian National Congress** was organized in 1885. The hope of its founders, according to the first chairperson, was "to be governed according to the ideas of government prevalent in Europe" and "was in no way incompatible with their thorough loyalty to the British government." Because of this professed loyalty, the British government did nothing to discourage the operations of the Indian National Congress.

At this early period in its history, the Indian National Congress set modest goals for itself. Its leaders did not call for complete self-government (home rule), nor did they clamor for independence. Most of the members believed that mutually helpful relationships between Britain and the subcontinent would be fostered in time. Moreover, their demands hardly were revolutionary. They simply asked for more good jobs and more responsibility in government. The leaders of the Congress were convinced that such goals could be achieved within the framework of the existing government.

A vocal minority in the Congress, however, questioned the wisdom of relying on British promises. This minority refused to believe that the imperial homeland intended to relax its grip on the subcontinent's government. They were convinced that Britain was interested in the subcontinent only for the sake of profits. To this minority, even reform measures were prompted by selfish British motives.

The foremost critic in the Congress was a talented writer named Bal Gangadhar Tilak (TEE-lahk). A fiery nationalist, Tilak has been dubbed "the Father of Indian Unrest." Equally dissatisfied with British policies and with the moderate views of fellow nationalists, Tilak openly advocated rapid change—by revolution if necessary. Tilak's anti-British activities on the subcontinent led to his imprisonment. After being released, however, Tilak became even more aggressive in his fight for home rule. In 1906 Tilak and his followers left the Indian National Congress to form their own nationalist group. Later they returned to the Indian National Congress and helped swing the then moderate organization into a more aggressive position regarding self-government.

Muslim Suspicions

A more serious threat to national unity than Tilak's extremist position was the large Muslim population of the subcontinent. Few Muslims felt comfortable in the Congress, which was dominated by Hindus and which appealed more to teachers, writers, business people, lawyers, and other professionals. Muslims were so devoted to preserving the traditional ways of Islam that few of them attended Western-style schools. Consequently, not many Muslims acquired the education needed to fill government posts or to enter modern professions.

An early Muslim leader in the Hindu–Muslim rivalry was Sayyid Ahmad Khan (1817–1898). Although he was descended from Mogul officials, Sayyid Ahmad Khan did not turn his back on Western culture. While urging his fellow Muslims to take pride in their Islamic heritage, he also advocated the study of Western science. To advance his ideas, Sayyid Ahmad Khan helped found Aligarh University, an **institution** that was to become the foremost seat of Muslim learning in the subcontinent. Sayyid Ahmad Khan's leadership of the Muslim community was an important influence in limiting Muslim membership in the Congress, which he distrusted, viewing it as an institution associated with the Hindu faith.

Muslim suspicion of the Congress was heightened even further when the Congress advocated extending voting rights to people of the subcontinent. It was obvious to Muslims that Muslim candidates would win few seats in any election to a legislature because most voters would be Hindus. Muslims became advocates of **communal representation,** a plan that would reserve a specified number of political offices for each religious and ethnic community. To protect its interests and to further the idea of communal representation, the Islamic minority formed the **Muslim League** in 1906. In time, Mohammed Ali Jinnah (JIHN-ah), a Western-educated lawyer, emerged as the leader of the Muslim League. He maintained this position until his death in 1948.

The Partition of Bengal

Shortly before the organization of the Muslim League, the British took a step that greatly upset the people of the subcontinent. This step was the partition of Bengal in 1905. Because of its great area and large population, Bengal had been a difficult province to administer. The partition created an East Bengal of 31 million people and a West Bengal of 47 million. Undoubtedly the partition of Bengal facilitated its administration, but the partition also provoked a fierce and unexpected reaction on the part of Hindus.

The furor arose because the British had completely ignored social divisions in making the partition. Hindus were upset because they became a minority in East Bengal, which was predominantly Muslim. Bengalese in West Bengal were unhappy because, with the addition of Bihar and Orissa to the new province of West Bengal, they became a minority in their own land. Throughout the subcontinent an outcry arose for reunification of Bengal. By ignoring the demand for the reunification of

Bengal, the British caused the nationalist movement to gather speed and force.

British Concessions

In 1909 the British Parliament enacted the Morley–Minto Reforms, a program that was designed to quiet the rising discontent. The Reforms opened numerous high positions in the Indian Civil Service to qualified local candidates. The Morley–Minto Reforms stopped short, however, of giving subcontinentals positions that would enable them to exercise any degree of effective control over the government. Most members of the Congress realized that the Morley–Minto Reforms had barely touched on the many grievances they had forwarded to Parliament. Nonetheless the moderates viewed the Morley–Minto Reforms as a step in the right direction.

In 1911 the British took further steps to appease the subcontinent. During the visit of King George V to India, the British made several important announcements, among them the decision to reunite Bengal. The British also revealed their plan to move the capital of the government from Calcutta to Delhi, the old capital of the Mogul Empire and a city rich in traditions. Both decisions were popular with nationalists. Still these moves did little to dampen the demands of the nationalists for greater responsibility in government.

Check Your Understanding

1. **a.** How did Western-style education influence attitudes in the subcontinent? **b.** Why did some people reject Western influences? **c.** Why were few Muslims influenced by Western attitudes?
2. **a.** Why was the Indian National Congress formed?
   b. What were its goals during its early period?
   c. Who opposed its early goals and why?
3. **a.** Why did the partition of Bengal greatly upset Hindus? **b.** Why did it upset the Bengalese?
4. **a.** What were the results of the Morley–Minto Reforms? **b.** What other concession pleased the nationalists?
5. *Thinking Critically:* Why were Muslims suspicious of the Indian National Congress? How did they protect their minority interests?

2. Indian Nationalism During World War I

Because the subcontinent was part of the British Empire, it was drawn into World War I. In a sense, the subcontinent responded loyally. Thousands of volunteers took part in crucial military campaigns in Europe and the Middle East. The factories of the subcontinent became a vital source of supplies for the Allied cause. The wealthy, especially the rulers of native states, responded generously to the appeal for war bonds. Yet, the subcontinent continued to seethe with unrest. By the time World War I had ended, the people of the subcontinent were seeking self-government.

Coolness Toward the British Raj

Despite their apparent support of the British war effort, subcontinentals had not rejected nationalism. They expected and even demanded concessions for services rendered. To all requests for change, however, the British always gave the same response— "After the war." Under these circumstances nationalists in the subcontinent became increasingly impatient with British rule and the British refusal to listen to their demands.

The war also diminished the people's respect for their imperial ruler. British power seemed less awesome as people came to realize that Great Britain was but one of a number of powerful nations. People of the subcontinent also lost respect for Western culture in general. Seeing the violence and bloodshed brought on by World War I, the people of the subcontinent wondered how the culture of the West could be superior to theirs. After experiencing rejection in their demands for more responsibility in government and having lost respect for their imperial ruler, the people of the subcontinent became even more committed to their nationalist goals.

Formation of a Hindu–Muslim United Front

For years the fear of losing their identity in the huge Hindu population of the subcontinent had kept Muslims loyal to the British raj. But during World War I, Muslims became increasingly upset by policies of the British. The British government was playing a leading role in the destruction of the Ottoman Empire, long the leading Muslim state. An attack on the Ottoman Empire was also an attack on the caliph, the spiritual leader of the Muslim world. Many Muslims in the subcontinent and elsewhere began to consider the war a British conspiracy against their religion.

The increasing militancy of the nationalist cause, together with growing disenchantment with British rule on the part of the Muslims, combined to bring the Muslims into the Hindu-dominated nationalist movement. Bal Gangadhar Tilak, who had been imprisoned for his active resistance to British rule, emerged from prison to find a favorable climate for his brand of nationalism. (See page 142.) In 1916, under Tilak's leadership, the Indian National Congress took a step that was calculated to attract Muslims to the nationalist cause. With this step, the Congress declared itself in favor of communal representation—long a goal of Muslim leaders. The strategy worked. Soon Hindus and Muslims were presenting a united front to the British government in demanding complete self-rule.

A Promise Not Fulfilled

A promise made by Great Britain near the end of World War I seemed to indicate that Britain was ready to meet the demands of the nationalists. On August 20, 1917, Edwin Montagu, the Secretary of State for India, made an important announcement. He stated that Great Britain would take steps toward the "increasing association of Indians [subcontinentals] in every branch of Indian administration, and the gradual development of self-governing institutions, with a view to the progressive realization of responsible government in British India as an integral part of the Empire." Clearly, this was a promise of self-rule for the subcontinent.

Unfortunately this was a hollow promise. Instead the first postwar acts of the British government brought further repression. During World War I, militant nationalists had resorted to acts of violence to register their protests against the policies of the British raj. Because of such acts of protest, the British government passed the two Rowlatt Acts in 1918 and 1919. These measures empowered British authorities to arrest and try in secret those protestors accused of political crimes. In effect, by these measures the accused were denied legal counsel and trial by jury. To people educated in British-controlled schools, the Rowlatt Acts were a clear violation of rights guaranteed under the British judicial system.

Heightened Antagonism

The Rowlatt Acts aroused great indignation among nationalists in the subcontinent. At the urging of Mahatma Gandhi, many people began staging **hartals,** one-day strikes in which all commercial activity ceased. (See page 148.) Throughout the subcon-

INFLUENTIAL LEADERS. Both Jinnah (left) and Gandhi (right) were influenced by the Western way of life. In time Gandhi renounced Western ways for the simple life and dress of a peasant.

tinent's history the hartal had been a favorite nonviolent method of registering dissatisfaction. But in postwar times, the hartal led to riots, which provoked further repressive measures from the British. As a result, antagonism between the British and the nationalists heightened.

The most serious incident between the British and the nationalists occurred at Amritsar, a town in the province of Punjab. Although forbidden to gather for political purposes by the British, hundreds of people had gathered in a wall-enclosed park to listen to political speeches. Suddenly a unit of British troops appeared and fired repeated volleys into the unarmed crowd, killing almost 400 people and wounding 1,200 more. Later General Dyer, who had ordered the action, was censured by an investigating committee and ordered to return to Great Britain. But the House of Lords, the upper house of the British Parliament, officially approved his action and even established a fund in his behalf. The Amritsar incident caused many people on the subcontinent to lose whatever faith they had in the British system of justice.

The Montagu–Chelmsford Reforms

The British, however, were attempting to fulfill their wartime promise even while taking repressive action. In 1919 the British

S IDELIGHT TO HISTORY

Gandhi—Champion of Equal Rights

During the early years of the nationalist movement, the man most commonly associated with the independence movement of the subcontinent, Mohandas K. Gandhi, was fighting for the rights of Indian nationals in South Africa. Born in the western part of the subcontinent, Gandhi was a Vaishya and a son of the prime minister of a small native state. At the age of 19, Gandhi went to London to study law. After completing his studies, he practiced law in Bombay. In 1893 the young lawyer went to South Africa, a part of the British Empire to which many subcontinentals had migrated. Local authorities had adopted various measures not only to restrict the immigration of Asians but also to limit their citizenship rights. Gandhi became a leader in the movement to ensure fair treatment for all subcontinentals. It was in South Africa that Gandhi formulated his theory of using **civil disobedience** and passive resistance to fight discrimination and injustice.

Gandhi, with a well-established reputation as a foe of discrimination, returned to the subcontinent in 1915 just after the outbreak of World War I. Given the title of *Mahatma*, meaning "great soul," by the poet Rabindranath Tagore, Gandhi wisely decided not to participate in any divisive nationalist activity for the length of the conflict. But after the war, when Britain failed to extend generous rights of self-government to the subcontinent, Gandhi's goal became self-rule free of all foreign control. To achieve self-rule Gandhi advocated nonviolence and noncooperation with the British. Blamed for disorders throughout the subcontinent, Gandhi was imprisoned in 1920.

Upon his release in 1922, he retired to his *ashram*, or religious retreat. To the ashram came leaders from all parts of the world. While leading a discussion, Gandhi often spun thread on a traditional spinning wheel. Even before Gandhi resumed active leadership of the nationalist movement in 1930, the spinning wheel had become the symbol of the struggle for independence and was emblazoned on the Congress Party flag. From the time of his "March to the Sea" in 1930 until his death in 1948, Gandhi worked ceaselessly for the subcontinent's independence, but always in a nonviolent way.

The Amritsar Massacre took place within this enclosure. Hundreds of people were killed or wounded when the British troops fired into a crowd gathered to protest British policies.

announced the Montagu–Chelmsford Reforms, a program that was designed to provide a larger role for subcontinentals in the administration of their own land. These Reforms did not limit Great Britain's control over subcontinental affairs. In fact, the viceroy in Delhi continued to have the last word in matters that affected the subcontinent as a whole. But three local representatives were to serve on the viceroy's advisory council of seven members, and a two-house or **bicameral legislature** was to be established.

In both houses of the legislature more members were to be elected by voters in the subcontinent than were to be appointed by the British government. Local representatives thus were placed in positions of influence. Moreover, the representatives were provided a forum where they could express their grievances openly.

The Montagu–Chelmsford Reforms also provided for changes at the provincial level. The governor of each province, who was appointed by the British Crown, was to be responsible for law and order and for matters that involved revenue. A one-house or **unicameral legislature** was to be established in each of the provinces. A majority of the members in each legislature was to be chosen by the eligible voters in an election. These legislatures were assigned responsibility for such "nation-building" affairs as education, public health, and local self-government. But just as the viceroy was to have the last word at the national level, the governor was given final authority at the provincial level.

Gandhi's ashram was always filled with people seeking advice or inspiration. Sometimes they waited for days as Gandhi sat wordlessly at his spinning wheel, thinking about the problems of his native land.

The Montagu–Chelmsford Reforms went into effect in 1921. From the point of view of the British, the Reforms were a major concession. That the people were not satisfied with the Reforms is an indication of the great change that had taken place in their attitude since the beginning of World War I. Nationalists in the subcontinent had begun to regard themselves as equals of the British. They believed that self-rule was a right, not a favor to be granted by others. In the political climate of the new nationalism, even a major concession was considered too little. Consequently the implementation of the Montagu–Chelmsford Reforms did little to quiet unrest.

Gandhi's Leadership

Before 1918 Gandhi had shared the hope of moderate nationalist leaders that at the end of World War I Britain would extend generous rights of self-government to the subcontinent. But disillusioned by the Rowlatt Acts and outraged by the Amritsar Massacre, Gandhi had lost patience with Great Britain. The "beneficent institutions of the British Government," he concluded, "are like the fabled snake with the brilliant jewel on its head, but which has fangs full of poison. . . ."

Even while the Montagu–Chelmsford Reforms were being discussed, Gandhi rejected them as nothing more than piecemeal concessions. Without waiting to judge the effectiveness of the reforms, Gandhi began his campaign to achieve **swaraj.** But Gandhi firmly believed in *ahimsa,* the doctrine of non-injury to living creatures. Gandhi's program of protests called for civil disobedience, but it also called for nonviolence.

In 1920 Gandhi called for a peaceful boycott of governmental agencies and services. Thousands of students responded to Gandhi's call by staying away from their classes in government schools. Many of the eligible voters refused to vote when the elections were called to implement the Montagu–Chelmsford Reforms. Some people of the subcontinent even went so far as to resign from the Civil Service. The unrest that was created by the boycott of governmental agencies and services led to riots in some parts of the subcontinent. The British blamed Gandhi for the disorders, arrested him, and sentenced him to a prison term of six years. But he was released two years later.

In 1924 Gandhi began another boycott, this one against British goods. He urged the people not to buy and use British-manufactured textiles. Instead Gandhi sought to popularize homemade cloth, spinning thread to make the cloth on his own traditional spinning wheel. Gandhi's example in spinning thread for his own needs was followed by tens of thousands of people, including members of the wealthy classes. Gandhi, however, was waiting for the right moment to assume the leadership of the nationalist movement.

Check Your Understanding

1. **a.** How did World War I increase tensions between Great Britain and nationalists in the subcontinent?
   b. How did the war help produce a Hindu–Muslim united front?
2. How did the passage of the Rowlatt Acts lead to the massacre at Amritsar?
3. **a.** What were the Montagu–Chelmsford Reforms?
   b. Why were these reforms considered too little and too late by nationalists?
4. ***Thinking Critically:*** How did Mahatma Gandhi come to symbolize the movement for self-government?

3. The Shift to Independence As a Goal

A new class of Indian leaders had arisen after the Sepoy Rebellion, and another group arose after World War I. As stubborn as their predecessors, the new post-World-War-I leaders sought goals different from those pursued by the older generation. Just as nationalist demands at an earlier period had changed from more responsibility in government to complete responsibility, they now evolved into demands for independence. Bombarded with criticism and protests from the nationalists, the British continued to wrestle with the problem of formulating an acceptable system of government for the subcontinent. It seemed to the British that no program could satisfy this new highly vocal generation of nationalist leaders.

Nehru's Leadership

Beginning in the late 1920's when Mahatma Gandhi began his withdrawal from active leadership, the burden of leadership in the nationalist movement fell increasingly on the shoulders of Jawaharlal Nehru. Born in 1889, Nehru, the son of a prosperous lawyer, grew up in luxurious surroundings. The Nehru family was Brahmin and traced its ancestry to the province of Kashmir in the subcontinent's far north. Like his father, Nehru studied law in Great Britain.

For many years Nehru kept himself apart from the activities of the nationalist movement. Although he joined the Congress in 1916, he did not commit himself to political affairs until after the Amritsar Massacre. How Nehru discovered what came to be the central purpose in his life has been dramatically recounted in his autobiography *Toward Freedom.*

> . . .Gandhiji [Gandhi] took the leadership in his first all-India agitation. He started the *Satyagraha Sabha,* the members of which were pledged to disobey the Rowlatt Act, if it was applied to them, as well as other objectionable laws to be specified from time to time. In other words, they were to court jail openly and deliberately. When I first read about this proposal in the newspapers, my reaction was one of tremendous relief. Here at last was a way out of the tangle, a method of action which was straight and open and possibly effective. I was afire with enthusiasm and wanted to join the *Satyagraha Sabha* immediately. I hardly thought of the consequences—law breaking, jail-going, etc., and if I thought of them I did not care.

Jawaharlal Nehru joined the Indian National Congress at age 27. He did not become active in the Congress, however, until he was nearing age 40. This picture shows him about the time he was achieving prominence as a leader in the independence movement. In what ways did Nehru and Gandhi differ?

Differing Views

Despite his admiration for Gandhi, Nehru did not always follow Gandhi's views. Gandhi would not accept an elective post in any nationalist organization because he wanted to be free to work outside an organization whenever the occasion so demanded. Nehru provided the political leadership that Gandhi shunned, eventually serving four terms as president of the Indian National Congress. Gandhi and Nehru also took different positions on the question of independence. By the late 1920's both were advocating independence for the subcontinent. Gandhi, however, would have been satisfied with **dominion status** as a self-governing member of the British Commonwealth and linked to other dominions by allegiance to the British Crown. Nehru wished to sever all political ties with Great Britain. Gandhi eventually accepted complete independence as the goal. He also gave his full support to Nehru—an important factor in Nehru's position of permanent leadership of the independence movement.

Nehru and Gandhi also differed over solutions to social and economic problems. In 1927 Nehru visited the Soviet Union to see the experiments in **socialism** that were taking place in that country. He returned to the subcontinent with the conviction that many of its problems could be solved by turning to socialism. Gandhi's ideas, although frequently startling, could hardly be called socialistic. In his autobiography *Toward Freedom*, Nehru described Gandhi's outlook.

India's salvation [according to Gandhi] consists . . . in unlearning what [it] has learned during the last fifty years. The railways, telegraphs, hospitals, lawyers, doctors, and suchlike have all to go; and the so-called upper classes have to learn consciously, religiously, and deliberately the simple peasant life, knowing it to be a life giving true happiness.

Nehru then showed how his own philosophy differed from that of Gandhi.

Personally, I dislike the praise of poverty and suffering. I do not think they are at all desirable, and they ought to be abolished. . . . Nor do I appreciate in the least the idealization of the 'simple peasant life.' I have almost a horror of it, and instead of submitting to it myself I want to drag . . . the peasantry from it, not to urbanization, but to the spread of urban cultural facilities to rural areas. Far from . . . giving me true happiness, it [the life of a peasant] would be almost as bad as imprisonment for me. What is there in "The Man with the Hoe" to idealize over? Crushed and exploited for innumerable generations, he is only little removed from the animals who keep him company.

The Simon Commission

Nehru became prominent when Parliament appointed a commission to evaluate the Montagu–Chelmsford Reforms. The Act of 1919, which called for the Montagu–Chelmsford Reforms, also provided for a review of the program after 10 years. As a gesture of goodwill toward the subcontinent, Parliament decided to hold the review in 1927, two years early. A commission of Parliament members headed by Sir John Simon came to the subcontinent to examine the situation. But to its surprise, instead of finding a grateful subcontinent, the Simon Commission met outrage everywhere. Offended because no one from the subcontinent had been asked to serve, both the National Congress and the Indian Legislative Assembly boycotted the Simon Commission conference. Wherever they went, Sir Simon and his fellow members of Parliament encountered hostile demonstrations and lack of cooperation.

The seriousness of Parliament's mistake soon became evident. At the urging of Nehru and other "young radicals," the Indian National Congress issued a demand for independence. To work out the details, the Congress proposed a round-table conference involving British and local leaders. Thoroughly

154

alarmed, the British government agreed to call the conference and announce that the "attainment of dominion status" was a goal for the subcontinent. Few nationalists, however, believed that the British were sincere.

After the demand of the Congress for independence, Gandhi came out of his retreat and rejoined the group to lead the opposition to British rule. To dramatize discontent he organized the civil disobedience movement, a plan to openly but peacefully defy British regulations. As his first target, Gandhi chose the British monopoly on the manufacture of salt. For many years the people of the subcontinent had resented the tax they had to pay on all salt produced in the subcontinent. In 1930 Gandhi marched 60 miles to the sea. There on the beach he distilled salt from the water and used it.

Gandhi's march started widespread demonstrations against British policies. Protest marches, hartals, and riots occurred. At least 100,000 people, including Gandhi himself, were arrested and jailed. These protests proved to the British that the Indian problem was getting out of hand.

Round–Table Conferences

Between 1930 and 1932 the British Parliament held the promised round-table discussions. The recommendations of the Simon Commission were discussed by members of Parliament and leaders from the subcontinent at three conferences in London. Hoping to include every interest group in the subcontinent, the British invited representatives of the Indian National Congress, the various Hindu castes, the Untouchables, the Muslims, and the native states, as well as leaders from the subcontinent's industrial community.

The Round–Table Conferences were complete failures. Claiming that the British called in the many groups simply to confuse the issue, the Indian National Congress boycotted the meetings. Gandhi attended the second conference as the sole Congress delegate, but his presence did nothing to bring about an agreement. He demanded that the Congress dominate whatever new system of government was devised. The Muslims, however, refused to budge from their demand for communal representation. Only if they had a guaranteed number of seats in government, they reasoned, could they protect their interests. The various native rulers objected to any plan that might limit their powers or threaten their privileged position in the subcontinent. If the British learned anything from the three Round–Table Conferences, it was that they could never satisfy all parties.

Widening of the Hindu–Muslim Rift

Muslim distrust of the Hindu **majority** had never disappeared despite the wartime pledge of the Congress that it would support communal representation. During and after the Round–Table Conferences, the views expressed by Hindu political leaders did nothing to dispel Muslim distrust. Beginning in the early 1930's, Muslim nationalists advanced proposal after proposal to ensure that Muslim rights would not be trampled on by either the British or the Hindus. Many Muslim suggestions went further than earlier demands for separate electorates.

Sir Mohammed Iqbal, a widely respected scholar, was one of the most vocal Muslim nationalists of this period. Iqbal was also known as a poet. Some of his most often quoted lines promoted Muslim nationalism and condemned Western imperialism. In 1930, in his presidential address before the Muslim League, he called for the establishment of an **autonomous** Muslim state in the subcontinent's northwest. Although Iqbal did not go so far as to advocate a separate nation for Muslims, other followers of Islam soon began to champion the idea.

The Government of India Act

Despite the discouraging outcome of the Round–Table Conferences and the continuing antagonism between Hindus and Muslims, Parliament passed the Government of India Act in 1935. The new plan of government was based largely on the report of the Simon Commission. The goal of the Government of India Act was to establish a partnership between the people of the subcontinent and the British government that eventually would lead to dominion status.

Under the Government of India Act the 11 provinces would elect their own governments. These would be subject to British intervention only in time of emergency. At the national level there was to be a bicameral legislature. This body, while having extensive powers, was to be kept in check by the British Viceroy. Muslims and other minority groups were to have no more than their proportionate share of seats in the legislature. The native states were given the option of joining or not joining the new **federation.**

Problems with the New System

The leaders of the Indian National Congress were not happy with the political system worked out by the British government. The system failed to give the subcontinent complete independence,

THE INDEPENDENCE MOVEMENT. The Round—Table Conferences of 1930–1932 were held at a time when civil disobedience was being practiced. In Gandhi's famous March to the Sea (above), thousands of people joined in a protest against the salt tax. After the March, nationalists supported Gandhi's program for staging hartals. Workers (below) are pondering whether to defy a hartal by walking over the outstretched bodies and reporting to work. British officials stand by to maintain order. Why was civil disobedience attractive to Hindus?

One of the native rulers who refused to join the proposed federation was the Nizam of Hyderabad. A Muslim, he ruled over a state that was 85 percent Hindu.

and it did not ensure a Congress monopoly of the government. Neither were the Muslims satisfied. Although they received the communal representation they had asked for, they discovered that in only a few small provinces would the plan ensure them effective control. Furthermore, the native rulers were reluctant to join the proposed federation. As a result, the federal provisions of the Act could not be put into effect. Despite these problems, elections to fill seats in the provincial legislatures were scheduled for 1937. After much discussion, both the Indian National Congress and the Muslim League decided to participate. The Indian National Congress of prewar days became the Indian Congress Party when it began competing in elections.

The Congress Party scored a major victory in the provincial elections, winning a majority of the seats in six provinces and a **plurality** in three others. This outcome seemed to justify Muslim fears of Hindu domination. Congress Party ministries were formed in eight of the provinces. The Congress Party refused to include non-members of the Congress Party in these ministries and decided not to participate in coalition ministries in provinces where no party had a majority. As a result, the Congress Party further aroused the resentment of the Muslim League. Mohammed Ali Jinnah, who had hoped to work with the Congress Party in establishing cooperative governments, now began to attack the Congress Party with all his might. From this time until the British withdrew in 1947, neither the Muslim League nor the Congress Party would make a concession to the other. This refusal to compromise made it clear that the two organizations could never work together in a united way.

The British spent the years between 1937 and the outbreak of World War II attempting to bring the native states into the new federation. The native rulers, however, held back, fearing that in the proposed federation they would lose their special

158

privileges. Meanwhile the new system of government provided Congress Party members with first-hand political experience.

Check Your Understanding

1. How did Nehru and Gandhi differ in their goals for the subcontinent?
2. **a.** Why did the appointment of the Simon Commission anger people? **b.** How did Gandhi dramatize the subcontinent's discontent?
3. Why did differences between Hindus and Muslims widen during the 1930's?
4. *Thinking Critically:* How did the Government of India Act attempt to satisfy Hindu and Muslim demands? How did the provincial elections prove the Muslim's worst fears to be true?

4. Friction During World War II

In 1939 Britain declared war on Nazi Germany. Immediately the viceroy of India proclaimed the subcontinent to be in a state of war. Members of the Congress Party were incensed because the people of the subcontinent had been thrust into a war without any say in the matter. They also fully realized that Britain would be too busy with the war to grant self-government. Perhaps unwisely, the Congress Party refused to cooperate in the war effort unless independence was granted.

Refusal to Cooperate

The Muslim League and all other political parties expressed their willingness to help the British. But the Congress Party, in a resolution written mainly by Nehru, made clear its position:

> If this war is to defend the status quo, imperialist possessions, colonies, vested interests and privileges, then India can have nothing to do with it. If, however, the issue is democracy and a world order based on democracy, then India is intensely interested in it. And if Great Britain fights for maintenance and extension of democracy then [it] must necessarily end imperialism in [its] own possessions, establish full democracy in India, and the Indian people [subcontinentals] must have the right of self-determination—and must guide their own policy. . . . [Quoted in: Frank Moraes, *Jawaharlal Nehru: A Biography.*]

This declaration by the Congress Party leaders placed them in opposition to their imperial rulers in Great Britain. Nehru and his colleagues were determined to withhold all support for Britain's war effort unless their demands for an independent and undivided India were met immediately. The British government thought it unwise to give independence to the subcontinent during wartime. The British feared that confusion and strife would be the outcome at the very time when harmony and cooperation were especially needed. Locked in the struggle with Hitler, Britain's leaders stressed the urgency of getting on with the war. But instead of giving the British government the wartime cooperation it requested, the Congress Party instructed its members to resign their posts in the provincial ministries.

Call for an Independent Pakistan

The Muslim League, headed by Mohammed Ali Jinnah, took comfort from the growing friction between Great Britain and the Congress Party. The League regarded the withdrawal of the Congress Party members from political office as a golden opportunity to further Muslim interests. At its meeting in March 1940 the Muslim League issued a momentous declaration that changed the course of subcontinental politics. It called for the division of the subcontinent into two parts, one part to be an independent nation for the Muslims. The idea of a nation called Pakistan, which originally was to consist of the Punjab, Kashmir, and Sind, thus became a stated goal after years of informal discussion. (See page 165.) Because the Muslim League remained loyal to Britain, the League's leaders were hopeful that Britain would listen to their request. Also because the Congress Party was out of favor with the British government, Muslim League leaders thought that Britain might favor the Muslim League in any postwar partition of the subcontinent.

Britain's War Efforts

In the summer of 1940 Hitler's armies overran much of Western Europe. It seemed that nothing short of a miracle could save Britain from defeat. In the summer and fall, therefore, the British government tried to gain the support of the Congress Party. Again, as in World War I, all promises were to be fulfilled "after the war." These long-range promises failed to satisfy Nehru and other Congress Party leaders. The British attempt to reach an agreement with the Party ended in failure.

Gandhi revealed his displeasure with Britain's unwillingness to act by launching another campaign of nonvilent noncoopera-

The Meaning of "Pakistan"

Since the call for an independent Muslim nation on the subcontinent, the origin of the word *Pakistan* has been in dispute. A widely accepted view is that the name was coined by a group of Muslim students at Britain's Oxford University in 1933. Supposedly these students coined an acronym, a word made from the initials of other words, by listing the names of their homelands. You can see how the students arrived at the name of Pakistan by reading this list:

P for Punjab
A for Afghana (the Northwest Frontier Province)
K for Kashmir
I for Iran
S for Sind
T for Tukharistan
A for Afghanistan
N for the last letter in Baluchistan

tion. Many nationalists were imprisoned for taking part in the campaign. Nehru and Gandhi were among the nationalist leaders who were jailed, but they refused to budge from their position of noncooperation with the war effort.

The Royal Navy and Air Force saved Britain from an invasion by Nazi armies. Then when Great Britain was reeling from night raids by Nazi airplanes, Hitler decided to attack the Soviet Union before he had overcome the stubborn British resistance. With the Nazi forces divided between eastern and western fronts, the pressure on Great Britain was greatly relaxed. But in December 1941, Great Britain had to face another powerful enemy. While Japan was striking American bases in Hawaii and the Philippines, it was also opening a front against British holdings in Southeast Asia.

The winter of 1941–1942 was a long nightmare for the British in Asia. Japanese troops quickly overran the Malay Peninsula, then continued their advance to overwhelm the British naval base at Singapore. Next the Japanese pushed into Burma and again defeated British defenders. Difficult terrain, long supply lines, and spirited opposition, however, prevented the Japanese

Even though India's influential Congress Party took a stance of noncooperation with Britain during World War II, Indian troops were dispatched to North Africa to reinforce the Allied forces there.

from invading the subcontinent. Faced with a hostile Japan at the very door of the subcontinent, Great Britain needed the full cooperation of all parties.

The Cripps Mission

In March 1942 Sir Stafford Cripps was sent to the subcontinent to seek a settlement with the Congress Party leaders. Cripps made what the British government considered to be a generous offer. The Cripps Mission proposed dominion status for India, to be granted at the end of the war. Moreover, each province and each state could choose between joining a union of Indian states or becoming a separate dominion. The British also offered to renegotiate treaties with the native states and to take all necessary steps to protect the interests of Muslims and other minority groups. In addition to these long-range promises, the British were willing to grant immediately one important concession—the filling of all posts on the viceroy's Council of Ministers with local candidates. Thus the people would be given a larger role in the administration of their land. With respect to the war, however, the British insisted that they would remain in complete control.

The Cripps Mission ended in failure. At first it seemed that Congress Party leaders would accept the plan, but then Gandhi brought his influence to bear on the proposal. He objected to the Cripps program because it did not give the people of the subcontinent immediate control over their own affairs. Gandhi wanted the Council of Ministers to be a policy-making body, not an advisory board that could be ignored by the Viceroy. Remembering disappointments during World War I, most nationalist leaders went along with Gandhi. No one in the nationalist movement wanted to risk a second failure.

The "Quit India" Campaign

After the Congress Party had rejected the terms proposed by the Cripps Mission, Gandhi started a drive to win immediate independence. He told British officials that he would direct another campaign of noncooperation if Britain did not immediately withdraw from the subcontinent. Nehru and other Congress Party leaders backed Gandhi's plan. The British were understandably angered and, before the "Quit India" movement could gain momentum, they arrested Gandhi, Nehru, and 60,000 of their followers. Gandhi and most of the other nationalists were released before the end of the war, but Nehru was among hundreds who spent the rest of the war in jail.

During his long period of imprisonment, Nehru wrote many letters to his daughter Indira, who as Indira Gandhi became the third prime minister of the Republic of India and mother of the fourth prime minister. In these letters Nehru evaluated the long history and the rich culture of the people of the subcontinent. Eventually these letters were published in the book *The Discovery of India*. Nehru's book was not an objective history, nor did it even pretend to be. Above all, *The Discovery of India* was an articulation of the emotions and the influences that compelled the people of the subcontinent to revolt against their British masters.

Participation in the War Effort

Despite the lack of support from the Congress Party, Britain found the subcontinent valuable in its struggle for victory. Early in the war, troops from the subcontinent were used to reinforce British and imperial units in North Africa, Singapore, and Hong Kong. Industrialists in the subcontinent adapted their factories to meet the demands of military production, and sent military supplies to the various war fronts. Shipbuilders built naval vessels, and shipyards were used for repairing British ships damaged in battle. A general lack of enthusiasm for war in the subcontinent did not prevent Britain from utilizing the resources of its great colony.

The subcontinent also provided an important base for military operations. Without this base the British war effort in Asia would have been severely handicapped. The subcontinent was also important to the military activities of the United States. American troops were trained in the subcontinent for the recapture of Burma. At the same time Chinese troops underwent training by American officers, and supplies were transported into China from the northeastern part of the subcontinent. This aid enabled Chiang Kai-shek, the Chinese leader, to hold out against Japanese aggression until Japan surrendered in 1945.

Independence for the Subcontinent

As World War II drew to a close, it became clear that Britain could not hope to retain its prewar empire. British holdings everywhere were showing signs of nationalist unrest. Moreover, the British were too exhausted from the war to resist independence movements. Viewing the situation realistically, Britain resigned itself to granting independence to its colonial possessions. Foremost among these possessions was the subcontinent of India, a land where millions of people were anxiously awaiting the fulfillment of British wartime promises.

Independence for the subcontinent was speeded by elections in 1945 in Great Britain, which resulted in the victory of the Labour Party and the defeat of Prime Minister Winston Churchill and the Conservative Party. Churchill, an outspoken defender of Great Britain's imperial policies, had stated earlier that he had not become "His Majesty's First Prime Minister in order to preside over the liquidation of the British Empire." The Labour Party, however, was more willing than the Conservative Party to allow the various peoples under the British flag to go their independent ways.

Like the Conservatives, the Labourites soon found themselves searching for a formula that would smooth the transfer of power and still be acceptable to all groups on the subcontinent. For months the road to independence was blocked by differences between the Congress Party and the Muslim League. Each organization, realizing that a turning point in the history of the subcontinent was at hand, sought the maximum advantage. Various plans were put forward by the British, but none met the approval of both Hindus and Muslims. While the discussions were going on, restless nationalists began to take matters

164

into their own hands. Riots and demonstrations Provoked by nationalists occurred daily in various parts of the subcontinent. Finally the British decided they could wait no longer for the groups to settle their differences. In February 1947 Britain announced that it would withdraw from the subcontinent. A few months later Britain proclaimed its plan for creating the two nations of India and Pakistan.

Check Your Understanding

1. When World War II broke out, what stand was taken: **a.** by the Congress Party? **b.** by the Muslim League?
2. Why did the Muslim League issue its call for an independent Pakistan?
3. **a.** What was the purpose of the Cripps Mission? **b.** Why did it end in failure? **c.** What response did Britain give to Gandhi's "Quit India" Campaign?
4. *Thinking Critically:* How were efforts toward independence for the subcontinent hampered by World War II? How were they furthered by the demands that the war made on Britain?

5. Independence for India and Pakistan

On August 15, 1947, Britain officially withdrew from the subcontinent. Two new nations, India and Pakistan, had been born. Ordinarily the birth of a new nation is an occasion for rejoicing, but such was not the case when India and Pakistan achieved nationhood. Even as independence was being proclaimed, unprecedented waves of violence and bloodshed were sweeping over large areas of the subcontinent.

A Hasty Partition

British and subcontinental leaders had spent years in fruitless negotiations, but once the fact of independence was agreed on, the British wasted no time in withdrawing from the subcontinent. Six months after Britain had announced its intention, it turned over all its properties and powers in the subcontinent to Indian and Pakistani officials. A viceroy remained for a time, but was merely an adviser. As of midnight August 14, 1947,

August 15, Independence Day, is India's most important holiday. Here Nehru is pictured speaking to an overflow crowd in Delhi on Independence Day, 1960.

India and Pakistan were free to chart their own courses as independent nations.

Under a plan worked out beforehand, the provinces and native states rapidly aligned themselves with one or the other country. Outwardly simple, the plan called for each province under direct British rule to join the country with the religion that was accepted by most of its residents. Thus provinces inhabited mainly by Hindus became part of India, while those with largely Muslim populations joined Pakistan. The rulers of native states were free to surrender their states to the country of their choice. Almost all the rulers respected the religious views of their subjects in arranging the transfer of power.

The partition plan created a "divided" Pakistan. One part of the country, which was called West Pakistan at the time, lay in the northwest part of the subcontinent. The second part of the divided nation lay in the eastern portion of the subcontinent and was called East Pakistan. It is this part that later became the independent nation of Bangladesh.

Violence in the Punjab and Bengal

The speed of the partition caused great suffering for millions of people throughout the subcontinent. This was particularly true for those people who were living in the heavily populated provinces of the Punjab and Bengal.

At the time of partition, large numbers of both Hindus and Muslims lived in the Punjab and Bengal. For this reason, British officials had divided each province between India and Pakistan. The portion of the Punjab where Muslims were in the majority became part of West Pakistan. The Muslim part of Bengal was included in East Pakistan. During the negotiations preceding the division, long-smoldering religious hatreds erupted, bringing on massacres, looting, and burning in Bengal and the Punjab. Muslims persecuted and attacked Hindus living in Muslim areas, and Hindus persecuted and attacked Muslims living in their areas. The Sikhs, whose land had been divided between India and West Pakistan, joined Hindus in the mistreatment of Muslims. In turn, Sikhs were the victims of Muslim reprisals. Before the disorders ended, at least 500,000 Hindus, Muslims, and Sikhs had been killed. Some 5.5 million Hindus and Sikhs fled from Pakistan into India, and even more Muslims moved from India to Pakistan.

Actions by Native States

By offering generous settlements and exerting economic and political pressure, the Indian and Pakistani governments persuaded all but two rulers of native states to surrender their independence and become an integral part of the nation. One holdout was the Maharaja of Kashmir, ruler of a large state on the India–Pakistan border. Although Kashmir was 70 percent Muslim, the Maharaja was Hindu and he refused to transfer his domain to Pakistan. At the same time he was also reluctant to join India. Only when Kashmir was invaded by Pathan troops from Pakistan did the Maharaja agree to cooperate with officials from India. At the Maharaja's request, troops from India entered Kashmir. In return for their services, the Maharaja agreed to join the Indian federation. The action of the Maharaja, however, did not bring peace to Kashmir, which continues to be an area of contention between the two nations to this day.

The other holdout was the Nizam of Hyderabad. A Muslim, the Nizam rejected the idea that Hyderabad should join India even though most of the inhabitants were Hindus. Like the Maharaja of Kashmir, the Nizam refused to join either country. The infuriated Indians settled the issue by force. In 1948 an Indian army occupied Hyderabad, pensioned off the ruler, and divided it along linguistic lines among the Deccan states of India.

BLEAK CONDITIONS.   India's first Independence Day was not a time for rejoicing. Whole villages lay in ruins because of conflicts that had erupted between Hindus and Muslims. Refugee camps were crowded with Hindus who had fled from Muslim Pakistan. Conditions in Pakistan were equally bleak. What caused these conditions?

Disruption of Government Service

In addition to causing the conflicts between Hindus and Muslims, partition brought chaos to many services developed under British rule. The British had provided extensive transportation, communications, and irrigation systems, all of which had to be divided. The division of services, property, and assets led to endless disputes.

Perhaps the most serious problems that stemmed from the division of property concerned the British-built irrigation and railroad systems. Most of the thousands of miles of irrigation canals built by the British were in the Punjab, a province divided between India and Pakistan. Partition left sources of water in one country and many of the distribution canals in another. The railroad system, which was the best in Asia, had been built long before partition became an issue. Because Pakistan and India were far from friendly with each other, neither country was willing to accept joint operation of the irrigation and railroad networks. The problem of dividing railroad and irrigation systems plagued Indian and Pakistani officials for many years. Although a division of irrigation and railroad networks was finally made, the efficiency of both systems was badly hurt.

Partition also caused a disruption in such government services as mail delivery, the administration of health services and schools, and law enforcement. The assets of and the responsibility for these government-administered services had to be divided between India and Pakistan. Many months passed before satisfactory arrangements for partition could be made. The inconvenience and delay in settling problems that arose from partition further increased discontent among people in both countries.

The Assassination of Gandhi

No Indian was more distressed by the disorders and violence accompanying partition than Mahatma Gandhi. During the widespread upheavals, the aged leader (Gandhi was 78) pleaded for humane behavior toward others by both Hindus and Muslims. Unfortunately his pleas went unheeded. Then in January 1948, Gandhi was shot to death by a fellow Hindu. Disturbed by the consideration that Gandhi had shown for Muslims, this Hindu fanatic assassinated Gandhi, charging that Gandhi had been a traitor to his religion. Gandhi's death was mourned throughout the subcontinent by Hindu and Muslim alike, as well as by admirers throughout the world. A tearful Nehru expressed the shock and sorrow of millions of Indians. "A light," he said, "has gone out of our lives."

Check Your Understanding

1. Describe the plan of partition that divided the sub-continent into the two nations of India and Pakistan.
2. Why did partition lead to violence and bloodshed?
3. How did the rulers of native states respond to the plan of partition?
4. What other problems were posed by the plan of partition?
5. *Thinking Critically:* Use information from the textbook to prove or disprove the statement: Discrimination by a majority group toward minority groups was at the heart of the partition problem in the Indian subcontinent.

CHAPTER REVIEW

■ **Chapter Summary**

Section 1. A new class of political leaders emerged in the subcontinent in the years after the Sepoy Rebellion. Often educated in British universities and familiar with the British traditions of self-government and political rights, these leaders wanted a greater share in the government of their own land. The Indian National Congress, founded in 1885, was designed to help the new leaders achieve this objective. But before the National Congress could achieve success, it was split by differences over the best method of achieving its political goals. Some members were willing to rely on British promises that greater responsibility in government would be granted in time to the people of the subcontinent. Others, such as Tilak, were unwilling to rely on British promises and urged rapid change. Meanwhile, Muslims became advocates of communal representation. To protect its interests and to further the ideal of communal representation, Muslims withdrew from the National Congress and formed the Muslim League, a group organized to protect Muslims against Hindu domination. When the British ignored minority interests in the partition of Bengal, nationalism gathered speed and force.

Section 2. The Indian nationalist movement began to change from a passive, patient movement to an aggressive, demanding one during and after World War I. Disappointed by Britain's rejection of their wartime requests for additional rights, and outraged by the passage of the Rowlatt Acts and by the tragic Amritsar Massacre, nationalists undertook a series of one-day strikes, or hartals, to emphasize their demands. The Montagu–Chelmsford Reforms established national and provincial legislatures, giving the people of the subcontinent a larger share in their government. But the reforms only partially satisfied the nationalists, and under the leadership of Gandhi the clamor for self-government continued. Gandhi transformed the nationalist movement into a struggle against British rule. Popular with Hindus because of his religious and moral qualities, Gandhi was also a masterful political strategist, who is remembered as much for his success in awakening the people to their need for self-government as for his humanitarianism.

Section 3. After World War I nationalist goals changed, especially under Nehru, who provided the political leadership that Gandhi shunned. While Gandhi and Nehru sometimes differed on the means to achieving their goals, they were in complete agreement on their goal—complete independence from British rule. Gandhi demonstrated his opposition to British rule through his civil disobedience campaign and his March to the Sea. Through a series of Round–Table Conferences held in London, Great Britain tried unsuccessfully to satisfy the conflicting demands and interest of the Congress Party, the Muslim League, the rulers of native states, and other groups. Increasingly suspicious of Hindu motives, Muslims began to discuss the possibility of a separate Muslim nation. In the Government of India Act, passed in 1935, Great Britain attempted to quiet nationalist unrest but was only partially successful.

Section 4. During World War II, the subcontinent participated in Britain's struggles to resist German and Japanese aggressions. At the same time, friction between the British government and nationalist groups in the subcontinent increased. The Muslim League offered Great Britain its fullest cooperation in the war effort, but it also issued a call for a separate Muslim state. Incensed because the Viceroy of India had declared the subcontinent to be in a state of war without consulting them, the Congress Party leadership refused to participate in the war effort unless its demands for immediate independence were met. Displeased with plans for another nonviolent, noncooperative campaign, the British jailed Gandhi, Nehru, and thousands of their supporters.

Later Britain attempted to appease the nationalists with the Cripps Mission proposals. As the war drew to a close, Britain realized that it could not hope to keep its Indian Empire, and in February 1947 it announced plans to withdraw from the subcontinent and to create two separate nations—the Hindu-dominated nation of India and the Muslim-dominated nation of Pakistan.

Section 5.   With the birth of India and Pakistan, the subcontinent's long-simmering antagonism between Hindus and Muslims came to a boil. Under the partition of the subcontinent, the Punjab and Bengal were divided between India and Pakistan. This division created a Pakistan of two sections—West Pakistan in the northwest and East Pakistan in the northeast. Rulers of native states were to align themselves with either India or Pakistan, depending on the wishes of their religious majority. Great suffering and discrimination ensued as the majority group of an area abused the minorities who were their neighbors. Two native states—Kashmir and Hyderabad—became battlegrounds for control between Pakistan and India. Disruption of major services throughout the subcontinent also occurred. Gandhi himself became a victim when a Hindu fanatic shot him because he was too kind to Muslims.

■ **Vocabulary Review**

Define: home rule, sahib, Indian National Congress, institution, communal representation, Muslim League, hartal, civil disobedience, bicameral legislature, unicameral legislature, swaraj, dominion status, socialism, majority, autonomous, federation, plurality

■ **Places to Locate**

Locate: Bengal, Bihar, Orissa, Amritsar, Punjab, Pakistan, India, Kashmir, Hyderabad

■ **People to Know**

Identify: Mohandas K. Gandhi, Allan O. Hume, Bal Gangadhar Tilak, Sayyid Ahmad Khan, Mohammed Ali Jinnah, Edwin Montagu, Jawaharlal Nehru, Sir John Simon, Sir Mohammed Iqbal, Sir Stafford Cripps, Indira Gandhi, Winston Churchill, the Nizam of Hyderabad

■ **Thinking Critically**

1. Discuss each of the following, indicating its role in contributing to the growth of nationalism in the subcontinent: attitudes toward the West, formation of the Indian National Congress and the Muslim League, the partition of Bengal, and the Morley–Minto Reforms.
2. Compare Gandhi's stand toward Britain in World War I with his stand in World War II. Why were the two positions so different?
3. For what movement is Gandhi most widely known? How effective was this movement in bringing independence to the subcontinent?
4. How did nationalist thinking change between World War I and World War II? Why did it change?
5. How did the proclaiming of independence bring sadness and suffering to the people of the subcontinent? Could this suffering have been avoided? Why or why not?

■ **Extending and Applying Your Knowledge**

1. Many books provide an insight into Gandhi's philosophy of nonviolent resistance. Use the card catalog of your local or school library to locate one of these books. Read the book to find out about Gandhi's implementation of his philosophy, reporting to the class about its effectiveness.
2. Prepare a chronology or timeline of events that show the subcontinent's progress toward independence from the founding of the Indian National Congress to the Proclamation of Independence for India and Pakistan. Display your timeline on the class bulletin board.

7

Independent India

After independence, India had a multitude of problems that it had to learn how to solve. India had to form a government, expand industry, lift the masses from poverty, improve the health of the people, and make good on its promises of social equality for all. The nation also had to find a place for itself in world affairs, no easy task on a globe divided by conflicting **ideologies.** National leaders soon found that the struggle to establish a strong and secure nation was even more demanding than the fight to break away from British rule.

India's leaders have not found easy answers to their problems. Year after year, grinding poverty has prevented the majority of Indians from enjoying their status as independent people. India's leaders, realizing that domestic concerns need to take priority, have largely withdrawn from competition for world leadership. They have trimmed expectations regarding industrialization and have tried to launch social reforms for the betterment of the people.

Given the stage of its development at the time of independence, India has made considerable progress in bringing a stable government to India, in expanding its industrial development, and in making inroads in social reform. India, however, must speed up the pace of reform as it moves into the twenty-first century if the country is to meet the needs of its ever-expanding population.

1. Politics of India

The leaders of newly independent India faced the task of creating order out of turmoil. Although the initial violence had ended, the problem of stabilizing the shaky political situation remained. Jawaharlal Nehru, leader of the new India, made it unmistakably clear that the country was to be a **democracy** that was committed to the advancement of the people's welfare. The lengthy **constitution** that went into effect in 1950 set forth in detail the plan for a democratic political system. The constitution emphasized that India's social system was based on full equality. The constitution also established a program for eliminating poverty and establishing a sound economy.

The Indian Constitution

The ideas of many political systems and philosophies are found in the Indian constitution. Especially noticeable in the constitution are ideas that reflect Nehru's socialist leanings. So, too, are principles borrowed from the United States Constitution. For example, India's bill of rights strongly resembles the one found in the United States Constitution. India's constitution also reflects extensive borrowings from British law and tradition, with the basic plan of Indian government patterned after that of Great Britain.

India's constitution is unusual in that it devotes considerable space to social problems. It includes a ban on caste distinctions. The constitution also guarantees free and compulsory education for all children to age 14, a living wage for all, equal pay for equal work, and public assistance for the needy. These various social welfare provisions reflect the long-range ideals and goals that the leaders of India had for their people. India's leaders knew that the goals and ideals contained in the constitution would take some time to be implemented. They further knew that India first had to overcome many challenges before significant improvement in social welfare could be achieved.

The constitution of 1950 established India as a **democratic federal republic,** setting up a central government whose officials were representatives of the people elected by popular vote. The former provinces, which became states, surrendered certain powers to the central government and retained other powers. Thus according to the constitution, India became a federation of equal self-governing states. The major amount of power, however, was placed in the central government.

(Continued on page 178)

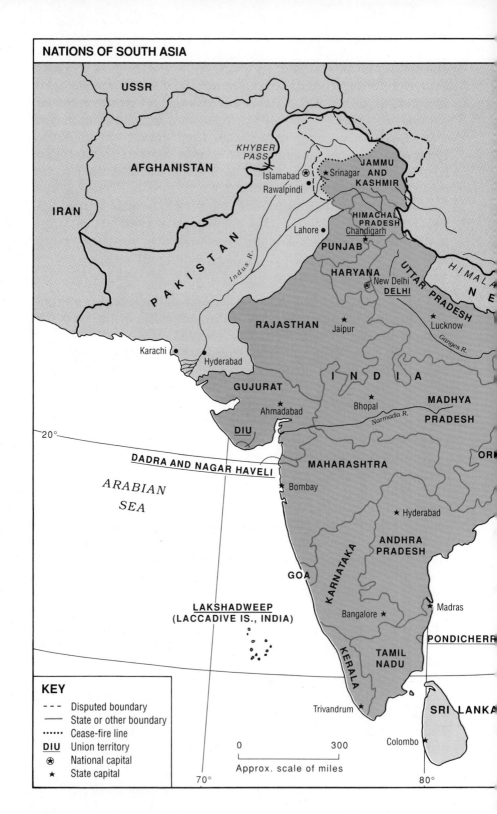

NATIONS OF SOUTH ASIA

USSR

AFGHANISTAN

KHYBER PASS

Islamabad ⊛
Rawalpindi ●

JAMMU AND KASHMIR
★ Srinagar

IRAN

PAKISTAN

Indus R.

Lahore ●

HIMACHAL PRADESH
Chandigarh
★
PUNJAB

HARYANA

New Delhi ⊛
DELHI

HIMALA
N E

UTTAR PRADESH
Lucknow ★

RAJASTHAN
★
Jaipur

Ganges R.

Karachi ●
● Hyderabad

I N D I A

GUJURAT
★
Ahmadabad

Bhopal ★

MADHYA
PRADESH

Narmada R.

DIU

—20°—

DADRA AND NAGAR HAVELI

ARABIAN SEA

Bombay ★

MAHARASHTRA

OR

★ Hyderabad

ANDHRA
PRADESH

GOA

KARNATAKA

LAKSHADWEEP
(LACCADIVE IS., INDIA)

Bangalore ★

★ Madras

PONDICHERR

KERALA

TAMIL
NADU

KEY

- - - Disputed boundary
——— State or other boundary
······ Cease-fire line
DIU Union territory
⊛ National capital
★ State capital

Trivandrum ★

SRI LANKA

Colombo ★

0   300

Approx. scale of miles

70°   80°

176

PLACE: THE NATIONS OF SOUTH ASIA. In 1947 South Asia was partitioned into two independent nations—India and Pakistan. Pakistan at the time was split into two predominantly Muslim sections—West Pakistan and East Pakistan. In the early 1970's East Pakistan began a separatist movement that India supported. The resulting war ended with East Pakistan receiving its independence as the nation of Bangladesh. The official name of India is the Republic of India. Pakistan's is The Islamic Republic of Pakistan. The official name of Bangladesh is People's Republic of Bangladesh. The island nation at India's southern tip is the Democratic Socialist Republic of Sri Lanka. Total population of these four nations of South Asia in 1990 was estimated to be 1.1 billion.

India Since Independence

1947	Partition of India
1947–1948	India's first war with Pakistan
1947–1964	Nehru's years as prime minister
1948	Assassination of Mahatma Gandhi
1950	Adoption of the Constitution
1951	Beginning of first Five–Year Plan
1954	Sino–Indian agreement
1956	Kashmir claimed as permanent part of India
1962	Border skirmishes with China
1964–1966	Shastri's years as prime minister
1965	India's second war with Pakistan
1966–1977; 1980–1984	Indira Gandhi's years as prime minister
1971	India's third war with Pakistan Formation of Bangladesh
1975	Annexation of Sikkim
1984	Assassination of Indira Gandhi
1984–1989	Rajiv Gandhi as prime minister
1985	Beginning of seventh Five–Year Plan
1987	Sending of Indian troops to Sri Lanka
1989–	V. P. Singh as prime minister

India's System of Government

India, like Britain, has a **parliament** consisting of an upper and a lower house. The upper house, the *Rajya Sabha* (RUHJ-yuh SUB-huh), or Council of States, with no more than 250 members has very little power. Members of the Council of States serve for six years, with a third of its 238 elected members being elected every two years by the state legislatures. The president of India, who is the country's constitutional head of state, appoints 12 members to the Council of States. These appointed members are usually distinguished writers, artists, scholars, and scientists. The real lawmaking body in India is the lower house, the *Lok Sabha* (LAHK SUB-huh), or House of the People. Its 546 members may serve for the five years prescribed by the constitution, or less if the president dissolves parliament and calls for new elections. Of its total membership 532 must be elected by qualified voters. The other members represent the union territories and are chosen in a manner prescribed by parliament.

Executive and Judicial Functions

The constitution states that "the executive power . . . shall be vested in the president." In practice, however, the president exercises power only upon the request of the prime minister, who is the actual head of the Indian government. India's president is elected jointly by parliament and the state legislatures for a term of five years. The president formally appoints the prime minister, has the power to dissolve parliament and to call for a new election, and constitutionally has broad powers over the state governments.

The prime minister, who is the leader of the majority party in the lower house of parliament, chooses an advisory council from party members in parliament. The prime minister and the advisory council perform all of the other executive functions of government.

Unlike the United States, which has both federal and state courts, India has only federal courts. The judges of these courts have a large measure of independence and cannot easily be influenced by the executive and legislative branches.

State Governments

The state governments are modeled on the national system, each having a legislative assembly and a legislative council. The nominal head of each of the 25 states is a governor appointed by the president of India. The governor of each state appoints a chief minister, who is the leader of the majority party in the state legislative assembly. The head of the legislative council is the chief minister. Members of the legislative council are appointed by the governor on the advice of the chief minister. Most states have bicameral legislative assemblies, but some have single-house legislative assemblies. State legislators are chosen by direct election. Membership in state legislative assemblies varies from as few as 60 to as many as 500 members.

In addition to the 25 states, India has seven union territories. These territories, administered by the central government, have less autonomy than the states. Their people do not elect legislative assemblies, but they do elect members of legislative councils.

S IDELIGHT TO HISTORY

India's Constitution

India is often described as the world's largest democracy. Like the British system, India's constitution set up a parliamentary system of government, with a prime minister serving as the actual head of government. Like the United States system, the constitution of India created a system of federalism and provided for a Supreme Court with the power of judicial review. The constitution of India also emphasizes human rights and equality. Its preamble closely models that of the United States:

> WE, THE PEOPLE OF INDIA, having solemnly resolved to constitute India into a SOVEREIGN, DEMOCRATIC REPUBLIC and to secure to all its citizens:
>
> JUSTICE, social, economic, and political;
>
> LIBERTY of thought, expression, belief, faith and worship;
>
> EQUALITY of status and opportunity; and to promote among them all
>
> FRATERNITY assuring the dignity of the individual and the unity of the nation;
>
> IN OUR CONSTITUENT ASSEMBLY . . . do HEREBY ADOPT, ENACT, AND GIVE TO OURSELVES THIS CONSTITUTION.

The constitution was adopted on January 26, 1950. The Republic of India remains a full member of the British Commonwealth and accepts Britain's monarch as "the symbol of the free association of its independent member nations and, as such, the head of the Commonwealth." Since its adoption, the constitution has been amended 57 times.

Like the British parliamentary system, the head of the party that wins a majority in a national election becomes the prime minister. While the constitution specifies that the term of election is five years, the prime minister through the president must call for a new election any time that the legislature gives the ruling party a vote of "no confidence." The prime minister also has the right to call for a new election whenever the situation seems to demand it. So far the call has seldom been requested.

CONSTITUTIONAL GOVERNMENT IN INDIA

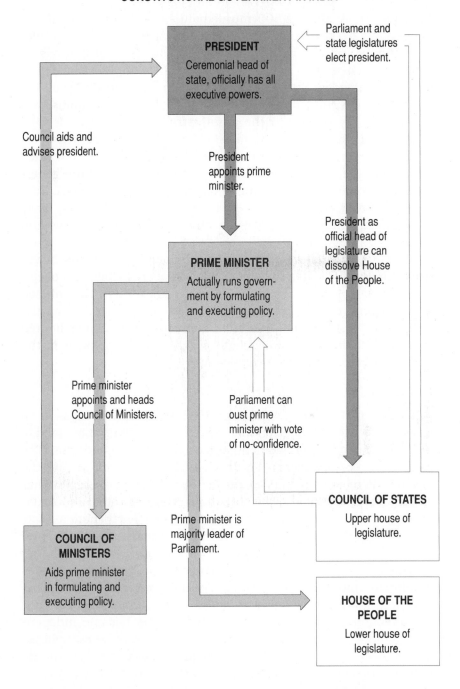

PRESIDENT
Ceremonial head of state, officially has all executive powers.

Parliament and state legislatures elect president.

Council aids and advises president.

President appoints prime minister.

President as official head of legislature can dissolve House of the People.

PRIME MINISTER
Actually runs government by formulating and executing policy.

Prime minister appoints and heads Council of Ministers.

Parliament can oust prime minister with vote of no-confidence.

COUNCIL OF STATES
Upper house of legislature.

COUNCIL OF MINISTERS
Aids prime minister in formulating and executing policy.

Prime minister is majority leader of Parliament.

HOUSE OF THE PEOPLE
Lower house of legislature.

FUNCTIONS OF GOVERNMENT. The chart above shows the flow of legislative and executive responsibility and authority as determined by the constitution of India.

Local Government

India has more than 2,500 municipalities and other city units, most of which are ruled by elected municipal councils under the sanction of the state governments. In the rural areas of India, the district is a major political subdivision. Most of India's states are divided into districts, a system inherited from the days of British rule. Under British rule, the district commissioner was the key official in the administrative system. Under the constitution, the district commissioners remain the most important government officials in rural India. The offices are now filled by presidential appointment. The commissioners have the general responsibility for developing projects to further economic development and social welfare in their respective districts. They also collect revenue and have authority to maintain law and order.

Within each district are hundreds or even thousands of villages. Each village has an official who is responsible for collecting revenue and keeping order in the community. This official is a member of the panchayat, the governing council of the village. For millions of peasants, many of whom have limited contact with the state and federal system, the panchayat is the most important unit of government.

Congress Party Domination

India has had many political parties, but until its loss of a majority in the 1989 elections the Congress Party has held a near monopoly on government offices since independence. The leaders of the Congress Party were in the forefront of the nation's struggle for independence. Their names were familiar to millions of Indians, many of whom knew nothing about national politics. Moreover, only the Congress Party had a truly nationwide organization with branches in every major city and town.

The rivals of the Congress Party represented many shades of political opinion. Some political groups, such as the Socialists and the Communists, had been active before independence. Other opposition parties were founded after India became independent. Among competitors of the Congress Party were political parties seeking to preserve Hinduism, parties devoted to the interests of factory workers, organizations concerned with the special problems of farmers, and parties that advocated rapid social change. But for many years no party was able to make a significant showing against the firmly entrenched Congress Party.

Although almost a quarter of a billion people were eligible to vote in postwar India, only about half that number exercised this right in the early elections. One of the major obstacles to voting was widespread illiteracy. This problem was solved by continuing a practice devised during British times. In this practice, parties and their candidates used familiar symbols to identify themselves. Thus, in campaign materials and on the ballot the Congress Party was represented by a pair of yoked bullocks (young bulls). The Communist Party was identified by ears of corn and a sickle. The Socialists used a hut for their symbol. The Jan Sangh (JUHN SUNG), representing orthodox Hindus, was identified by a lamp.

Over the years Indian voters have become increasingly more concerned about government. Because Indian voters now weigh political choices with even greater care than when independence was first declared, candidates of the incumbent party need to campaign vigorously to be reelected and kept in power. Every political party, for example, has experienced ups and downs in popularity among the voters, depending primarily on its stand on domestic issues.

Nehru's Influence

In the postwar era, Nehru towered above all other Indian leaders. From independence until his death in 1964, Jawaharlal Nehru remained at the helm of India's national government. The leader of the National Congress Party, he led it to parliamentary majorities in three successive national elections. Nehru was India's first prime minister, and as long as he lived no other Indian could aspire to party leadership in order to gain that office.

Nehru was the only Indian leader to gain respect and popularity approaching that held by Mahatma Gandhi. Nehru exercised enormous power, though perhaps not so much as some of his critics contended. Nehru admitted that he made mistakes in governing India. Whatever progress India made during the early years of independence, however, must be credited to the leadership of Nehru, who retained the confidence of the Indian people until his death. Nehru's passing marked a turning point in the politics of modern India. Nehru was the symbol of the generation that had struggled for independence. But by the final years of his life, a new generation had arisen, one that had taken no part in the nationalist movement. While these young men and women admired Nehru, they were less enchanted with some of the older nationalist leaders. While these leaders retained control of the party's power structure after Nehru's death, they showed no inclination to share positions of leadership with the new generation of voters. Moreover, the Congress Party was split into factions, and only Nehru's magnetism had kept the huge organization reasonably united. Excluded from the power structure of the Congress Party and disillusioned by its lack of real unity, the new generation of voters turned increasingly to other political parties.

Even before Nehru's death, the Congress Party's popularity had begun to wane. With Nehru's death, the party's decline became more rapid. Lal Bahadur Shastri (lul buh-HUH-door SHUHS-tree), a veteran in the fight for independence, became prime minister. Shastri lacked Nehru's stature in leadership and popularity. During Shastri's brief period as leader of the Congress Party and prime minister of India, the split in party ranks widened. Still, the Congress Party maintained its firm control of the Indian government.

The Rise of Indira Gandhi

Indira Gandhi breathed new life into the Congress Party when, on Shastri's death in 1966, she became prime minister of India. Indira Gandhi, who was born in 1917, was Nehru's only child. After attending college in India, she went to Britain in 1937 to study at Oxford University. Shortly after her return to India, Indira Nehru married a lawyer and journalist named Feroze Gandhi, who was no relation to the Mahatma. The Gandhis had two sons, but the marriage was not a happy one and, after a few years, the Gandhis separated.

When Nehru became prime minister, Indira Gandhi served as his official hostess. (Nehru's wife died in 1936, and he did not remarry.) Soon Gandhi became active in the Congress Party and in 1959–1960 served as its president. In 1964 she was appointed India's Minister for Information and Broadcasting in Shastri's government.

Despite Indira Gandhi's efforts to restore unity, the Congress Party continued its quarrels over issues of leadership and policies. In the national elections of 1967 the party suffered a serious decline. It lost almost one quarter of its seats in the lower house of parliament, and fully half the states voted the Congress Party out of office. At no time since the winning of independence had the power and prestige of the Congress Party sunk so low. These political setbacks convinced Gandhi that the Congress Party had to be revitalized. Even at the cost of further splitting the party, she launched a basic shakeup in leadership.

184

Change in Policies

For several years turmoil raged within the party, but Gandhi succeeded in keeping the upper hand. In the national elections held in 1971, her supporters, running as the New Congress Party, captured more than two thirds of the seats in the lower house of parliament. This landslide victory firmly established Gandhi's power and popularity with the voters of India.

Gandhi's popularity began to wane when the economy faltered in the mid–1970's. Upset by the economic decline, voters staged nationwide protests, demanding her resignation. Claiming that order was breaking down, the government issued the Proclamation of Emergency under Article 352 of the constitution in June 1975. Under the state of emergency formalized by the proclamation, opposition politicians were arrested, press censorship was imposed, and many civil rights were suspended. More than 100,000 people were arrested and held without trial. The state of emergency lasted 21 months. When nationwide elections were finally held in March 1977, the result was a decisive victory for the Janata Party, a coalition of opposition parties. Soon thereafter, Mararji Desai (mohr-AHR-jee DEE-SIGH) became prime minister.

The Janata Party, which had never been more than a loose coalition, was in power for only a brief time. Shortly after coming into power, its various factions began squabbling with one another. Desai was forced out of office in 1979. Charan Singh, who formed an interim government, followed him. Meanwhile, Indira Gandhi had been elected to parliament from where she planned her return to power. She eventually hoped to have Sanjay, the favorite of her two sons, succeed her. But Sanjay died in a plane crash in 1980. The elections in January 1980 gave Indira Gandhi and the New Congress Party a sweeping victory. Rajiv (rah-JEEV), Gandhi's other son, won election to his brother's seat in parliament. Indira Gandhi then appointed Rajiv to a high post in the New Congress Party, intending that he gain political experience.

In 1984 a group of Sikh separatists were using the Golden Temple at Amritsar, the Sikh's holiest shrine, as a base from which to send out raiders into the countryside. Indira Gandhi ordered the Indian army into the temple. The 14 million Sikhs in India were outraged at the invasion of the temple and the killing of fellow Sikhs. Later in the year, Indira Gandhi was assassinated by two Sikhs who were part of her bodyguard. Needing a figure who could rally the nation, the members of her government turned to Rajiv.

Rajiv Gandhi

Unlike Sanjay, Rajiv Gandhi had not been groomed for a political career and, in fact, had been quite happy to stay out of politics. But when his brother died, he willingly sacrificed his own wishes to continue his family's political tradition. Several weeks after Rajiv assumed the post of prime minister, he led the New Congress Party to an impressive triumph in the 1985 national elections as millions of Indians remained loyal to the Nehru–Indira Gandhi dynasty. Rajiv contributed to his victory by promising to weed out corruption in government and to enhance government efficiency.

Religious and Ethnic Strife

Rajiv inherited a number of problems. Perhaps his most serious challenge was ethnic unrest and regional demands for greater autonomy. He also had to cope with the ongoing conflict among Hindus, Sikhs, and Muslims. Since 1985, the year Rajiv Gandhi assumed the post of prime minister, Sikh terrorists have murdered several thousand people. Extremist Hindu organizations also have been formed and have engaged in terrorist activities. Following Indira Gandhi's death, at least 3,000 Sikhs were murdered by Hindus. While many of these attacks were organized by local Congress Party bosses, Rajiv Gandhi never expressed any outrage to his public.

The amount of Hindu–Muslim violence that has long plagued India has probably not increased during the 1980's. However, religious and ethnic strife has spread to parts of the country that previously had not experienced it. Large numbers of Hindus actually fear that the Muslims will once again dominate India as they did during the time of Aurangzeb. (See pages 92–93.) The fear is largely unwarranted. Although India has more Muslims than any other country except Indonesia and Bangladesh, Hindus in India are overwhelmingly in the majority, representing about 83 percent of the population.

On their part, many Muslims fear either that they will be absorbed into Hindu society or that they will be annihilated. Muslims also complain about discrimination in business and government service. They argue that Muslims own few of India's businesses and that Muslims are underrepresented in public service jobs. Muslims, however, have seldom attempted to acquire the type of education that would enable them to pass successfully the civil service exams that qualify them for public service jobs. Still, discrimination of one religious or ethnic group toward another is deeply ingrained in Indian society.

A FAMILY'S LEADERSHIP IN INDIA.   Mrs. Indira Gandhi, who served as India's prime minister two different times (1966–1977; 1980–1984), is shown with her prime minister father (1947–1964), Jawaharlal Nehru (top left), and her prime minister son (1984–1989), Rajiv Gandhi (top right). Rajiv (below) campaigns for the job in 1984 after his mother's assassination.

Violence has also occurred in several of India's border areas when foreigners have moved in, usually in search of work. In Tripura, a state in northeastern India, a number of immigrants from Bangladesh have been murdered. There are also separatist movements taking place. The Gurkhas living in West Bengal have demanded a separate state within India. Some of the Gurkahs have resorted to terrorism and other violence. Another separatist movement existed in Tamil Nadu in southern India for a number of years, but separatism there has apparently died down. However, a separatist movement among Muslims has been developed in Kashmir.

Gandhi's Political Future

Rajiv Gandhi's popularity eroded after its high point in 1984 and 1985. At that time he was widely regarded as a person who would root out government corruption. He spoke out forcefully against the unholy alliance of business people, bureaucrats, and politicians—a "license-permit raj"—as many people called it. Business people contributed to political campaigns and paid off politicians and bureaucrats. In return, the government gave out favors to certain businesses and protected them from competition, both domestic and foreign. In the process the economy improved slowly, consumers suffered, and democracy was undermined.

As prime minister, Gandhi did not move forcefully enough against corruption, perhaps because he feared antagonizing those who benefited from the current system. More seriously, his own administration became engulfed in charges of corruption. In spring 1987 information came to light that government officials had accepted enormous bribes from a Swedish arms manufacturer. As the months passed, growing numbers of Indians concluded that the government was engaged in a massive cover-up of scandal and corruption.

When India held elections for the lower house at the end of 1989, Gandhi and the Congress Party won more seats than any other single party. But the Congress Party failed to win a majority. Following the clear mandate for change expressed by the voters, the president of India asked V. P. Singh, a former member of Gandhi's cabinet and a leader of the National Front coalition to be prime minister. The naming of Singh brought to a halt rule by the Congress Party, which had been in power for all but three years since independence. Nehru, his daughter, and his grandson had ruled India for all but five years of the Congress Party's rule.

188

Supporters greet V. P. Singh outside his home in New Delhi just before his nomination as prime minister.

The Indian people, however, had many reasons for wanting a change in party leadership. Many were deeply troubled by the corruption in their society, and large numbers of them held Gandhi and the Congress Party responsible. Many were convinced that Gandhi himself was involved. Many Hindus complained that Gandhi had not stood up to Muslim fundamentalists and Sikhs. Finally, few Indians gave Gandhi credit for India's economic boom of the late 1980's.

Until the election campaign, Singh—nicknamed "the Raja"—was a distant figure to many Indians. His success as prime minister hinged on his ability to keep the National Front coalition united behind him.

Check Your Understanding

1. **a.** How does India's constitution give it a government that resembles the government of Great Britain? **b.** In what ways does the constitution reflect democratic ideals of the United States?
2. Why is the government of India a federation?
3. Why is the panchayat the most important unit of government on the local level?
4. *Thinking Critically:* Why has the Congress Party dominated politics in India since independence? What characteristics of India and of Indian politics have accounted for the lack of opposition?

2. India's Economic Headway

Nehru and his lieutenants recognized the urgency of strengthening India's economy. Among the major nations of the world, none had a poorer **standard of living** than India. At the time of independence in 1947, India's **per capita income** was estimated to be about $50. Because this sum is an average, that meant millions of Indians were living on less. Consequently, stimulating economic growth and raising the standard of living for the majority of Indians was the most important task facing the new government. The challenge was overwhelming. More than 40 years after independence, however, India has developed a growing industrial sector. Millions of Indians belong to a growing and prosperous middle class. Still, the majority of Indians live in poverty. In the late 1980's India's annual per capita income was only about $270 a year, a reflection of the meager circumstances in which most Indians live.

A Growing Economy

India's leaders were determined to raise their country's standard of living but did not agree on how to accomplish this. Many top-ranking members of the Congress Party were industrialists and businesspeople. They believed that India could best make economic progress by encouraging **free enterprise.** If the system made them wealthy, they reasoned, it could make others wealthy. They were also thinking in terms of protecting their own interests. They pointed to Great Britain and the United States as examples of countries that had built healthy economies by encouraging the development of free enterprise. But Nehru and his supporters blamed Britain and its economic system for many of India's problems. Also, Nehru was convinced that **capitalism** could not work in a **Third World** country because of the lack of available capital to develop new industries. He believed that socialism and **central planning** were the path to India's economic future.

India's leaders finally established a **mixed economy,** one that combined free enterprise and socialism. Both private capital and public funds were to be used to develop industry, mining, and farming. The government, however, prepared the master plan for developing the nation's resources, giving India's economy a socialist framework. That master plan was implemented in a series of five-year plans. The first Five–Year Plan went into effect in 1951. The seventh plan went into effect in 1985, and the eighth Five–Year Plan took effect in 1990.

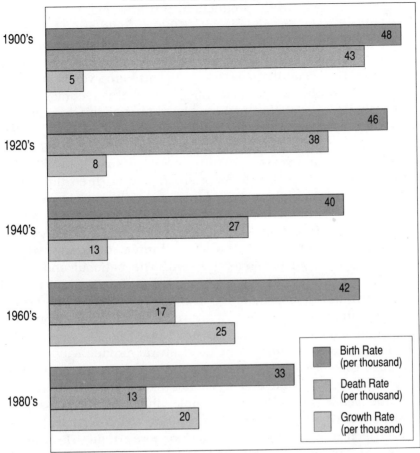

POPULATION GROWTH IN INDIA

1900's	Birth: 48, Death: 43, Growth: 5
1920's	Birth: 46, Death: 38, Growth: 8
1940's	Birth: 40, Death: 27, Growth: 13
1960's	Birth: 42, Death: 17, Growth: 25
1980's	Birth: 33, Death: 13, Growth: 20

Birth Rate (per thousand)
Death Rate (per thousand)
Growth Rate (per thousand)

POPULATION GROWTH. The graph above shows the average rate of growth for every 1,000 people (birth rate minus death rate) in India from the 1900's to the 1980's. Note that although the birth rate generally decreased from the 1900's to the 1980's, the average rate of growth was much higher in the 1980's than it was in the early part of the century. Why is this?

Agricultural Production

Nehru believed that the nation needed to give the highest priority to boosting the output of food. At the time of independence, the crop yield per acre in India was one of the lowest in the world. Farmers were too poor to buy fertilizer or to invest in improved seeds and insecticides. Farming methods were out of date, with peasants continuing to use methods developed by their ancestors centuries ago. Moreover, landholdings were small. The average farm was five acres, but millions of peasants had only an acre or two.

During the Nehru years, India made considerable progress in expanding agricultural production. But even more rapid gains were beginning in the mid– to late–1960's. India and a number of other countries experienced a **green revolution,** an impressive expansion of agricultural productivity. Through the green revolution, these countries were able to raise crop yields dramatically through the use of scientific agricultural techniques. In some cases countries that had long been food importers suddenly became food exporters. In India the amount of land under cultivation increased by 10 percent between 1961 and 1981. Yet during these same years agricultural output soared by 50 percent. By the mid–1980's grain production was three times the 1951 level. Farmers planted newly developed high-yield varieties of wheat, rice, and other grains and made increasing use of fertilizers. The irrigation system was expanded and improved. Irrigation frequently made possible **double cropping** where single cropping had previously existed. The national and state governments in India were also very active in funding agricultural research and in disseminating useful information to the farming population. By 1990, agriculture accounted for about 40 percent of India's gross national product (GNP).

The dramatic expansion in agricultural productivity helped minimize the threat of famine from the ever-present possibility of drought, a condition that India has experienced many times over the years. In 1965, for example, India suffered a severe drought. Faced with the threat of famine, the government purchased food from abroad and asked for foreign aid. The United States sent thousands of bushels of wheat. When the drought continued into the next year, India made a new appeal for help. Again the United States responded.

In the late 1980's, however, India experienced an even worse drought. This time there was no famine and no need to plead for foreign help. The reason was the large surpluses that the government had managed to accumulate through its increases in food production. The government used these surpluses to distribute food to people in need, thus preventing famine and starvation.

Nonetheless, India's agricultural problems are not over. The nation's population continues to expand at too fast a rate. After partition, India's population was about 345 million. The population reached 392 million in 1957 and passed the half-billion mark in the mid–1960's. In 1990 India's population was estimated to be about 833 million. Eventually, increases in population will outstrip increases in the food supply. In addition, too many people still work the land, with agricultural workers making up about 70 percent of India's work force. Between 1961 and 1981, India's rural population increased by about 166 million, while the amount of land under cultivation increased by only 10 percent.

Industrial Expansion

In 1948 when it became independent, India had a modest industrial system. But in terms of its size and large population, India's industrial development was quite inadequate. One of the reasons was India's place in the British system of **mercantilism.** Britain, being a highly industrialized nation, turned out many products that it needed to sell in its colonial markets. Not wanting competition for its finished goods, Britain had slowed India's **industrialization** by developing India as a market for British products. Once in charge of its own destiny, however, India began to encourage industrialization and made notable strides in that direction. Still in terms of India's enormous population, manufacturing output has remained very small.

Problems of Economic Expansion

India's road to industrialization has been slow and difficult. A continuing problem has been the lack of investment capital. Without capital India cannot develop new industries nor can it expand established ones. Part of the problem has been caused by the extensive restrictions that India has placed on foreign investments. These restrictions have existed mainly because India has been deeply concerned about foreign economic exploitation and domination. In addition, Indian business people have wanted to monopolize all of the economic opportunities in their own country.

Another reason for the lack of capital available for full industrialization has been the priority given to defense spending. In 1962 a border dispute with China erupted into a brief war that ended with India experiencing a humiliating defeat. The government's response was to divert a larger portion of the national budget into military expenditures. In 1965 and again in 1971 India went to war with Pakistan. Although India won these wars easily, its military needs put a strain on the economy. During the 1970's and 1980's India has continued to spend heavily on its military establishment.

Until Rajiv Gandhi became prime minister, Indian manufacturing was heavily regulated by the state. Many of the industries underwent **nationalization.** In the 1970's Indira Gandhi nation-

193

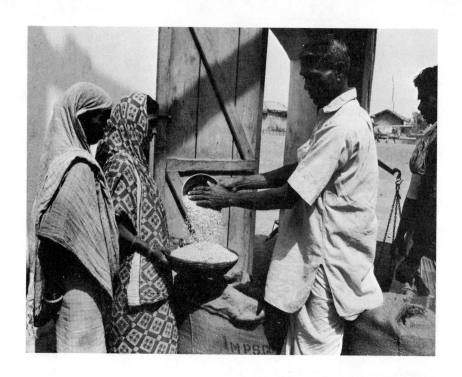

THE FOOD PROBLEM.
During the severe drought of the late 1980's, the government was able to distribute food to the needy (above) from its large store of surplus grains. Crop experts at an Indian university (right) study seeds of high-yield varieties of corn. Why must India continue to improve its crop production?

alized the banking and insurance industries and imposed even stiffer limitations on foreign business people who were interested in investing in India. The private sector was limited largely to the manufacture of consumer goods. An owner of a factory in the private sector could not expand production, build a new facility, or close down an existing one without receiving permission from the government.

In the years since independence an extensive and cumbersome system of regulations and controls was developed. An enormous **bureaucracy** evolved in order to implement and police the government's economic policy. The people who staffed the bureaucracy frequently used their power to obtain illegal payments from the business community. Connections and the payment of bribes, not market forces, determined which businesses thrived and which did not.

India's large number of government-owned industries, particularly in the heavy industrial sector of steel, transport, mining, power, and fertilizers, were incredibly inefficient. The coal mines, for example, employed 700,000 workers. This vast work force produced as much coal as Australia, yet Australia had a work force of only 30,000 miners. Thousands of government enterprises ran at a loss.

Relaxation of Controls

Massive government interference in the economy slowed the growth rate. Corruption was pervasive. Consumers complained about shortages, lack of choice, and **inflation.** During the late 1970's and early 1980's many influential Indians began to criticize the government's economic policies. Very slowly, Indira Gandhi began to relax some of the business controls. This policy was expanded in the 1980's, when Rajiv Gandhi became prime minister. He reduced the restrictions that had been placed on foreign business people who wanted to invest in India. To Gandhi it seemed obvious that his country sorely needed Western capital and technology. He also made it easier for foreign goods to enter the Indian market. Because the government had erected a wall of **protectionism,** Indian industry did not have to worry about foreign competition. But the complacency that developed as a result of protectionism had discouraged manufacturers from becoming more efficient. The result was that consumers had to pay high prices for domestically made goods. Moreover, most Indian companies could not sell their products abroad. Rajiv Gandhi insisted that Indian industry modernize and become more competitive.

ECONOMIC GROWTH. Government relaxation of economic and business regulations has given the steel industry a boost, enabling factories like the one at the Tatu truck plant in Janshedpur (top left) to become more productive. India has also actively modernized its agricultural and industrial sectors. New varieties of high-yield crops (above right) have helped increase India's food supply. The privately owned electronics company (below) manufactures microchips and semiconductors.

India's Economic Future

Over the years India has developed a dual economy. A modern industrial and service economy exists in urban areas and a traditional economy exists in rural areas. While India has placed satellites in orbit and developed the technology to test an atomic bomb, at least one third of its rural citizens live in homes that lack electricity. In the large cities, stores are filled with advanced consumer electronics. Yet only about 10 to 15 percent of the Indian people can afford these products, and hundreds of millions of India's rural poor do not participate at all in the money economy.

As India's election of 1989 approached, the results of Rajiv Gandhi's policy changes were mixed. The private industrial sector had grown rapidly and exports had soared. A flood of new private investments had occurred. Many industries were producing surpluses for the first time. A wide variety of quality consumer products were now available in the stores. Tax revenues were up, but unemployment remained high. Furthermore, many businesses had been badly hurt by the increase in competition, and some had gone out of business. Although the drought of 1987 and 1988 never created a famine, it did hurt India's economic performance. The pace of economic reform slowed. Many people charged that the reforms had benefited only the rich. With the 1989 election bringing a new government to power, it is not clear how India's economic policies may change.

Check Your Understanding

1. Why did Nehru believe that socialism and central planning were better for India than free enterprise and capitalism?
2. Why is agricultural production still not sufficient to meet India's food needs?
3. **a.** Why does India have a lack of capital? **b.** How has lack of capital hindered India's progress toward full industrialization?
4. **a.** What were the results of Indira Gandhi's economic policies? **b.** What complaints did people have about these policies?
5. *Thinking Critically:* How has India departed from socialism and central planning in its efforts to expand agricultural production and industrialization?

3. India's Social Progress

For the long-suffering people of India, the new nation's leaders realized that more than food, clothing, and shelter were needed. Nehru and his successors hoped to raise the level of education, to improve public health, and to eliminate the social injustices that made many Indians second-class citizens. In short, government leaders wanted to create a way of life characterized by freedom and human dignity. Despite many handicaps, India has made progress in social reform.

Education in India

India can boast of a tradition of education dating back many centuries. Historically, Indian education was elitist and religious in nature. The few upper-class Hindus and Muslims who learned to read and write did so in connection with religious studies. These privileged individuals were only a tiny percentage of the population. The Western-style education introduced by the British also reached only a small number of people. At the time India became independent, only about 15 percent of the population could read and write.

In India's federal system of government, education is a shared responsibility of both the central government and the states. Primary education, the first four or five grades, is free. But education, except in a few states, is not compulsory, mostly because compulsory education does not make sense in a nation where the majority of the people need every hand to eke out a living. Still the leaders of the new India believed that literacy was needed to develop a modern democratic society. Consequently, expanding educational opportunities, especially on the primary school level, was a priority of the Indian government. This priority has also dramatically increased the number of teachers, schools, and students.

Although India has made great gains in education, the country still has a long way to go. As of the late 1980's, 64 percent of the Indian population is still illiterate. Of the millions of school-age children, 93 percent between the ages of 6 and 11 start school. The number drops to 52 percent for children attending school between the ages of 11 and 14. On average, about 40 percent stay in school until the fifth grade and about 25 percent reach the eighth grade. The dropout rate is far higher for girls than for boys and is higher in rural areas.

Since independence, many colleges and universities have been added to the institutions of higher learning that were founded during the British era. In the 1950 academic year, about 360,000 students were enrolled in higher education. By the late 1980's, the figure had risen to almost four million. Although this figure represents less than 1 percent of the people in India, competition is fierce for admission to first-rate colleges and universities. Even the less distinguished schools have more applicants than they can admit.

In the past, education has served as an avenue for advancement into middle and upper classes, but this is no longer the case. The Indian economy is simply unable to provide enough good jobs for all those with college degrees. As a result, many college graduates end up with low-paying jobs in the government bureaucracy or they leave the country to search for opportunities elsewhere.

The Brain Drain

Over the years, many talented people have left India. A number of university graduates have traveled to the United States and Europe for further training in their specialized fields. After completing their studies, a majority have decided not to return home, attracted by the higher salaries and better living conditions that are available overseas. Also, Indians in specialized occupations, such as doctors and scientists, find that the West has the research laboratories and sophisticated equipment they need to carry on their studies.

The "brain drain," as this loss of talented people is called, afflicts many poor countries, including Pakistan and Bangladesh, and produces an ironic situation for them. On the one hand, **less developed countries** desperately need the services of their educated citizens. On the other hand, the public and private sectors of less developed countries are not able to make effective use of all the graduates of higher education who do stay home.

The Language Issue

The issue of a national language was raised as soon as India's leaders had organized the new government. The issue was controversial because so many languages and dialects are spoken on the subcontinent. Most leaders spoke and wrote English, but few of them thought it should be the national language. For many people, English was the symbol of British imperial rule, something many of them had fought against for years.

The most logical choice for a national language was Hindi, the native language of about 38 percent of the people. Accord-

Developing nations often cannot offer their educated citizens the opportunities they can find overseas. Unfortunately most students, like the ones in this rural primary school, will not receive a secondary education.

ingly, the leaders of the new India added a provision to the constitution that made Hindi India's official language, effective in 1965. Many people, however, opposed the naming of Hindi as India's official language. Most speakers of Hindi lived in north India, and residents of other regions feared that the use of Hindi would weaken their cultures. In an effort to satisfy everyone, the constitution gave 14 other languages, plus English, official status. (See graph, page 18.)

The expansion of official languages has failed to extinguish the language controversy. Feelings against making Hindi the national language have been so strong that the government has not tried to force its acceptance. The opponents of Hindi argue that the non-Hindi speakers will never accept Hindi as the national language. These opponents further point out that although English is spoken by only 3 percent of the people, it is understood by most of India's leaders and can therefore be used for all official purposes. The opponents of Hindi as an official single national language see no reason for changing the current system of regional languages. On the other hand, the backers of Hindi complain about the use of English, which continues to bridge the barrier between India's many languages. The backers of Hindi as a single national language say that neither Hindi nor any other language will become a national language as long as English is used.

Improvements in Health Care

Over the centuries India has repeatedly suffered epidemics of such fatal diseases as malaria, smallpox, typhoid fever, cholera, and tuberculosis. Many Indians have also died from supposedly "non-fatal" illnesses, such as intestinal and respiratory ailments. Diseases related to malnutrition have been fatal for many of India's poor and homeless. The introduction of modern medicine during the British era greatly reduced the death rate in India by slowing down the epidemics that periodically broke out in various parts of the subcontinent. But it could scarcely be said that the Indian people enjoyed good health during the centuries of British rule.

Since independence, health improvement has been a major goal of the Indian government. Among the campaigns launched for this purpose have been efforts to get the villagers to avoid polluting water supplies and programs that will eliminate such animal carriers of disease as rats and other vermin. The government has paid for the education and training of doctors and nurses. It has also built hospitals and clinics and has sponsored medical research. India's health programs have also been aided by other countries and by the World Health Organization of the United Nations.

India's efforts have resulted in a certain amount of progress. The country no longer suffers, for example, from outbreaks of smallpox and typhoid fever. In the late 1980's and early 1990's, life expectancy was still only 50 years for Indian males who were born in 1981 and 52 for females born the same year. In contrast the life expectancy in Great Britain was 70 for males and 76 for females. The infant mortality rate remains unusually high, 104 per 1,000 births. In contrast, the infant mortality rates in the nations of Europe range from a low of 8 to a high of 19 for every 1,000 births.

India's leaders have realized that disease cannot be eliminated simply by providing doctors and nurses, medical equipment, and medicine. People's attitudes and behavior must also be modified. One factor working against a major modification of attitudes and behavior is India's widespread poverty. Poor people often cannot afford to alter their diets or to make other changes that have been proposed by health-care professionals. According to a recent study, for example, 50 to 70 percent of Indian children 10 years of age and under receive a daily intake of calories that is insufficient to maintain their health. An even larger percentage of young children receive an insufficient daily intake of protein.

Population Problems

Since the 1950's, India's population has been growing at an alarming rate. In earlier decades, the high birth rate had been offset by a high death rate and, as a result, the population had expanded at a much slower rate. Today with the improved knowledge and techniques of modern medicine, especially mass inoculations to prevent disease, the death rate has steadily declined. At the same time, however, the birth rate, while lowered, has remained stubbornly high. (See graph, page 191.)

The Indian government first began sponsoring family planning programs in the 1950's. By the late 1960's, the government concluded that the population explosion was the single greatest obstacle to India's economic development. Slowing down the population growth rate became a national priority. The government then started a campaign to introduce family planning programs and to educate people in the use of those programs.

The impact of family planning programs on India's population growth rate has not been great. Many Indians have ignored such programs. Moreover, a lack of qualified health-care professionals has hindered the distribution of family planning programs, and thus their effectiveness. Another problem is that many Indian women marry young, typically by their early 20's, thus expanding their child-bearing years. Furthermore, families to whom daughters are born continue having children until they have at least one son. Actually many Indian families want more than one son because they fear the high mortality rates for infants and young children. According to Hindu and Muslim traditions, sons are more important than daughters because sons carry on the family name. Also, sons are expected to take care of their parents in old age.

Status of the Untouchables

Perhaps India's oldest problem is the plight of the Untouchables, or the **Scheduled Castes,** as the constitution and other official documents refer to them. To help Untouchables overcome their many handicaps, the framers of India's constitution have officially outlawed Untouchability. The Scheduled Castes have been given equal access to government buildings, institutions, and services. Advisory councils and departments for promoting their welfare have been set up in all the states. Blocs of seats in parliament and in the state legislatures have also been reserved for the Scheduled Castes.

In the decades since the constitution was written, parliament has given additional help to the Scheduled Castes. Penalties for

POPULATION DENSITY

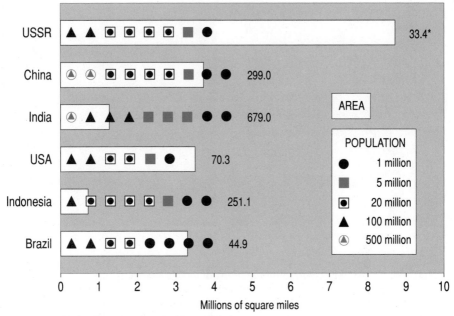

	Millions of square miles
USSR	33.4*
China	299.0
India	679.0
USA	70.3
Indonesia	251.1
Brazil	44.9

AREA

POPULATION
- ● 1 million
- ■ 5 million
- ◉ 20 million
- ▲ 100 million
- ◉ 500 million

Source: *The 1990 Information Please Almanac*
*Note: Figures indicate number of people per square mile.

COMPARING POPULATION DENSITIES.   Of the six most heavily populated nations, India has the highest population density, as shown in the graph by
the number of people per square mile. Where does India rank in land area?
Where does it rank in size of population?

discrimination have been provided and laws have been passed
assuring Untouchables a certain proportion of government jobs.
Also, universities have been required to admit a certain number
of applicants from this group. Because the economic condition
of the Scheduled Caste students is lower than the national average, the government has provided them with financial aid. In
recent years, several other groups have demanded legal status
as disadvantaged minorities.

The condition of India's millions of Untouchables is better
than it once was. Some Untouchables have found places in political life and have filled jobs previously closed to them. But the
majority of Untouchables have experienced little change in society's attitudes toward them. Legislation on their behalf is one
thing. Society's acceptance of change in their status is another.
As a result, legislation has been unable to sweep away
deep-rooted attitudes and customs that have been part of Indian
life for centuries.

SOCIAL CHANGE.　At the root of many of India's problems are illiteracy and a soaring population. To combat these problems, the Indian government has opened hundreds of new schools (above, left) and family planning clinics (below). Another area that has seen considerable change is the status of women. The woman at the upper right, employed in a high-technology factory, is an example of the increasing opportunities available for women outside the home.

The Status of Women

A very obvious advance in India has been the improved legal status of women. For many centuries women held an inferior position in Indian life. For example, women could not inherit property. At the death of a husband, his estate went to a son or brother rather than to his widow. In some regions, a widow could be deprived of her children. Marriage laws were also strongly weighted in favor of the husband.

The leaders of the new India have passed laws to give women equality in marriage, property rights, and other matters. Moreover, positions in public life and in private industry have been opened to women. Today many Indian women pursue careers in government, education, medicine, and the arts. Indira Gandhi's rise to the position of prime minister is proof that new opportunities are available to Indian women.

But actual change for India's women has occurred more slowly than the passage of legislation suggests. Furthermore, Indira Gandhi's status is far from typical. Men still hold the large majority of important positions in the government, the bureaucracy, business, and the professions. In most homes, women retain the entire responsibility for homemaking and taking care of the children.

While women in India have made progress toward achieving equality, much still needs to be done to change traditional ways of thinking. Examples of practices that Indian leaders want to abolish are child marriages and "dowry murder."

Already forbidden by law, parentally arranged marriages of children—sometimes as young as four and five years of age—are still common. Often, both bride and groom are young. On other occasions only the bride is a child. Such marriages are often arranged to cement relations between two families or to improve the status of one of the families, usually the groom's. Married children continue to live with their parents.

Discrimination against women is practiced through dowry murder. Dowry murders are committed by the wife's husband or his parents when the bride's dowry is smaller than expected. Often severe harassment is inflicted on the wife to force her family to offer further gifts to the husband. Sometimes women in this situation commit suicide so their families no longer have to sacrifice to make dowry payments. Perhaps several thousand dowry murders take place every year. Not all guilty parties are brought to justice. Many people feel that the government needs to enforce violations of the laws against dowry murder with greater energy and determination.

1. **a.** How has education in India changed since the days of British imperial rule? **b.** Why is primary education in India compulsory in only a few states?
2. **a.** Why does India have a language controversy? **b.** What is the nature of this controversy? **c.** What is a likely solution to it?
3. **a.** In what ways has the status of Untouchables changed in modern India? **b.** In what ways has their status remained the same?
4. How are traditional attitudes in India a major stumbling block to women's equality and advancement?
5. *Thinking Critically:* How are India's population size, language diversity, standard of living, and religious traditions bound up with its slow progress in social reform?

4. India's Place in the World Order

When India received its independence from Great Britain in 1947, shortly after the end of World War II, the balance of political power in the world was shifting. Germany and Japan, the former Axis nations, had been defeated in war and were no longer great powers. A Communist government was about to be established in mainland China. In the West, a number of Eastern European nations were coming under the domination of the Soviet Union. The once mighty empires of Britain and France were collapsing as former colonies began to agitate for independence. India, of course, was one of the first British colonies to achieve its independence.

From the ashes of World War II, a new order was emerging in international affairs. Eventually the new order would consist of three power **blocs.** One bloc was the Communist world, consisting of the Soviet Union and its satellite nations in Eastern Europe. Another bloc was the Western world, made up of the United States, its allies in Western Europe, and friends elsewhere. The third bloc, which became known as the Third World, consisted of many less developed and newly independent nations of Africa and Asia that officially followed a policy of **nonalignment** with either of the two **superpowers.** India had to decide which of these three blocs to join and what kind of role to play within the bloc of its choice.

India's Policy of Nonalignment

The Indian government from Nehru onward tried to pursue a policy of nonalignment with the two major superpowers. For India, the avoidance of entangling **alliances** was a way to maintain its own independence. Nonalignment did not mean neutrality or national isolation to India. With respect to the struggle between the Communist and Western blocs, nonalignment meant that India refused to become involved in issues that were of no direct concern to it. The Indian government insisted that it hold to a policy of judging each international issue on its own merits. India's critics at home and abroad, however, have argued that the government has been too quick to support the Soviet Union.

India's struggle for independence made it a foe of imperialism. From the beginning of the new nation, Nehru put India forward as a champion of Asian and African peoples who wanted freedom from colonial rule. By 1964 many of the former colonial possessions had achieved their independence. For India, anti-imperialism meant not only political freedom for colonial possessions but also the elimination of all remnants of foreign rule. In keeping with this attitude, India often spoke out against foreign economic domination and exploitation. India also demanded full equality for all peoples.

Relations with Pakistan

Since partition, India and Pakistan have fought three wars—in 1947–1948, 1965, and 1971. Central to the ongoing tension between the two countries has been a dispute over Muslim Kashmir, one of two provinces in the present-day state of Jammu and Kashmir. This state was important to both countries as a **buffer zone** against the other and against China. Kashmir was also a valuable prize because its rivers supplied water for the Indus irrigation system, which was used by both India and Pakistan. Each country was afraid that the other would monopolize the water if it controlled the source.

When a Muslim revolt flared up in Kashmir after partition, the Hindu ruler of the state fled to India and placed his state under India's rule. India flew troops to the state's capital to do battle with the Muslim rebels, who were supported by Pakistan. Fighting continued for two years, until the United Nations brought about a cease-fire and a division of Kashmir between India and Pakistan along the cease-fire line. In 1953 a legislative assembly in Kashmir voted for incorporation into India. The incorporation was delayed because of further disagreements between the two nations and the United Nations' disapproval of the annexation without a **plebiscite.**

Shortly after agreeing to the plebiscite, India retracted its pledge. Muslims greatly outnumbered Hindus in Kashmir, and Indian officials knew all too well how such a plebiscite would turn out. In 1956 India proclaimed that the part of Kashmir it was occupying was a permanent part of Indian territory. Tension over the Kashmir issue built up steadily until large-scale fighting between the two countries finally erupted in 1965. The fighting ended when a United Nations peace-keeping team negotiated another cease-fire along a new line that showed the inroads India had made into Pakistani-held territory.

In 1971, after fighting erupted between West and East Pakistan when the latter tried to secede, India and Pakistan again clashed in Kashmir. Again India made some gains in Pakistani-held territory. In December 1972 a new cease-fire took place. The new cease-fire line extended further into Kashmir.

In 1987 the possibility of a fourth war between these two countries was averted. The crisis occurred because both sides interpreted the other's military exercises as a prelude to an attack. In December 1988, Benazir Bhutto, Pakistan's new prime minister, met with Rajiv Gandhi. The two leaders agreed that their countries would not attack the other. Today relations are

The 1962 border dispute between India and China took place in some of the most rugged area on the subcontinent. The rugged terrain made it difficult to send in troops and supplies, which often had to be moved over narrow trails where few mechanized vehicles could travel. The fighting has since ended, but the borders between the two countries remain in dispute.

still tense, but the situation is somewhat less hostile than it was in 1987. The Kashmir dispute remains a major source of tension between these two countries.

The 1971 fighting had another result—the formation of the independent nation of Bangladesh from the Pakistani territory known as East Pakistan. For many reasons the people of East Pakistan, who made up 56 percent of Pakistan's total population, were discontented with their incorporation into Pakistan. (See page 221.) When civil war broke out in March 1971, India joined the fighting in support of East Pakistan's bid for independence, which was finally recognized by Pakistan in 1974. India entered the war because it wanted to create a friendly independent nation on its eastern border.

Annexation of Foreign Enclaves

Many of Nehru's foreign critics charged that India ignored its professed ideals of nonalignment and peaceful means to a solution whenever its own national interests were at stake. This argument gained additional supporters when India took steps to annex several small European possessions along the coast. These **foreign enclaves** were the last remnants of Portuguese and French power in India. None of them, with the possible exception of Portuguese-held Goa, had much strategic or economic importance. But these foreign enclaves reminded Indians of their country's former colonial status. Because of national pride as much as anything else, India's leaders decided that the enclaves had to be eliminated.

France put up little opposition when India demanded the **cession** of its possessions on the subcontinent. In 1954 France surrendered its five small holdings on India's east coast. Portugal, however, having held its three small territories for more than 400 years, refused to give them up. Finally, in 1961, India sent troops into the Portuguese enclaves. This militant action shocked many of India's supporters, who had heard Indian leaders condemn force as a means of settling international disputes.

Sino–Indian Relations

When the Communists came to power in China in 1949, Nehru was confident that India could maintain peaceful relations with the new government. India was one of the first countries to break off relations with the defeated Chinese Nationalist government and to recognize the People's Republic of China. India consistently led the annual attempt to have Communist China seated in the United Nations. In 1954 Nehru and the Chinese foreign minister, Zhou Enlai (JOE en-LIE), agreed on "Five Principles of Peaceful Coexistence," a pledge of peaceful and neighborly relations between India and China.

After China occupied Tibet in 1950, India began to be disturbed by the presence of Chinese forces along the borders of India, Bhutan, and Nepal. In 1959 Sino–Indian relations worsened when a widespread rebellion in Tibet was cruelly suppressed by the Chinese. The Dalai Lama, the spiritual leader of Tibet, and some 13,000 of his followers sought sanctuary in India. Over the next few years, skirmishes between Indian and Chinese troops occurred from time to time along the frontier. In 1962 heavy fighting suddenly broke out, and Chinese troops advanced into Indian border areas. Before a full-scale war could erupt, however, the Chinese withdrew from many of the areas they had occupied. China had made its point, namely that it did not recognize India's claim to **sovereignty** over the disputed frontier territories.

For about 14 years after 1962, relations between India and China remained tense. While maintaining diplomatic relations with each other, the two nations recalled their ambassadors. Contact between India and China was limited. India continued to insist that a satisfactory settlement of the border dispute was a condition for any real improvement in relations.

Only in the mid–1970's did Sino–Indian relations begin to improve, and then only gradually. In 1976 both countries once again exchanged ambassadors. Cultural and scientific exchanges grew, and trade began to expand slowly. In 1983 India and China held discussions regarding the disputed border territories, but nothing was resolved.

In December 1988, Rajiv Gandhi traveled to Beijing, becoming the first Indian prime minister to visit China in 34 years. Relations between the two countries, however, have remained distant. The Indian people did not want to surrender any Indian territory. For its part, China sees little to gain from improved relations with India.

Relations with the Soviet Union

Although India has refused to join either of the two great power blocs, it has been consistently friendly with the Soviet Union. For many years Indian leaders were inspired by the success of the Soviet Union in modernizing its industry within a socialist framework. During the 1950's and 1960's, the Soviet Union occasionally granted India economic, technical, and military aid. Although less substantial than similar programs of foreign aid

In 1989 the Dalai Lama, Tibet's ex-iled spiritual and political leader, received the Nobel Peace Prize for his nonviolent efforts to free Tibet from nearly 40 years of Chinese control. Enthroned in 1940 at the age of 5, he is the 14th Dalai Lama, or "high monk." China denounced the award and accused the Nobel committee of interference in China's internal affairs.

from the United States, Soviet aid was deeply appreciated in India.

The foreign policies of India, the Soviet Union, China, and Pakistan demonstrate the old diplomatic adage "my enemy's enemy is my friend." During the 1960's a widening split between the Soviet Union and China tended to draw India and the Soviet Union closer together, especially because Chinese leaders were directing propaganda attacks against both countries. It took some time, however, before India and the Soviet Union solidified their ties. Finally, in 1971, the two nations signed a 20-year treaty of "Peace, Friendship, and Cooperation." Meanwhile, China and Pakistan developed close ties of their own. When war flared up between India and Pakistan late in 1971, Soviet Russia shipped military supplies to India.

Although Soviet–Indian ties have remained close since 1971, India has never given blanket approval to Soviet actions. Indira Gandhi, for example, spoke out, although not forcefully, against the Soviet invasion of Afghanistan. Rajiv Gandhi, while maintaining the alliance, has tried to put some distance between India and the Soviet Union. At no time has India been willing to allow Soviet warships to use Indian ports as bases. Furthermore, India has always insisted that its relationship with the Soviet Union would not stop it from improving relations between India and any other country, including China.

Relations with the United States

Relations between India and the United States have been friendly but formal for many years. Americans felt deep sympathy for India, and Nehru had many admirers in the United States. As

American concern over Asian affairs mounted, the volume of aid to India increased. American funds for economic development and technical assistance and credits for the purchase of food played a vital role in India's early five-year plans. Nevertheless, India turned down offers of American military aid to remain nonaligned in foreign affairs.

When Chinese military ventures along the frontier exposed glaring weaknesses in India's defenses, Nehru, and later Shastri, had to turn to the United States for military aid. But when Indian and Pakistani troops clashed in 1965, the United States suspended arms shipments to both sides.

India as a Regional Power

Many South Asians and some people within India contend that India has come to regard itself as the protector of South Asia. On numerous occasions India has interfered with other nations, ostensibly to maintain the peace, but in reality to advance Indian national interests. In 1971 India supported Bengali secessionists. Then in 1975, India simply annexed the small Himalayan nation of Sikkim. In the fall of 1988, India sent troops into the island nation of the Maldives to put down an attempted coup by mercenaries.

Since 1987, Indian troops also have been in Sri Lanka, an island nation of 16 million people that lies off the southern tip of India. About 75 percent of the population are Sinhalese, most of whom are Buddhists. About 18 percent of the population are Tamils, a largely Hindu group. In 1983 Tamil **insurgents,** who wanted to create a separate Tamil nation in the north and east of Sri Lanka, began clashing with the Sri Lankan army. At the time, the insurgents were given support by India. Since fighting began in 1983, thousands of Sri Lankans have lost their lives and hundreds of thousands have become refugees in areas where they have sought safety.

By 1987, India had changed its attitude toward the civil war. Given the separatist movements that have plagued their own nation, India's leaders have concluded that they should think twice about supporting separatist movements abroad. Hoping to bring an end to the violence, India has sent troops to Sri Lanka with the agreement of the government there. India insisted that any settlement between the Sri Lankan government and the Tamil insurgents should grant substantial local autonomy to the Tamils. Indian forces, however, have become bogged down fighting the Tamil guerrillas. At the same time, the Sri Lankan army has been trying to hold Sinhalese extremists in check.

Foreign Policy and the Future

Except for making a greater effort to improve relations with China, V. P. Singh has indicated that he does not intend to depart from the foreign policy India followed under Rajiv Gandhi. During the late 1980's, India has had to reorient its foreign policy. The great-power rivalries that originally brought the Soviet Union and India together are now changing. With Mikhail Gorbachev defusing tensions with the West and with China, India has had to reconsider its own foreign policy. Most of all, India has had to reevaluate its relationship with China in light of the improving relations between the Soviet Union and China. No longer can India consider the Soviet Union as a counterbalance to China.

Check Your Understanding

1. **a.** How did the nations of the world align themselves after World War II? **b.** With what bloc has India aligned itself? **c.** Why do some people criticize India's foreign policy?
2. **a.** How did most of Kashmir become a part of India rather than Pakistan? **b.** Why is a fourth war between India and Pakistan over Kashmir still a possibility?
3. Why did India annex the foreign enclaves on the subcontinent?
4. What problems exist in the relationship between China and India?
5. What actions has India taken to show that it regards itself as the protector of other nations in South Asia?
6. **Thinking Critically:** How does the statement *"My enemy's enemy is my friend"* apply to relations between India and the Soviet Union?

CHAPTER REVIEW

■ Chapter Summary

Section 1. With the acceptance of its constitution in 1950, India officially became a democratic federal republic with a parliamentary system of government. The nation consists of 25 states and 7 union territories. The actual leadership of India rests with the prime minister, the leader of the majority party. Since independence, with the exception of a few years, India's leadership has come from the Congress Party, which has been dominated by the Nehru–Indira Gandhi dynasty. Rajiv Gandhi, Indira's son, was India's prime minister between 1985 and 1989. In elections held in November 1989, the Congress Party failed to win a majority of seats in the lower house. As a result, V. P. Singh emerged as the leader of the National Front coalition and was named prime minister.

Section 2. India has made considerable economic headway since independence in 1947. India's leaders established a mixed economy that operated within a public sector framework of socialism, central planning, and nationalization of heavy industries. These were combined with free enterprise in the private sector through a series of five-year plans. India's greatest economic gains were in agricultural productivity, which has helped minimize the threat of famine in recent years. But its agricultural productivity cannot keep pace with gains in population, which remains India's most serious concern for the future. India's industrialization has been hindered by lack of capital, which in turn has been hindered by too much emphasis on defense spending. Industrialization has also been limited by excessive bureaucratic regulations and by corruption. India's greatest need is to have its economic reforms benefit the poor as well as the wealthy.

Section 3. When independence occurred, India's new leaders wanted to provide the nation's people with a raised standard of living, a good system of education, and some measure of human dignity through social reforms. But 64 percent of India's people are still illiterate, and its average per capita income of $270 means that many of its people suffer from excessive poverty. Medical advances have helped reduce India's death rate, but the growth rate has not been stemmed, even though family planning programs operate throughout India. Discrimination toward women and the Scheduled Castes still exists despite legislation that emphasizes the equality of all people. India's leaders have found it easy to pass legislation to advance social reform but have found it difficult to change age-old attitudes. These attitudes are evident even in the language controversy that surrounds the continued use of English and the naming of Hindi as India's official language. To stem opposition, the government has given official status to 14 other languages.

Section 4. India emerged as an independent nation when the world political order was shifting into three blocs. Choosing the Third World bloc over the Communist or Western bloc, India has generally pursued a policy of nonalignment, except when it was in its own interests to do otherwise. Its most serious problems in foreign affairs have occurred with its neighbor Pakistan, with which it has fought three wars, and with China. It has consistently maintained friendly relations with the Soviet Union. With China it has had an ongoing border dispute that has resulted in distant relations. Its relations with the United States have been mostly friendly. Within its own region it considers itself a protector.

■ Vocabulary Review

Define: ideology, democracy, constitution, democratic federal republic, parliament, standard of living, per capita income, free enterprise, capitalism, Third World, central planning, mixed economy, green revolution, double cropping, mercantilism, industrialization, nationalization, bureaucracy, inflation, protectionism, less developed country, Scheduled Castes, bloc, nonalignment, superpower, alliance, buffer zone, plebiscite, foreign enclave, cession, sovereignty, insurgent

■ Places to Locate

Locate: Amritsar, Tripura, West Bengal, Tamil Nadu, Kashmir, Goa, Tibet, Sikkim, Sri Lanka

■ People to Identify

Identify: Jawaharlal Nehru, Lal Bahadur Shastri, V. P. Singh, Indira Gandhi, Morarji Desai, Sanjay Gandhi, Rajiv Gandhi, Benazir Bhutto

■ Thinking Critically

1. Explain how India's parliamentary system of government works. How is government connected to party politics? Why do you think India has rarely had strong opposition parties?
2. Why did Nehru think that socialism and central planning was the best framework for India's economic development? What changes took place between the 1950's and the 1990's that might be considered departures from central planning?
3. Why is education a crucial element in India's progress toward social reform? How is progress in education tied to economic reform?

4. Was India's establishment of a policy of nonalignment right for India? Why or why not?

■ **Extending and Applying Your Knowledge**

1. Find out more about one of India's states or union territories, using such reference books as *The Statesman's Year–Book,* latest edition. Prepare either an oral or a written report on its history, its area and population, language, constitution and government, and natural resources. In conclusion give an estimate of its importance to India's future progress.

2. *The Information Please Almanac* provides a table of the world's largest cities that lists for each a recent population figure, a projected population figure for the year 2000, area in square miles, and population density. Use the table to make a chart of India's largest cities. Display the chart to illustrate the severity of India's population problems.

8

Pakistan and Bangladesh After Independence

In the case of some nations, such as Pakistan, new developments seem to overshadow the past. For other nations, such as Bangladesh, change seems to come very slowly, and the past continues to dominate the present—and possibly the future.

Pakistan has experienced a number of very basic changes over the last several decades. Industry has developed, the agricultural sector has become more productive, and international trade has increased. Political changes have been even more dramatic, beginning with the secession and independence of Bangladesh (formerly East Pakistan) and continuing through the recent restoration of democracy after several years of dictatorial rule. With the restoration of democracy, Pakistanis chose a woman to be the new prime minister, the first female leader of a Muslim nation in modern times.

While Pakistan has undergone changes, much of the nation has remained largely as it once was—terribly poor and illiterate. Population increases have undone many of the benefits provided by economic expansion. Finally Pakistan's foreign policy has continued to revolve around its hostile relationship with India.

For Bangladesh, however, change has come so slowly that it seems as if time has stood still. The very same problems that thwarted economic development in 1971 still exist today. The country has also been a dictatorship almost from its day of independence to the present.

1. Politics in Independent Pakistan

For years before the partition of the British Empire on the Indian subcontinent, Muslim leaders dreamed about a separate nation of their own. That dream became a reality with the creation of the independent state of Pakistan. Pakistan, however, was even less ready for independence than India. Not only did partition leave particularly deep scars in Pakistan, but the new nation also had little on which to base a spirit of national unity. Moreover, Pakistan was a very poor nation, especially its eastern portion.

A Difficult Start

Few states of the postwar world were founded under such harsh conditions as Pakistan. The first unmistakably difficult condition was the division of the country into the two sections of West Pakistan and East Pakistan and their separation by 1,000 miles. (See map, page 176.) Most messages and goods passing from one section to the other had to follow air and sea routes that avoided India, the unfriendly nation that lay between the two Pakistani sections. The second difficult condition was the existence of a distinctive culture in each section, a factor that greatly hindered the development of any national unity between the two sections. Even the languages were different, with most people in West Pakistan speaking Urdu, while in East Pakistan, most people spoke Bengali. The most important bonds between the two sections of Pakistan were the mutual distrust of India and the Muslim religion, although their religious bonds differed slightly. West Pakistan looked to the Muslim nations of the Arab Middle East for inspiration, while East Pakistan had closer ties with the Muslim nations of Southeast Asia.

The third trying condition had to do with the resettlement of the more than six million Muslims who fled from India into West Pakistan after partition. One out of every five persons in newly independent Pakistan was a refugee. Families had to be resettled in new homes and new jobs had to be found for them so they could become self-supporting. In the meantime, their needs drained Pakistan's meager resources. The fourth difficult condition had to do with defense. Because India had absorbed most of the British military system, Pakistan was left with almost no military establishment of its own. Further, Pakistan had lost most of its merchants, moneylenders, and civil servants as well as many doctors, lawyers, and teachers. Most of these people were Hindus who had fled to India after partition.

218

Pakistan After Independence

1947	Pakistan's creation and independence
1948	Death of Mohammed Ali Jinnah
1950	Adoption of constitution
1955	Adoption of first Five–Year Plan
1956	Adoption of second constitution
1958–1969	Government of Ayub Khan
1962	Adoption of third constitution
1965	War with India over Kashmir
1966	Tashkent Declaration
1969–1971	Government of Yahya Khan
1971	War with India
	Independence of Bangladesh
1971–1977	Government of Ali Bhutto
1973	Adoption of fourth constitution
1977–1988	Government of Zia
1979	Beginning of war in Afghanistan
1988–	Government of Benazir Bhutto

Bangladesh After Independence

1971	Independence of Bangladesh
1972	Adoption of constitution
1972–1975	Government of Mujibur
1976–1981	Government of Ziaur
1976	Establishment of diplomatic ties with Pakistan
1982–	Government of Ershad
1988	Adoption of Islam as state's official religion

An Unsettled Political Situation

Like India, Pakistan also had to create a new central government. India had been able to build on its experience with the British governmental system, but the people in the areas that became Pakistan had experience only with the provincial level of government. They had to create and adopt a constitution for a central government, a process that was finalized in 1950 with the adoption of the nation's first constitution. The people had to learn how to organize a central legislature that operated effectively. The legislators, for example, had to learn how to work with a central executive. The government had to develop a foreign policy and establish an agency to handle economic development. For the first decade of its existence, Pakistan learned through trial and error, finding it difficult simply to survive.

India had the firmly established Congress Party to guide its destiny. But Pakistan had no strong political party to take it through the critical early years. Especially devastating to the new nation was the death in 1948 of Mohammed Ali Jinnah, the leader of the Muslim League, and the assassination in 1951 of the nation's first prime minister. If these two able leaders had lived, they might have brought a measure of stability to the land. At the time of independence, Jinnah had virtually taken over Pakistan's new government and had kept it from falling apart.

The passing of Mohammed Ali Jinnah led to bitter political struggles. Intense rivalries between leaders and parties threatened to tear the state apart. Cooperation between East and West Pakistan proved difficult because each was afraid of being dominated by the other. For a number of years Pakistan changed leaders with confusing frequency. Not even the adoption of a new constitution in 1956 and the establishment of Pakistan as an Islamic Republic within the British Commonwealth helped to eliminate political unrest. Paskistan withdrew from the Commonwealth in 1972.

The Start of Dictatorial Rule

In 1958 a strong political leader emerged to take control of the government. Army leaders had suspended the constitution and had declared **martial law.** Soon General Mohammed Ayub Khan (AH-yoob KAHN) became supreme. Taking the title of president, Ayub governed firmly. He removed corrupt officials, curbed economic abuses, and started social reforms. In 1962 a new constitution granted the president almost unlimited powers. One of the president's first acts was the lifting of martial law. In 1965 when presidential elections were held, the popular Ayub easily won. Many Pakistanis credited Ayub Khan with saving the nation from disaster, mainly because Pakistan was so divided that an effective government probably could not have been formed under a fully democratic process.

Political Differences with East Pakistan

Despite the benefits of efficient government, in 1969 simmering opposition to Ayub Khan's strong rule led to rebellion in East Pakistan and the establishment of an independent Bangladesh. Faced with continued riots and protest demonstrations, Ayub resigned from the presidency. His place as head of state was taken by General Agha Mohammed Yahya Khan (YAH-yah KAHN), the commander-in-chief of the Pakistani army, who proclaimed another state of martial law.

Yahya Khan made a serious effort to satisfy the demands of the government's critics. He relaxed many of the military controls over Pakistani life, cracked down on corruption by state officials, and permitted greater freedom of political expression. He also promised to hold elections for the parliament, which had been dissolved several months before. When the elections were held in 1970, an East Pakistani political party called the **Awami League** scored a landslide victory, winning all the parliamentary seats allotted to East Pakistan. The election sweep gave the Awami League a powerful base from which to continue its agitation for greater self-rule for East Pakistan. The Pakistan People's Party (PPP), a socialist group led by Zulfikar Ali Bhutto (BOO-toh), won many of the parliamentary seats in West Pakistan. The first responsibility of the newly elected parliament was to draw up a new constitution for the nation.

Yahya Khan twice postponed the first session of the new parliament. When leaders of the Awami League protested and rioting broke out, the government sent armed forces into East Pakistan to enforce its authority. The confrontation between Yahya Khan's regime and the East Pakistani protesters led to a continuous wave of violence. Finally, in December 1971, India entered the tragic conflict. In a short but bitterly fought war, the Indian army overwhelmed the Pakistani forces that were trying to suppress the revolt in East Pakistan.

As a result of India's military victory, East Pakistan established itself as the newly independent country of Bangladesh. Pakistan thus lost about one sixth of its territory and more than half of its population. In Pakistan, Yahya Khan was held responsible for the defeat, and he resigned the presidency in disgrace in December 1971.

The Ali Bhutto Years

Ali Bhutto, whose Pakistan People's Party was by then the largest political party in West Pakistan, succeeded Yahya Khan as president. Although Bhutto had the support of some wealthy

FORCEFUL LEADERS. Under Ayub Khan (right) Pakistan had a period of stability, but mounting unrest forced him to resign. Following the independence of Bangladesh in 1971, Ali Bhutto (left) took charge of the Pakistani government. His daughter Benazir, who followed him into public life, can be seen behind him. What contributions did each leader make to Pakistan?

Pakistanis, he made his strongest appeal to the rural and urban poor. He nationalized many industries, including banking, and raised wages for industrial workers. He also made a largely unsuccessful attempt to redistribute the land.

In 1973, Pakistan adopted a new constitution that provided for a two-house legislature consisting of an upper house called the Senate and a lower house called the National Assembly. Bhutto became the prime minister, with all executive power vested in that office. At Bhutto's direction, the constitution was written in such a way that it was virtually impossible for the National Assembly to remove the prime minister.

During his years in office, Bhutto moved away from policies of **egalitarianism** and became far more supportive of the wealthy elements in society. Although Bhutto spoke of his commitment to democracy, his political style over the years became increasingly **authoritarian.** He jailed thousands of political opponents inside and outside his party, and removed those in the bureaucracy and the military who dared to disagree with him. Many Pakistanis began to question his leadership.

222

In 1977 Bhutto announced that elections for the National Assembly would be held. Nine opposition parties formed a coalition—the Pakistan National Alliance (PNA). The PNA's campaign focused on the issues of government inefficiency and corruption. In the elections that followed, Bhutto's Pakistan People's Party (PPP) won two thirds of the seats in the National Assembly. The PNA charged fraud and demanded new elections, but Bhutto refused. Following widespread rioting and other acts of violence, Bhutto arrested the PNA leaders. In many parts of the country the army was called in to restore order. Then in July 1977 the army removed Bhutto from power by a military **coup** and declared still another period of martial law. Although Bhutto fell from power in disgrace, he is still remembered in Pakistan as a friend of the poor.

A Change in Leadership

General Mohammed Zia (ZEE-ah) ul-Haq, an army leader, became Chief Martial Law Administrator (CMLA). He first promised to hold elections in 90 days, but later decided to postpone the elections. He also initiated criminal investigations of Bhutto and other leaders of the PPP. Bhutto was tried and convicted of conspiracy to murder a political opponent and was executed in 1979.

Zia ruled Pakistan for 11 years until his death in the summer of 1988. Few people thought that Zia would rule Pakistan for very long because he seemed so politically unskilled and indecisive. But Zia learned quickly. He was also very lucky. Good weather brought high crop yields to Pakistan's farmers. Also, many Pakistanis flocked to the oil-rich gulf states of the Middle East in search of work. The money they sent home took care of their families and helped to fuel Pakistan's economy during the Zia years.

Zia also benefited from the war in Afghanistan, a poor Muslim country to the northwest. In December 1979, the Soviet Union sent troops into Afghanistan to prop up the Communist government there. With the Soviet Union moving into Afghanistan, Pakistan became very important to the United States, which funneled military aid through Pakistan to the Afghan guerrillas who were fighting the Communists. In addition, the United States sent billions of dollars in military and economic aid to Pakistan.

In other ways, however, the people of Pakistan suffered because of their country's role in the Afghanistan war. The Soviet-backed Afghan government countered with acts of terrorism against Pakistan. Guns and drugs entered Pakistan along with the Afghan guerrillas crossing back and forth between Afghanistan and Pakistan. More than three million Afghan refugees fled to Pakistan seeking safety and assistance.

The Influence of Islam

Like many people in the army, Zia regarded political parties and their leaders as unpatriotic because they focused their activities upon their own narrow self-interests rather than upon the needs of the nation. On the other hand, Zia believed that he and the country needed to be surrounded by the framework of a civilian, democratic government.

When Zia first took power, he had no natural allies outside of the army. Because he was a deeply religious Muslim, he sought to attract conservative Islamic support. He gave the conservatives television time, enforced Islamic prohibitions against the use of alcoholic beverages, and put himself forward as the defender of Islam in the war in Afghanistan, which he considered a jihad, or holy war. Zia also regulated the behavior of women according to traditional Islamic precepts. Women were told to wear a dupatta, a cloth wrapped around the shoulders, and a chador, or veil. Court proceedings followed traditional Islamic law for cases involving theft, adultery, rape, and drunkenness. Adultery and rape were given equal status and the testimony of two female witnesses was given the same weight as only one male. During the Zia years Pakistan society became more male-dominated than before.

The Coming of Free Elections

In 1978 Zia assumed the office of president, but kept his position as Chief Martial Law Administrator. The following year he once again postponed elections and also banned political activity. The General feared that in a free election Bhutto's Pakistan People's Party (PPP) would win. In response, the PPP and a number of other political parties formed the Movement for the Restoration of Democracy (MRD). The MRD demanded that Zia step down, that martial law be ended, and that free elections be held. Finally, in 1983 Zia announced that he would soon lift martial law and that elections would be held by March 1985. At the same time that Zia made this announcement, he also proclaimed his intention to strengthen the power of the presidency through a revision of the constitution.

In December 1984, Zia held a **referendum** to determine whether or not the people approved of his policies and wanted him to continue in office. In the referendum, he won over 90 percent of the vote, but the MRD and other opposition groups claimed that the election had been rigged. Zia announced that national and local elections would be held in February 1985, but that candidates for office had to run on a nonpartisan basis, or without affiliation to any political party. Although the MRD boycotted the elections, several religious and conservative parties and many politicians from the MRD decided to participate in the elections, which were generally free from fraud.

Lifting of Martial Law

Following Zia's wishes, the new National Assembly unanimously selected Mohammed Khan Junejo, a Muslim League member, to be prime minister. Zia lifted martial law on December 30, 1985. Contrary to Zia's expectations, however, Junejo often acted independently, resulting in the development of a tense relationship between the two men. Junejo began to remove Zia's supporters in the cabinet and relaxed restrictions on opposition politicians. Zia was determined to support the Afghan rebels until they toppled the Soviet-backed government. Junejo wanted to settle the Afghan issue even if it meant compromising with the Soviets.

In spring 1988, Zia retreated on his promise to move his country toward democracy. At this time he suddenly dismissed Prime Minister Junejo, the cabinet, and the National Assembly, promising to hold new elections in 90 days. On August 17, 1988, a plane carrying Zia and several of his generals mysteriously blew up. A Pakistani investigation concluded that the explosion had been an assassination rather than an accident and that the Soviet Union had probably been behind the attack. Because Pakistan is Asia's largest producer and trafficker in illegal drugs, another possibility was that Pakistani drug barons had been responsible. Regardless of who was to blame, Zia's death gave Pakistan an opportunity to restore democracy. When the acting president promised elections in the fall, the opposition demanded a free and fair election. To the surprise of many, the army decided to abide by the constitution and to allow elections to take place.

The Rise of Benazir Bhutto

Ali Bhutto's Pakistan People's Party was now headed by his daughter Benazir Bhutto. Zia had done everything he could to weaken the PPP, but the party had changed over the years and managed to keep its following. In the election campaign that

Pakistan's prime minister Benazir Bhutto is not only the first Muslim woman to be elected to lead a nation, she is also the first elected leader in modern times to give birth while in office. Her second child, a daughter, was born in January 1990.

followed, Benazir Bhutto and her supporters moderated the earlier **radicalism** of the PPP. The PPP still claimed to be the champion of the poor, but it avoided any mention of socialism. Rather, Bhutto and other PPP leaders spoke of making Pakistan a "developed nation, free of exploitation, poverty, and injustice." They promised the voters more schools, a minimum wage, and better health care. But they refrained from talking about nationalizing industry or redistributing land to the poor. The PPP also avoided any position similar to its past anti-Americanism.

Benazir Bhutto As Prime Minister

In December 1988, the PPP won a plurality in the elections. Soon after 35-year-old Benazir Bhutto, as leader of the PPP, was chosen as prime minister of Pakistan's first democratically elected government in 11 years. She was also the first woman in modern times to lead a Muslim nation. This was much to the dismay of many conservative Muslim clerics, who insisted that it was unseemly for a woman to rule a Muslim nation.

Like Indira Gandhi and her son Rajiv, Benazir Bhutto is heir to a political dynasty. She was Western-educated, having received bachelor's degrees from both Radcliffe in the United States and Oxford in Great Britain. As prime minister, Bhutto faced daunting tasks. To begin with, she had to placate the army, which had a long tradition of interfering in the political process. Bhutto also had to be particularly careful in charting her policy towards Afghanistan. Furthermore, the PPP held only a plurality of seats in the National Assembly. With her position as head of a coalition government, Bhutto and the PPP had to rely on the cooperation of other parties to fulfill their campaign promises.

During Bhutto's first years in office, change occurred slowly. The economy remained stagnant and bureaucratic corruption still abounded. Most foreign investors continued to shy away from Pakistan. While Bhutto promised to repeal Islamic fundamentalist laws opposed by many women, she has had difficulty in gathering the necessary support in the National Assembly.

Check Your Understanding

1. Why was it difficult for Pakistan to survive in the first decades after independence?
2. How did the death of Jinnah contribute to an unstable political situation?
3. Why was martial law imposed in 1958?
4. **a.** How did Benazir Bhutto come to power? **b.** What problems did she face on becoming prime minister?
5. *Thinking Critically:* Pakistan's experience shows that a fully democratic system of government is not always the best form of government for a newly independent nation to adopt. Do you agree or disagree with this statement? Support your opinion with facts from the section.

2. Pakistan's Economy and Society

Of the three nations on the Indian subcontinent, Pakistan has the highest standard of living. Still, Pakistan is ranked among the poorer countries in the world. Although the country has made good economic progress during the 1980's, its prospects for progress in the future remain clouded. Although the government has made some very wise decisions, it has also made some that were not so wise.

The Agricultural Situation

When Pakistan received its independence in 1947, its economic situation was very bleak. National income was unequally distributed. There were a few wealthy families and a small middle

COMPARING NATIONAL PROFILES

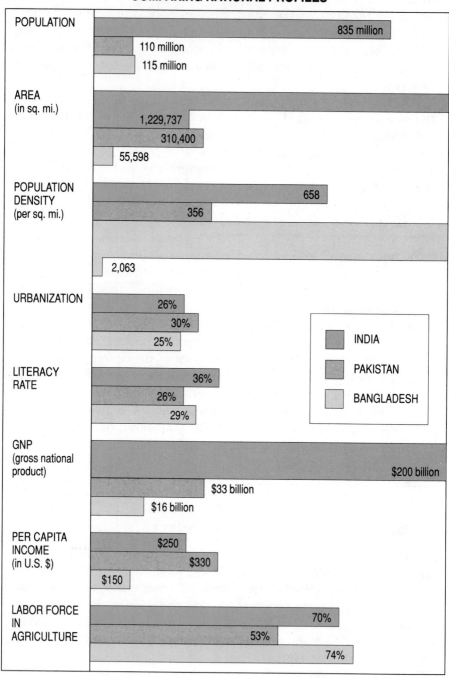

POPULATION
- 835 million
- 110 million
- 115 million

AREA (in sq. mi.)
- 1,229,737
- 310,400
- 55,598

POPULATION DENSITY (per sq. mi.)
- 658
- 356
- 2,063

URBANIZATION
- 26%
- 30%
- 25%

LITERACY RATE
- 36%
- 26%
- 29%

GNP (gross national product)
- $200 billion
- $33 billion
- $16 billion

PER CAPITA INCOME (in U.S. $)
- $250
- $330
- $150

LABOR FORCE IN AGRICULTURE
- 70%
- 53%
- 74%

Legend:
- INDIA
- PAKISTAN
- BANGLADESH

Source: *Information Please Almanac, World Almanac and Book of Facts.*

228

class. The majority of the people, however, were extremely poor. Farms averaged about five acres. Most of the peasants owned no land, working either as tenant farmers or as day laborers. Agriculture was the mainstay of the nation's economy because industry was almost nonexistent.

Agriculture has remained the largest part of the economy. Currently agriculture has accounted for about 25 percent of Pakistan's gross national product (GNP) and has utilized 53 percent of the nation's work force. With an abundance of fertile land and an adequate water supply, yield per acre has increased, especially with the use of high-yield seeds and fertilizer. The agricultural sector, however, has never lived up to its potential, mainly because Pakistan has lagged behind in agricultural research and in teaching enough farmers new agricultural methods.

Industrial Growth

In the years since independence, Pakistan's economy has undergone many changes. At independence Pakistan had almost no modern industry. The mills that had processed Pakistan's cotton and jute had been lost to India in the partition. Moreover, the areas inherited by Pakistan were poor in industrial resources such as coal and iron ore. To establish its economy, Pakistan, like India, used central planning, expanding its industry through a series of five-year plans. The first one began in 1955. But the leaders of the new Pakistan also relied on free enterprise and the private sector. The government encouraged businesspeople to develop needed industries by making credit available to them, by providing tax incentives, and by promoting investments by foreign capitalists.

Year after year Pakistan has continued to make steady strides in industrial development. Many plants and mills have been built to replace those taken over by India at the time of partition. Modest starts have been made in establishing plants and factories to produce iron and steel, railroad equipment, light machinery, cement, glass, paper, and a wide variety of consumer goods. Moreover, all this has been done at relatively little expense to the government. Much of the capital invested in the five-year plans has come from private business. For its part, the government has created necessary facilities such as power plants and transportation and communication systems. Although some state-run industries have been set up, it has often happened that whenever one of the industries began to function efficiently, it was sold to a private company.

ECONOMIC DEVELOPMENT. Pakistan has made great progress in developing irrigation systems (top left), industry, and job-training programs. One reason for its success as an "economic showcase" has been its job-training programs, which have made it possible for thousands of workers to join the industrial labor force. A trainee learns welding (top right). In a silk mill (below), a worker tends one of the weaving machines that turns out the textiles that are a major export of Pakistan.

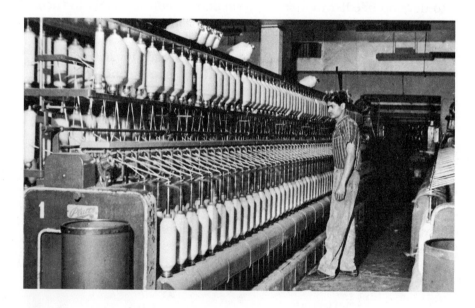

At the time of Zia's death, Pakistan seemed to have made more progress toward industrialization than India. Per capita income in Pakistan was higher than in India. Pakistan had also become more urbanized than India. Proportionally speaking, manufacturing and services had become a more important component of Pakistan's economy than of India's.

However, several economic problems trouble the nation of Pakistan today. Benazir Bhutto claims that the country has edged close to bankruptcy. Inflation has been high. Military expenditures have consumed almost half of the nation's budget. Foreign debt has remained large, and the country has experienced an annual **trade deficit**. Finally, the tax base has shrunk. Although Pakistan has more than 100 million people, only one million people have regularly paid taxes. Thus, the government has not received the revenue needed to repair essential facilities, to expand industries, or to improve education.

Illiteracy in Pakistan

When a nation industrializes, a number of changes usually precede or accompany the process. Education becomes more widespread, the population growth rate slows down, health care improves, and women achieve greater equality. But for Pakistan, only a few of these changes have characterized its society since independence. Although the economy has enjoyed rapid growth, the country's social development has lagged. Many experts have concluded that Pakistan's economy will experience slower growth in the future as well.

Illiteracy remains a major problem in Pakistan. Three out of every four Pakistanis are illiterate. In addition, women are much more likely than men to remain illiterate. Only 7 percent of rural women are able to read and write. In comparison, many countries that are at a lower level of economic development have a higher literacy rate than Pakistan. In many ways, illiteracy has impeded economic development. Illiterate workers cannot operate complex equipment, and they are more likely to have accidents. It is difficult to introduce information about new agricultural techniques to illiterate farmers. Illiterate mothers learn little about modern nutrition, sanitation, or family planning.

Ethnic Divisions

As a society industrializes, regional, ethnic, and religious divisions usually tend to moderate. Pakistan was founded so that the Muslims could have their own country and not be dominated by Hindu India. Although the majority of Pakistanis are

Muslims, religious and other divisions have persisted since independence. About 75 to 80 percent of the Pakistani Muslim population belongs to the Sunni sect, while most other Muslim Pakistanis belong to the Shi'a sect. The differences between these two sects, which often spill over into violence, are both theological and political in nature.

Pakistan still has considerable nation-building to do. Most Pakistanis identify themselves in regional rather than national terms. Four ethnic or regional groups exist in Pakistan. The four regional groups are the Punjabis, Sindis, Pathans, and Baluchis. Each group has its own language and province. In addition, there are the Mohajirs, those people who migrated to Pakistan from India at the time of partition. The other four groups view the Mohajirs as outsiders, and have shown continuing resentment toward them.

Population Growth

Pakistan's population has been growing at an alarming rate. In 1947, the population of West Pakistan was about 32 million. By 1972, only 25 years later, the population had more than doubled to over 65 million. In 1989, Pakistan's population was estimated to be greater than 110 million. Some **demographers** predict that Pakistan's population might reach as high as 145 million people by the year 2000.

The population has expanded so rapidly over the last several decades because the birthrate has remained substantially unchanged while the death rate has decreased. This decrease has occurred generally because of improved medical practices and greater numbers of doctors. Still, life expectancy at birth has remained at 51 years. The people's poor state of health reflects their malnutrition, shortage of safe drinking water, and inadequate health-care system. Outside the large cities, modern medical care is largely unavailable.

Pakistan's large and rapidly growing population has placed a severe strain on the nation. The government has encouraged family planning, but has had scant success. The country simply has not had the resources to provide its citizens with adequate housing, food, health care, education, and electricity. Although the economy has expanded at a substantial rate, not enough jobs have been created to provide work for all the young people who enter the labor force each year. Pakistan's leaders have generally regarded the large number of unemployed young people as a potentially hazardous political situation.

The above picture shows a bustling, shop-filled street in Lahore, one of the largest cities in Pakistan. Note the woman walking with the bundle on her head, a traditional method of carrying heavy loads in many developing countries.

Women in Pakistani Society

Pakistanis have very strong views about the proper roles for women and men. Throughout the country, women and men have led very different, very unequal lives. Most men have believed that a woman's existence is supposed to center around the home, in keeping with an old saying that a woman enters her husband's home in a wedding dress and leaves it in a coffin. Many people, especially women, have objected to existing social conditions in Pakistan.

Islamic values have emphasized the need for women to maintain physical seclusion by not having any social contact with men who are not part of their families. Physical seclusion also extends to the workplace and jobs that involve contact with the public or that place women in close proximity to male workers. Most Pakistani women work at home or on the farm. Women who work outside the home or farm account for only about 4 percent of the paid labor force. Those who follow Islamic seclusion traditions wear the burga—a long, loose-fitting garment, when they leave their homes. However, more and more women have chosen to ignore the rules of physical seclusion as a way of protesting the inequality between men and women.

Check Your Understanding

1. Why has Pakistan's economy remained dependent on agriculture?
2. **a.** What advances has Pakistan made economically?
   b. What problems does it still have to overcome?
3. Why has Pakistan been unable to make much progress in modernizing social conditions?
4. *Thinking Critically:* What types of changes often characterize a nation moving toward industrialization? How does Pakistan's experience depart from this? Why is education a key element in progress toward industrialization?

3. Pakistan's Foreign Policy

Although Pakistan's foreign policy has remained remarkably consistent since independence, most of the same domestic and international forces that were at work 40 years ago are still operating today. Almost from the day of its independence, Pakistan has regarded India as its enemy. As a counterbalance to India's power, Pakistan has sought a close relationship with China, military aid from the United States, and worldwide Islamic solidarity. Pakistan's needs also led the nation to maintain a close relationship with the United States through most of the last 40 years.

The India Problem

Pakistan's foreign policy has consistently reflected fear of India. The Pakistanis have felt vulnerable not only because India is much larger and stronger, but also because their country's borders are difficult to defend, a fact illustrated by India's invasion and occupation of a large part of Kashmir. (See page 207.) Because Pakistan has not dared to relax its guard against India, its leaders have sought to make friends with nations that might help it in a conflict with India.

Unlike India, Pakistan has not pursued a policy of nonalignment. After receiving assurances of American military aid, Pakistan aligned itself with the United States in the **cold war** between the West and the Soviet Union. Pakistan also joined the Southeast Asia Treaty Organization (SEATO) and the Central Treaty Organization (CENTO), both now defunct. These international alliances had been formed at the encouragement of the United States for mutual defense against Communist expansion.

Pakistan joined these organizations not only because it feared the Soviet Union but also because it wanted to be well-armed in its quarrels with India. From 1954 to 1965, for example, the United States gave Pakistan $1.5 billion in military aid and a large amount of economic and technical assistance. The purpose of the United States aid was to strengthen Pakistan's defenses against the Soviet Union and also to maintain American radar stations and air bases in Pakistan. United States aid also enhanced Pakistan's military position against India. This aid has been deeply resented by India, which for many years has accepted only economic and technical assistance from the United States.

Pakistan and the United States

Many people had expected that some day India and Pakistan would go to war again over Kashmir. When a new war erupted in 1971, however, the issue that touched it off was the rebellion in East Pakistan. In the fighting that followed, the Soviet Union supported India, and Communist China supported Pakistan. The United States insisted that it was neutral, not wanting to offend either India or Pakistan. India, however, bitterly complained that United States policy favored Pakistan. Meanwhile, Pakistanis were angered that the United States was not more supportive of their nation.

Although the United States resumed arms shipments to Pakistan in 1975, relations between the two countries remained strained through the 1970's. In November 1979, a mob burned the United States embassy in Islamabad. The United States cultural centers in Lahore and Rawalpindi were also destroyed. Although the Pakistani government apologized, relations between the two countries deteriorated further.

In December 1979, Soviet forces invaded Afghanistan, an impoverished Muslim country to the south of the Soviet Union. As a result, Pakistan's relations with the United States began to improve. Both the United States and Pakistan, for different reasons, wished to support the Afghan resistance fighters. Both nations had a strong interest in maintaining stability and peace in the region. Understandably, the Pakistanis were very concerned about the extension of Soviet power into South Asia. Furthermore, Afghanistan is not only Pakistan's neighbor, it is also a Muslim country.

One issue dividing Pakistan and the United States has been nuclear weapons. In 1974 India tested a nuclear bomb and in subsequent years has carried on research into the development of a hydrogen bomb. By law the United States must discontinue aid to any country that has developed nuclear weapons. But Pakistan has assured the United States that it does not have nuclear weapons and is not making any. Bhutto has said that Pakistan would agree to inspection of any nuclear facilities by outside parties only if India also agrees to inspection. Because Pakistan pledged that it was not building nuclear weapons, and because vital American interests were involved, the United States Congress approved a multi-year military and economic aid package of $3.2 billion for Pakistan in 1981. In 1986, Pakistan and the United States agreed to a new $4.2 billion program to be distributed over six years.

Pakistan and the Soviet Union

The fighting in 1965 between India and Pakistan over Kashmir alarmed the Soviet Union, which had extended considerable aid to both countries. Soviet Premier Alexei Kosygin arranged for Prime Minister Shastri of India and President Ayub Khan of Pakistan to meet for peace talks in the Soviet city of Tashkent. Early in 1966 Pakistan and India signed the Tashkent Declaration. While this agreement did not settle the Kashmir dispute, it bound both countries to withdraw their forces from areas occupied during the war.

In the years after the 1965 war with India, when Pakistan began to cool its relations with the United States, the Pakistani government sought military and economic assistance from Communist states. Trade with the Soviet Union was gradually stepped up, and Soviet assistance to Pakistan increased. Even more notable was the improvement in Pakistan's relations with Communist China.

Pakistan and China

In 1962 the two countries of China and Pakistan began discussions aimed at settling a disagreement over their boundaries. The beginning of these talks coincided with the most serious phase of the border war between India and China. Early the next year, an agreement over the boundaries was reached. Thereafter, China not only supported Pakistan in the dispute with India over Kashmir but also supplied Pakistan with military equipment from time to time. When war between Pakistan and India broke out in 1965, China provoked incidents with India along its frontier, thus giving indirect assistance to Pakistan. Then in 1984, in a move to facilitate even closer relations, Pakistan and China built a highway that linked the two nations and speeded up trade between them. The two countries have regularly exchanged visits by high-level officials.

Relations with the Muslim World

Over the years the government of Pakistan has sought to encourage greater unity and cooperation among Muslim nations. Pakistan's leaders have hoped for the support of the Muslim community in any conflict with India. In addition, Pakistan has hoped for financial aid from the oil-rich Muslim nations of the Middle East in its struggle to develop economically, and some aid has been forthcoming.

In his role as the defender of Islam, Zia allowed equipment and other aid to the rebels in Afghanistan to be funneled through Pakistan. He also opened Pakistan to three million Afghans who fled the conflict and bloodshed. Bhutto's Afghan policy differs in one important respect from Zia's. The late dictator hoped to establish a fundamentalist Muslim regime in Afghanistan and was willing for Pakistan to make many sacrifices to achieve that goal. Bhutto would like to see the Communist government in Afghanistan fall. But she has been more willing to compromise to end the fighting so that the three million Afghan refugees can be sent home and her country can concentrate on its own domestic problems.

Check Your Understanding

1. Describe Pakistan's foreign policy with each of the following nations: **a.** the United States **b.** the Soviet Union **c.** China
2. What are Pakistan's relations with the Muslim world?
3. Why has Pakistan's foreign policy consistently reflected a fear of India? How has Pakistan's foreign policy generally differed from India's?
4. *Thinking Critically:* How, if at all, might Pakistan's relations with Muslim nations change in the future?

4. The Politics of Bangladesh

At the time of partition in 1947, Bengal—a key state in the British Indian Empire—was divided between India and Pakistan. The eastern two thirds of Bengal became East Pakistan. For many years after partition the people of East Pakistan had believed that the central government, which was located in West Pakistan, discriminated against them in the allotment of government funds and services. In the late 1960's the resentment of the East Pakistanis over this discrimination began to boil over into protests and rebellion. By the end of 1971 the people of East Pakistan had successfully revolted and had set up the newly independent nation of Bangladesh. Sheikh Mujibur Rahman (MOO-jee-BOOR rah-MAHN) became its leader.

As it came into being, Bangladesh faced gigantic problems. It was not simply that a new government had to be fashioned. An economic system capable of supporting a huge population somehow had to be created. In addition, resettling the refugees who had returned from India would require much time, patience, and sacrifice.

Mujibur's Early Leadership

The Bangladesh constitution of 1972 provided for a unicameral, or one-house, legislature, a prime minister, and an independent judiciary. Furthermore, the constitution proclaimed as state policy the Awami League's four principles of nationalism, secularism, socialism, and democracy. Although there were other separatist movements in the new country, most citizens enthusiastically embraced Bangladesh nationalism. At first the leaders of Bangladesh made the nation a secular state. But in 1988, the Bangladesh government established Islam as the state religion. With socialism as a stated goal, the new government nationalized many industries.

Mujibur's leadership was challenged throughout his rule by the problems of the new country. The economy, impoverished to begin with, had been ravaged by the war. Thousands of people had been killed, and many more were hungry and homeless. Returning refugees had to be cared for. The transportation and communication systems had to be repaired and improved. Law and order had to be restored. Corruption among officials also made the government's task all the more difficult. In addition, nationalization hampered rather than stimulated the economy, and democratic government turned out to be a short-lived experiment.

As the economic problems of the new nation mounted, civil disturbances became commonplace. In December 1974, Mujibur declared a state of emergency. Several months later the constitution was amended to establish a strong presidential office and to institute a one-party system of government. When Mujibur assumed the post of president, the government of Bangladesh became a dictatorship.

A Revolving Door of Leadership

In August 1975, Mujibur was assassinated by rebellious elements within the army. Following the assassination, a new civilian government was formed. But the real power of the government lay with those officers who had engineered the assassination and the military coup. After a short period of political instability, General Ziaur Rahman emerged as the country's new leader in November 1975. Martial law was declared, and the parliament was dissolved. A civilian government existed, but the real power was in the General's hands.

Ziaur sought to invigorate the country's economy and to eliminate government corruption. He traveled throughout Bangladesh to see his country's problems firsthand. Gradually he moved the country in the direction of constitutional government. In 1976, the government permitted political parties to organize and to participate in the political process, although only under government supervision. The next year Ziaur consolidated his power by assuming the position of president. He announced a program for economic expansion, especially in the production of food. He also emphasized the need to slow down the country's population growth rate.

In 1977, Ziaur held a referendum to determine whether or not he should continue in office. Almost 90 percent of the electorate voted, with the General receiving almost 99 percent of the vote. Everyone knew, however, that Ziaur had no intention of stepping down no matter what the vote. After the 1978 presidential election, in which Ziaur captured over 75 percent of the vote, the government removed the remaining restrictions on political parties.

But in 1979 Ziaur began to move away from constitutional government when he amended the constitution to give himself greater presidential power. Then, in 1981, Ziaur was assassinated by a group in the military who were trying to take over the government. The coup was put down by loyal officers within the army, which then named an acting president. That person was officially elected president in November 1981.

BIRTH OF A NATION. Celebrations (below) followed independence from Pakistan in 1971. But grim problems, including the resettlement of refugees (top left), faced Mujibar Rahman (top right), who is shown in a ceremony that symbolized the end of guerrilla activity in Bangladesh.

The new president's tenure in office, however, was short. Once again the army took charge of the political system, and in March 1982, General H. M. Ershad seized power, declared martial law, dissolved the parliament and the cabinet, and suspended the constitution. Ershad justified his actions by claiming that the government was corrupt and incompetent. He also insisted that the economy had been mismanaged and that law and order had broken down. Ershad announced his determination to deal with economic decay and to restore order. When conditions were ready, he said, power would be returned to a civilian government.

Leadership Under Ershad

In December 1983, Ershad became president of Bangladesh but kept his position within the army. He gradually relaxed martial law but did not lift it entirely until late in 1986. Meanwhile, he held elections in March 1985, but not because he was a believer in democracy. After all, he had deposed a democratically elected government. Ershad called for the election because he believed that the elections would give credibility to his right to rule. Opposition politicians, however, refused to participate in elections until martial law was ended.

After Ershad eased restrictions on political activity, several parties agreed to participate in the national elections scheduled for 1986. In elections for the parliament held in May 1986, Ershad's supporters won a slim majority. Opposition politicians and the foreign press charged voting fraud. Several months later elections were held for president. The two major opposition parties refused to put up candidates because martial law was still in effect and because they were convinced that the election would not be run fairly. Ershad retired from his military post and ran for president. Opposed by candidates from a number of minor parties, Ershad won almost 84 percent of the vote. Foreign observers and opposition leaders claimed there had been a lower turnout than government figures indicated. They also claimed widespread voting fraud. Shortly after the election, Ershad announced the end of martial law and the reinstatement of the constitution.

The following year was one of continuing strife. The numerous opposition parties demanded that Ershad resign. In fall 1987, the opposition parties organized strikes, marches, rallies, and other protests. Sometimes the demonstrations turned violent, and activity in the capital city of Dhaka would be brought to a standstill. In November 1987, Ershad declared a state of emergency. The legal rights of the citizenry were suspended, censorship was imposed, and political activity was restricted. Ershad described the opposition's behavior as "planned anarchy" and made it clear that he would not give in to "illegal and undemocratic pressure."

To demonstrate that the people of Bangladesh supported his regime, Ershad dissolved the parliament and called for new legislative elections in March 1988. These elections were boycotted by the two main opposition parties, the Awami League and the Bangladesh Nationalist Party. With the boycott in place, Ershad's Jatiyo Party won over 80 percent of the seats in the legislature. But the voter turnout was low and many observers complained that the elections were rigged. In April 1988, Ershad lifted the state of emergency.

Since then, Ershad has remained securely in control of Bangladesh's government. Only the army has the power to remove him, and so far it has shown no inclination to overthrow his leadership. When Ershad first came to power, many Bangladeshis regarded him as a patriot who was trying to save the country from chaos and poverty. Over the years, his reputation has seriously declined. Many people, Bangladeshis and foreigners alike, now contend that Ershad has been pursuing a contradictory policy. Over the years he has tried to integrate the opposition parties into the political process but without surrendering his control over the government. What keeps him in power is the support of the army and a weak and divided opposition. Indeed, there may be more political parties in Bangladesh than in any other country in the world.

Check Your Understanding

1. What were some of the conditions that made it difficult for Bangladesh to establish a stable democratic government?
2. **a.** How did Bangladesh become a dictatorship?
   b. Why did Ershad operate as a dictator, yet continue to call for elections?
3. Why might some people contend that Ershad pursued a contradictory domestic policy?
4. *Thinking Critically* Why can too many political parties be a hindrance to the establishment of stable democratic governments?

5. The Economic and Social Conditions of Bangladesh

Bangladesh has been called the "largest, poorest country in the world." During the 1970's and 1980's, Bangladesh received many billions of dollars in aid from private organizations, foreign countries, and such international organizations as the United Nations and the World Bank. Despite the large amounts of foreign aid, Bangladesh's economic and social conditions have changed very little, except for the size of its population, which has become much larger. Although agricultural production has increased and some industry has been developed, Bangladesh's population has continued to expand at an alarming rate.

Bangladesh has had two central and interrelated economic goals—to achieve self-sufficiency in food production and to slow the rate of population growth. The government has had some success in increasing domestic food production but not in containing the population. Each year there are many more mouths to feed and thus agricultural self-sufficiency has required ever higher levels of production.

Urban–Rural Differences

Bangladesh has remained largely a rural nation. Even though the country's population is well over 100 million, only two cities, Dhaka and Chittagong, have over one million inhabitants. Most people live in dire poverty in the thousands of farming villages that dot the countryside. Rural Bangladesh is severely overpopulated and unemployed. Over the last 30 years many people from the rural areas have moved to the cities in search of jobs and a better life. In 1961, about 5 percent of the population lived in cities. Today the figure is about 25 percent. Urban arrivals almost never make their way out of poverty because most do not have the kinds of skills that are needed in the cities. Moreover, the rapid expansion in the size of Bangladesh's cities has placed an enormous strain on services. The cities do not have the resources to take care of the poor.

Agricultural Conditions

About 80 percent of the people earn their livelihood from the land. The soil is fertile, the climate is warm year round, and water is abundant. The primary crops are rice, jute, and sugar. Wheat and tea are also grown. For years jute, which is used to make rope, sacks, and backings for carpets, has been the country's main export. Over the last few years, however, worldwide demand for jute has declined because foreign manufacturers have turned to synthetic materials.

Farms in Bangladesh are small. The average size in 1979 was only 3.5 acres. It is probably even less today. Moreover, many farms are composed of several individual parcels of land. According to a 1978 government study, 60 percent of rural households were either landless or owned less than one acre. Only a small percentage of rural families own sizable farms.

The government has had limited success in encouraging farmers to use modern agricultural methods. The green revolution, which had dramatically increased food production in India, has had a limited impact on Bangladesh, where many farmers are resistant to change. In addition, many of them do not have the money to buy high-yield seed or fertilizer, and the village moneylenders charge high interest rates for loans. The government is of little help because of its limited resources.

Industrial Growth

Successive governments in Bangladesh have tried to spur industrial development, but without much success. Major industries include the manufacture of jute products, textiles, leather goods, and the production of sugar, tea, and fertilizer. The Mujibur government nationalized many industries, but the government did not do a good job in running the businesses that it took over, and this hampered industrial growth.

To encourage foreign and domestic investors to establish businesses in Bangladesh, some of the previously nationalized industries have been returned to private hands. Beginning in 1982, the government began to ease restrictions on private investment. But few Bangladeshis have the money or the experience necessary to start a new business. The government has also been unable to attract foreign investors, who see few opportunities to make a profit in Bangladesh. They point to the unsettled political situation with its frequent disturbances and declarations of martial law and states of emergency. These conditions hardly reassure foreign businesspeople that their investments will be secure.

Wage rates are low, and most Bangladeshis are illiterate and unskilled. Furthermore, the country has few trained managers. Many of those who are educated or skilled have emigrated. Like India and Pakistan, Bangladesh has experienced a "brain drain." Some Bangladeshis have gone to the United States. Others have traveled to the oil-rich nations of the Middle East in search of work.

244

A devastating flood struck Bangladesh in 1988, displacing over 30 million people. This elderly man, in search of relief, has stuffed all his belongings into a boat, including a cow and a goat.

Population Pressures

Like India and Pakistan, Bangladesh has a severe population problem. Despite the continuing efforts of the Bangladesh government, the growth rate has remained very high. Between 1961 and 1981 the population surged from 50.8 to 87.1 million, a 70 percent increase. During the 1980's the country's annual growth rate has slowed somewhat, but Bangladesh's population has already reached an estimated 112 million.

Bangladesh has little likelihood of improving its standard of living unless the population growth is brought under control and it has some success in diversifying its economy and lessening its dependence on agriculture. Although the majority of Indians and Pakistanis continue to work on the land, many are employed in the growing industrial sector. Even with most people earning their livelihood directly or indirectly from the land, Bangladesh still must import food to feed its population. If the weather is poor, if floods cover the land, or if the price for their agricultural exports falls, the economy suffers.

Bangladesh must slow down its population growth rate. Unfortunately, government attempts to encourage family planning have been unable to overcome deeply ingrained cultural values. As in India and Pakistan, children are needed to take care of elderly parents. This is a major reason why resistance to family planning is strongest among the poor—those who can least af-

Sri Lanka, the Island Nation of South Asia

Sri Lanka, formerly Ceylon, lies in the Indian Ocean to the southeast of India. (See map, page 176.) The southernmost portion of the teardrop-shaped island almost touches the equator. In ancient times the island was known as Serendib, from which the English word *serendipity* comes, meaning "an ability to find nice things without searching for them." With its colorful landscape, breathtaking mountains, and inviting sandy beaches, many people consider Sri Lanka to be one of the most beautiful spots on earth.

The descendants of the Tamils, a minority on the island, came from southern India as early as 2600 B.C. Most Tamils continue to practice Hinduism. Today they represent about 18 percent of the population. The island's majority group, the Sinhalese, comprise about 74 percent of the population. Buddhism is the religion they practice.

Sri Lanka became a fully independent member of the British Commonwealth in 1948. In 1972, Sri Lanka became a republic, but still retained its Commonwealth affiliation. It was at this time that the nation changed its name from Ceylon to Sri Lanka. In 1978, another name change took place, this time to the Democratic Socialist Republic of Sri Lanka.

Like the many changes in its name, the nation has had a history of many changes in government. Sri Lanka's most serious political problem, however, is a civil war between the established government and the Tamil minority. (See page 212.) In their quest for a separate state in the northern and eastern portions of the island, the Tamil insurgents have clashed with the Sri Lankan army, resulting in much bloodshed and loss of life. India's attempts to mediate a peaceful solution have led to the presence of Indian troops on the island.

ford large families. By contrast, many wealthy Bangladeshis have limited the size of their families.

Education vs. Illiteracy

The illiteracy rate for women is 72 percent, and in rural areas it is much higher than that. No matter what the message—family planning, sanitation, new farming methods—it is hard to communicate with people who cannot read. While Bangladesh needs to spend far more money on education, its resources are limited and must be spread among many competing demands.

Complicating Bangladesh's education problem is the youthfulness of the country's population. About 45 percent of the population are 14 years of age or younger. Slightly more than 50 percent are in the age range of 15 to 59. The large percentage of young people places an enormous strain on the economy. The country has to take care of all these young people, including trying to educate them and give them jobs when they enter the job market.

Check Your Understanding

1. **a.** Why is Bangladesh largely considered a rural nation? **b.** Why does migration to the cities seldom relieve the poverty of Bangladesh's peasants?
2. How has the poverty of Bangladesh's farmers limited their ability to increase food production?
3. Why are foreign businesspeople unwilling to invest in Bangladesh?
4. *Thinking Critically:* If you were a leader of Bangladesh's government, would you continue to operate Bangladesh as an independent government or would you seek another solution? Explain your thinking.

6. The Foreign Policy of Bangladesh

As a country of little strategic concern to the great powers, Bangladesh has played a small role in the world of international diplomacy. Western involvement has been largely humanitarian in nature. After an initial flirtation, the Soviet Union has taken little interest in Bangladesh. The Bangladesh government, for its part, has tried to pursue a policy of nonalignment.

Most nations were slow to recognize Bangladesh's independence. Muslim countries did not want to offend Pakistan. Other nations that had their own separatist movements feared that recognition would lend credibility to these movements. By the mid–1970's, however, Bangladesh had managed to establish diplomatic relations with most countries of the world.

Bangladesh and India

Bangladesh's most important diplomatic relationship is with India. Not only is India the dominant power on the subcontinent, but almost all of Bangladesh's land border is with India. India and Bangladesh have close ties, although India tends to treat Bangladesh almost like a dependent, or satellite, nation. While the two nations are committed to resolving peacefully any differences between them, India has complained about ongoing illegal emigration from Bangladesh into the Indian state of Assam. The Bangladesh government denies that any illegal movement is taking place. Various border disputes have also taken place between the two countries, and these have not been resolved. The various disagreements notwithstanding, Bangladesh maintains friendly diplomatic and cultural ties with its powerful neighbor to the west.

Bangladesh and Pakistan

For about two years after the Indo–Pakistani war, relations between Bangladesh and Pakistan were hostile. Beginning in 1974, however, relations began to warm. Since 1976 when formal diplomatic ties were established, relations between the two countries have been close. Both Bangladesh and Pakistan have a vested interest in containing Indian influence over the subcontinent. The two countries have good relations with the United States and China and have been wary of Soviet power. Furthermore, both Bangladesh and Pakistan, as Muslim nations, have pursued many similar policies in foreign affairs. Both were particularly critical of the Soviet invasion of Afghanistan in 1979. In sympathy with other Muslims in the predominantly Arab Middle East, neither country has recognized Israel.

Bangladesh and the Islamic World

In deference to Pakistan, many Islamic states at first refused to recognize Bangladesh. An additional obstacle to recognition was that Bangladesh had declared itself to be a secular rather than an Islamic state. Some of the conservative Islamic countries, most notably Saudi Arabia, were disturbed by this secular orientation. But for most of Bangladesh's Muslims, religion was considered a personal matter, and the secular nature of the government did not disturb them. Moreover, one in six Bangladeshis were Hindus. As relations between Pakistan and Bangladesh healed, the Islamic countries began to extend diplomatic recognition to Bangladesh. Hoping for considerable economic and developmental aid from the oil-rich Islamic nations, Ershad began to stress his country's Muslim identity. Some foreign aid was forthcoming, much of it in the form of loans, but it was less than Bangladesh had hoped for.

Relations with the Major Powers

Relations between Bangladesh and the United States were initially strained because the United States and Pakistan were allies. Relations soon improved, however, and have continued to be cordial. The United States has had no strategic interest in Bangladesh and has looked at that country primarily from a humanitarian perspective. It rushed aid to the impoverished country when it received independence. Since then, it has supplemented Bangladesh's economic development with economic grants. In most years since 1972, the United States has been the largest donor of aid to Bangladesh. Nonprofit organizations in the United States have also sent millions of dollars of humanitarian relief.

The Soviet Union had supported India during the 1971 war with Pakistan and had been one of the first countries to recognize Bangladesh as an independent nation. For a brief time the Soviets contributed considerable foreign aid to the new nation. Their assistance in clearing the harbor of Chittagong was especially helpful. Many Bangladeshis, however, began to fear that the Soviet Union with its foreign aid would soon exert too much influence over their country. After the military came to power in the mid–1970's, a chill developed in Soviet–Bangladeshi relations. Two Soviet actions particularly troubled Bangladesh's government—the invasion of Afghanistan in 1979 and its support for Vietnam's invasion of Cambodia.

China supported Pakistan in its 1971 war with India and did not establish diplomatic relations with Bangladesh until 1975. Since that time, however, Bangladesh and China have had cordial relations. The two countries carry on some trading activity with each other, and China has extended to Bangladesh some military and economic aid. From time to time cultural exchanges take place between the two countries as well as visits by high-ranking officials.

Check Your Understanding

1. What relations has Bangladesh had with other nations on the subcontinent?
2. What has been Bangladesh's main goal in its relations with the Muslim world?
3. *Thinking Critically:* Why is it unlikely that Bangladesh will play a major role in world politics or international relations in the near future?

CHAPTER REVIEW

- **Chapter Summary**

Section 1. Few states of the postwar world were founded under such difficult conditions as Pakistan. Its people, however, survived very difficult early years to build a stable republic. The nation has had a series of strong leaders who sometimes found it necessary to assume dictatorial policies in pursuit of stability. Among these leaders were Ayub Khan, Ali Bhutto, General Zia, and Benazir Bhutto.

Section 2. Of the three nations on the subcontinent, Pakistan has the highest standard of living. Still it ranks among the poorest nations in the world with a per capita income of less than $400. The nation's economy depends on agriculture, which accounts for about 25 percent of its gross national product and utilizes about 53 percent of the work force. Pakistan has developed a growing industrial sector, but it still faces an uphill struggle in continuing its economic advancement. Hindering economic development is widespread illiteracy and a soaring population rate. Islamic values and traditions are still important to the majority of Pakistanis, making the achievement of equality for women difficult.

Section 3. Pakistan's foreign policy has remained remarkably stable since independence. India is regarded as its main enemy. As a counterbalance to India's power, Pakistan has sought close ties with China and with the United States, and has pursued cooperation and solidarity with the Muslim world. Pakistan has also received aid from the Soviet Union.

Section 4. The Independence of Bangladesh came in 1971 after India intervened militarily to help it defeat Pakistan. Guided by the principles of the Awami League, the nation developed a constitutional form of government that quickly gave way to a dictatorship under General Ershad.

Section 5. Bangladesh has been called the largest and poorest country in the world. Despite large amounts of foreign aid, its economic and social conditions have changed very little, except for population growth which has worsened. The increase in population has hindered the nation in achieving its goal of self-sufficiency in food production. Also slowing agricultural growth is the resistance of many people to change, as well as widespread illiteracy. The latter also hinders Bangladesh's industrial growth.

Section 6. Bangladesh has played a very minor role in world politics because it is of little strategic concern to the major powers. India has been a dominant influence on Bangladesh, assisting it both politically and economically. Since independence, relations with Pakistan have warmed, with formal diplomatic exchange taking place in 1976. The United States and the Soviet Union have given economic aid, and China has become a trading partner.

■ **Vocabulary Review**

Define: martial law, Awami League, egalitarianism, authoritarian, coup, referendum, radicalism, trade deficit, demographer, cold war

■ **Places to Locate**

Locate: East Pakistan (Bangladesh), West Pakistan, Afghanistan, Kashmir, Islamabad, Tashkent, Sri Lanka

■ **People to Know**

Identify: Ayub Khan, Yahya Khan, Ali Bhutto, General Zia, Mohammed Khan Junejo, Benazir Bhutto, Premier Kosygin, Mujibur Rahman, General Ziaur, General Ershad

■ **Thinking Critically**

1. Why has martial law been a frequent characteristic of political life in Pakistan?
2. How has Pakistan advanced its economic and social conditions since independence? What has been the greatest obstacle to its further development?
3. Why did Pakistan not pursue a policy of nonalignment?
4. How have Bangladesh's rulers used the trappings of democracy to further their own political ends?

5. Explain how illiteracy has slowed economic and social development in Bangladesh.

■ **Extending and Applying Your Knowledge**

1. Benazir Bhutto's rise to power and prominence is very unusual for a woman in a Muslim country. Using the *Readers' Guide to Periodical Literature*, research how she became the prime minister of Pakistan. Use this information to write a short biography.

2. Large-scale flooding continues to be a national problem in Bangladesh. Research the causes of such flooding, the frequency of floods, their costs in human lives and to the economy, and what is being done to control them. Using this information, prepare a timeline and charts to accompany a short oral report on flooding in Bangladesh.

APPENDIX

BIBLIOGRAPHY

General Works

Baxter, Craig. *Bangladesh: A New Nation in an Old Setting.* Westview Press, 1984. A brief but well done historical survey.

DeBary, William T., ed. *Sources of Indian Tradition.* Columbia University Press, 1964. A superb collection of selections from the Indian philosophical, religious, and literary heritage.

Er-Rashid, Haroun. *Geography of Bangladesh.* Westview Press, 1978. A detailed description and analysis of the geographical factors that influence the country.

Harle, J.C. *The Art and Architecture of the Indian Subcontinent.* Penguin Books, 1986. An illustrated survey of the subcontinent's art and architecture.

Keay, John. *India Discovered: The Achievement of the British Raj.* Windward, 1981. Illustrates part of India's cultural legacy.

Mackenzie, Donald A. *India.* Avenel Books, 1986. A rich collection of Indian myths and legends.

Massey, Reginald and Jamila Massey. *The Music of India.* Crescendo Publishing, 1977. A brief survey of India's musical heritage.

Myrdal, Gunnar. *Asian Drama: An Inquiry into the Poverty of Nations,* 3 vols. Pantheon, 1968. A dated but still very useful analysis of India's economy.

Radhakrishnan, S. *The Hindu View of Life.* Unwin Hyman, 1988. One of several brief works on Hinduism by the author.

Spear, Percival and Romila Thapar. *A History of India,* 2 vols. Penguin Books, 1966, 1975. One of the best general studies of Indian history.

Wolpert, Stanley. *A New History of India,* 2nd ed. Oxford University Press, 1982. A solid survey of Indian history by a leading expert in the field.

India to Partition *(Chapters 1-6)*

Basham, A.L. *The Wonder That Was India,* rev. ed. Hawthorn, 1963. A survey of subcontinental civilization from ancient times to the advent of Islam.

Bence-Jones, Mark. *Clive of India.* St. Martin's Press, 1974. A perceptive and well-balanced biography of Robert Clive.

DeBary, William T., ed. *Sources of Indian Tradition.* Columbia University Press, 1964. A superb collection of selections from the Indian philosophical, religious, and literary heritage.

Gandhi, Mohandas K. *Autobiography,* 2nd ed. Heinman, 1979. Must reading for anyone who wishes to understand the life and thought of India's great leader.

Gascoigne, Bamber. *The Great Moghuls.* Harper, 1971. An excellent study of the Mogul period, illustrated with many fine photographs.

Hansen, Waldermar. *The Peacock Throne*. Holt, Rinehart and Winston, 1972. A history of the Moguls, with emphasis on the key personalities of the period.

Lord, John. *The Maharajahs*. Random House, 1971. Fascinating accounts of the lives of some of India's most colorful princes.

Moon, Penderel. *Gandhi and Modern India*. W.W. Norton and Co., 1969. A solid political biography.

Piggot, Stuart. *Prehistoric India*. Barnes and Noble, 1962. An excellent introduction to ancient India.

Spear, Percival. *The Nabobs*, rev. ed. Oxford University Press, 1963. Rich sketches of the life and manners of the British in eighteenth-century India.

Spear, Percival and Romila Thapar. *A History of India*, 2 vols. Penguin Books, 1966, 1975. One of the best general studies of Indian history.

Tagore, Rabindranath. *A Tagore Reader*, ed. by Amiya Chakravarty. Beacon Press, 1966. Selections from the writings of India's Nobel Prize winner in literature.

Wiser, William and Charlotte Wiser. *Behind Mud Wall, 1930–1960*, rev. ed. University of California Press, 1972. A classic account of Indian village life by an American missionary couple.

Wolpert, Stanley. *A New History of India*, 2nd ed. Oxford University Press, 1982. A solid survey of Indian history by a leading expert in the field.

Woodruff, Philip. (pseud.) *The Men Who Ruled India*, 2 vols. Cape, 1963. An unusually illuminating study of the founders, builders, and rulers of the British Empire in India.

Independent India *(Chapter 7)*

Collins, Larry and Dominique Lapierre. *Freedom at Midnight*. Simon and Schuster, 1975. A gripping portrayal of the birth of independent India.

Fishlock, Trevor. *India File: Inside the Subcontinent*. Murray, 1983. A well-written and stimulating account of Indian political life.

Freeman, James M. *Untouchable: An Indian Life History*. Stanford University Press, 1979. An autobiography of an Untouchable as told to an anthropologist.

Gopal, Sarvepalli. *Jawaharlal Nehru: A Biography*, 3 vols. Harvard University Press, 1976, 1979, 1984. The definitive biography of Nehru, especially useful for reference purposes.

Markandaya, Kamala. *Nectar in a Sieve*. Jaico Publishing Co., 1980. A moving novel of life in modern India.

Mehta, Ved. *Face to Face*. Little Brown, 1957. The first of many fine works by a blind Indian writer.

Mehta, Ved. *A Family Affair: India Under Three Prime Ministers*. Oxford University Press, 1982. Particularly useful for the Emergency, the Janata period, and the return of Indira Gandhi in 1980.

Narayan, R.K. *The Financial Expert*. Michigan State University Press, 1963. A delightful novel by one of modern India's most gifted writers.

Nehru, Jawaharlal. *Toward Freedom*. Beacon Press, 1958. The reminiscences of India's great nationalist leader, particularly useful for the study of his early life and career.

Norman, Dorothy, ed. *Indira Gandhi: Letters to an American Friend, 1950–1984.* Harcourt Brace Jovanovich, Inc., 1985. A collection of letters from Indira Gandhi to the author.

Nyrop, Richard F. *India: A Country Study.* United States Government, 1985. A survey of contemporary India, with an extensive bibliography; good for reference purposes.

Sahgal, Nayantara. *Indira Gandhi: Her Road to Power.* Ungar, 1982. A critical study of the late prime minister.

Pakistan and Bangladesh After Independence   *(Chapter 8)*

Baxter, Craig. *Bangladesh: A New Nation in an Old Setting.* Westview Press, 1984. A well-done, though brief, historical survey.

Bhutto, Zulfikar Ali. *The Myth of Independence.* Oxford University Press, 1969. Sets forth in hard-hitting fashion some of the basic political beliefs of a major Pakistani leader.

Burki, Shahid Javed. *Pakistan: A Nation in the Making.* Westview Press, 1986. A well-written and thought-provoking history of modern Pakistan.

Er-Rashid, Haroun. *Geography of Bangladesh.* Westview Press, 1978. A detailed description and analysis of the geography of this impoverished nation.

Nyrop, Richard F., et al. *Area Handbook for Bangladesh.* United States Government, 1975. A dated but still very useful study of Bangladesh.

Nyrop, Richard F. *Pakistan: A Country Study.* United States Government, 1984. A wide-ranging survey of Pakistan since independence.

O'Donnell, Charles P. *Bangladesh: Biography of a Muslim Nation.* Westview Press, 1984. A study of Bangladesh's government, politics, and economy.

Reeves, Richard. *Passage to Peshawar: Pakistan Between the Hindu Kush and the Arabian Sea.* Simon and Schuster, 1984. A well-known American journalist offers a fascinating account of his 1983 visit to Pakistan.

Rushie, Salman. *Midnight's Children.* Oxford University Press, 1984. A prize-winning novel by one of the subcontinent's great writers.

Wolpert, Stanley A. *Jinnah of Pakistan.* Oxford University Press, 1984. The definitive biography of Jinnah.

Ziring, Lawrence. *The Ayub Khan Era: Politics in Pakistan, 1958–1969.* Syracuse University Press, 1971. A detailed review and analysis of political developments in Pakistan during Ayub's administration.

GLOSSARY

This Glossary contains definitions for the social studies terms used in this volume about South Asian history. These terms are printed in bold type the first time they appear in the text. The page number following each definition tells you the page on which the word is first used. Often words have more than one meaning. The definitions given below are the ones that will be most helpful to you in reading this book.

alliance association among nations based on mutual purpose, interest, or advantage (207)

authoritarian demanding total obedience (222)

autonomous having the right or power of self-government (156)

Awami League organization formed in East Bengal that led the fight for independence in Bangladesh (221)

bicameral legislature two-house lawmaking body (149)

bloc group united for a common purpose or action (206)

Brahma Hindu deity considered to be the Creator (64)

Brahmin priestly class of the Aryan religion (35)

British raj period of British rule in India (107)

Buddhism religion founded in India that is based on Siddartha Gautama's teachings (40)

buffer zone region or territory located between unfriendly powers that acts as a deterrent to war (207)

bureaucracy system of government administration by bureaus or departments (195)

burqa full-length veil worn by Muslim women when they leave the seclusion of their homes (102)

capital resources used to produce goods and services (134)

capitalism economic system in which businesses are privately owned and in which there is open competition in a free market (190)

capitalist practitioner of capitalism (134)

caste one of four main social classes in Hindu society (36)

caste system fixed social grouping in Hindu society based on class, occupation, and tradition (35)

central government kind of government in which authority is concentrated in a single organization or unit (76)

central planning process by which the government sets economic goals and oversees their implementation (190)

cession act of ceding territory to another country by treaty (209)

civil disobedience policy of passive, nonviolent resistance advocated by Mahatma Gandhi (148)

civil service system under which employees of the government are hired, trained, and regulated (118)

coalition union that is convenient and often temporary between parties with a common interest or goal (121)

cold war non-military conflicts between Communist and non-Communist countries in the post-World War II era (234)

communal representation plan advocated by Muslims to reserve a specified number of political offices and legislative seats for each religious and ethnic community (143)

compromise settlement of differences through concessions (99)

confederacy loose alliance of several states, communities, or cultural groups (97)

constitution document that sets forth the guiding principles and basic laws of a constitutional government (175)

cottage industry production of goods by family members working at home (135)

coup seizure of power from an established government through force (223)

cultural assimilation process by which the characteristics of one culture are acquired by a different culture (54)

cultural borrowing process similar to cultural assimilation (99)

cultural diffusion spread of cultural characteristics from one group to another (27)

democracy system of government in which citizens govern directly or through elected representatives (175)

democratic federal republic type of government formed by India in which states reserve certain powers for themselves while granting other powers to a central government (175)

demographer scientist who studies population growth (232)

distributary stream that carries water away from a river's main channel (14)

diwan provincial administrator (112)

dominion status position of a nation as a self-governing member of the British Commonwealth of Nations, linked to other members by allegiance to the British Crown (153)

double cropping   practice of growing a second crop within a
single growing season (192)

egalitarianism   policy that advocates equal treatment for all
people regardless of class or economic status (222)

federation   league or association of states (156)
floodplain   level area along a river or stream (11)
foreign enclave   territory within a nation that belongs to another nation (209)
Four Noble Truths   major principles by which a Buddhist
reaches enlightenment (40)
free enterprise   economic system in which individuals choose
and operate businesses and sell goods and services with a
minimum of government involvement (190)

Golden Horde   Mongol army of Genghis Khan that invaded Asia
in the 1200's (86)
green revolution   improvement in agriculture in India and other
parts of the Third World through the use of high-yield seeds,
fertilizers, new technology, and new methods of production (192)
guru   Hindu leader or teacher (93)

hartal   one-day strikes staged by Indian nationalists in an effort
to gain independence (146)
heavy industry   manufacture of steel, machines, transportation
equipment and the machinery to make these goods (135)
Hinduism   faith of most of India's people, characterized by the
goal of returning to Brahman through reincarnation (34)
home rule   a form of self-government granted to a protectorate
by an imperialist nation (139)

ideology   set of rigid or inflexible political beliefs (174)
imperialism   policy by which a nation extends its control over
other lands to gain an economic or political advantage (119)
India Act   legislation passed in 1784 by the British Parliament
that limited the East India Company to commercial activities,
thus stripping it of all its governing powers (117)
Indian National Congress   nationalist organization founded in
1885 that was dominant in bringing independence to India
(141)
Industrial Revolution   period of change in the production and
manufacture of goods that began in the 1700's brought on by

the invention of new machines and the discovery of new forms of power (116)

industrialization movement of an economy away from agriculture and trade toward industry and technological development (116)

inflation abnormal increase in price levels (195)

infidel term given to nonbelievers by Muslims (99)

institution relationship or behavioral pattern of lasting importance in the life of a nation or society; also an established organization (143)

insurgent person who revolts against an established government (212)

Islam monotheistic religion founded in the Arabian Peninsula by Mohammed during the seventh century A.D. (83)

jihad religious crusade waged by Muslims against infidels (99)

karma belief in Hindu society that the status of a person in any life is determined by behavior in a previous life (38)

Kshatriya class of Aryan rulers and warriors (35)

less developed country country, usually of the Third World, that is striving to industrialize (199)

majority that part of a group, society, or nation that makes up more than half of the membership or population (156)

martial law control of an area by military rule during which most civil rights are suspended (220)

mercantilism economic policy that stressed the founding of colonies and regulation of their trade in order to advance the interests of the homeland (193)

mercenary paid professional soldier (126)

minority any group that comprises less than half of a nation's total population (123)

mixed economy system that combines free enterprise with central planning (190)

monopoly control of a service or product and its price by a single group (86)

monsoon seasonal winds that cross southern Asia, producing wet and dry seasons (9)

Muslim League organization formed by Mohammed Ali Jinnah in 1906 to further the political interests of the Muslim minority in India (143)

mutiny open rebellion against authority (126)

nation   group of people organized under a single government (193)

nationalism   feeling of devotion to and pride in one's country (76)

nationalization   act of converting business ownership from private to government control (193)

nirvana   in Hinduism, the state of freedom from the cycle of rebirth, attained after extinguishing all attachment to the things of this world (42)

Noble Eightfold Path   practices by which a Buddhist reaches permanent peace, or nirvana (42)

nonalignment   condition of neutrality with respect to forming alliances with either the United States or the Soviet Union (206)

panchayat   village council (75)

parliament   lawmaking body (178)

partition   division into parts (14)

per capita income   the average income of all the people in a nation (190)

Permanent Settlement   change in Bengal's tax system in 1793 that ignored the rights of the cultivators by making zamindars owners of the lands from which they previously had collected taxes (118)

plebiscite   vote expressing an opinion for or against an issue, especially the formation of a government (208)

plurality   the number of votes in an election with several candidates in which the winning candidate has more votes than any of the opponents but less than half of the total votes cast (158)

protectionism   economic practice of protecting domestic industries from foreign competition (195)

protectorate   nation, state, or people that depend on a stronger country for defense and foreign affairs (6)

purdah   custom of wearing a veil observed by married Muslim women (102)

radicalism   policy that advocates revolutionary and extreme changes in government (226)

raja   title assumed by an overlord in post-Gupta times (73)

referendum   vote to express approval or disapproval of an issue or piece of legislation (224)

reincarnation   belief of Hinduism that the soul is reborn over and over in different bodies until it is purified (38)

ryot   peasant cultivator of the land (121)

262

ryotwari method of tax collection adopted in some parts of India (121)

sahib term used by a Muslim or Hindu in colonial India to describe a European (140)

Scheduled Caste (202) *See* Untouchable.

sepoy Indian soldier in Britain's Indian army (126)

Sepoy Rebellion revolt in 1858–1859 by sepoys that has been called India's "first war for independence" by Indian nationalists (126)

Shiva Hindu deity considered to be the Destroyer (64)

Shudra farm laborers, lowest ranking class in Aryan society (36)

Sikhism monotheistic religion of the Indian subcontinent founded in the 1500's that rejects caste (94)

socialism political and economic system under which the government owns and controls the means of production and operates them for the welfare of all citizens in society (153)

sovereignty supremacy of authority or rule (210)

standard of living general measure of the quality of life (190)

stupa Buddhist shrine (49)

subcontinent large landmass, such as India, that is geographically and culturally distinct from the rest of the continent (1)

superpower term often used since the 1950's in reference to the United States or the Soviet Union (206)

swaraj self-rule free of all foreign control, which was Gandhi's major goal for India (151)

tariff protection use of a tax on imports to make foreign goods more expensive than domestic goods (135)

Third World developing nations, usually nonaligned with either the United States or the Soviet Union (190)

trade deficit condition in which the value of a nation's imports exceeds the value of its exports, resulting in an unfavorable balance of trade (231)

tradition set of enduring customs and patterns from the past that influence the present (123)

tribute payment by a conquered region or ruler to a conqueror in exchange for protection or peace (72)

unicameral legislature lawmaking body with only one house (149)

Untouchable person excluded from one of the four main classes of Hindu society; also called Scheduled Caste (36)

Vaishya peasant class of Aryan society that later developed into a class of merchants and townspeople (36)

varna birth class of a Hindu (36)

Vedic Age first Aryan civilization, which lasted about 600 years (33)

viceroy administrator of a distant area during the Delhi Sultanate (84)

Vishnu Hindu deity considered to be the Preserver of Life (64)

zamindar hereditary tax collector (112)

ACKNOWLEDGMENTS

Text Credits

An Advanced History of India by R. C. Majundar. Copyright © 1946 by Macmillan Publishers Ltd. Reprinted by permission. *Asia: A Regional and Economic Geography* by L. Dudley Stamp. Copyright © 1962 by Metheun & Co. Reprinted by permission of Metheun & Co. *The Bhagavad Gita* translated by Swami Prabhavananda and Christopher Isherwood. Copyright © 1967 by Mentor Books. Reprinted by permission. *Britain and India* by Sir Reginald Copeland. © British Crown Copyright 1946. Reprinted by permission of the Controller of Her Brittanic Majesty's Stationery Office. *Jawaharlal Nehru: A Biography* by Frank Moraes. Copyright © 1956 by The Macmillan Company; copyright renewed © 1984. Reprinted by permissiom of Macmillan Publishing Company. *The Life of Buddha* translated by A. Ferdinand Herold and Paul Blum. Copyright © 1954 by Charles C. Tuttle Co. Reprinted by permission of Charles C. Tuttle Co. *The Oxford History of India* by Vincent A. Smith. Copyright © 1961 by Oxford University Press. Reprinted by permission. *Towards Freedom* by Jawaharlal Nehru. Copyright © 1957 by Jawaharlal Nehru. Reprinted by permission of The Nehru Memorial Fund. *The Wonder That Was India* by A. L. Basham. Copyright © 1963 by A. L. Basham. A Hawthorn Book. Reprinted by permission of Dutton, an imprint of New American Library, a division of Penguin Books, USA, Inc., and Sidgwick & Jackson Ltd.

Art Credits

Book designed by George McLean.
Cover concept and design by Hannus Design Associates.
Cover photograph: Gerard Champlong/The Image Bank.
Maps: Precision Graphics.
Title Page and Chapter Opener art: Marion Eldridge.

Photographs 10 *(top)* Government of India Information Service, *(center left)* UNESCO/Vaidya, *(center right)* Harrison Forman/World Photos, *(bottom)* Singer Media Corporation; **16** *(top)* Government of India Information Service, *(bottom)* P. N. Sharma/WHO; **19** *(top left)* Deane Dickson/Ewing Galloway, N.Y., *(top right)* Government of India Information Service, *(center left)* Robert Frerck/Odyssey Productions, *(center right)* United Nations *(bottom)* P. N. Sharma/WHO; **21** Wide World Photos; **29** *(top, bottom)* Harrison Forman/World Photos, *(center left, middle)* Archaeological Survey of India, Government of India, *(center right)* Government of India Information Service; **46** *(left)* UNESCO/Christopher Hills, *(right)* Government of India Information Service; **48** *(top)* Government of India Information Service, *(center)* Yale University Art Gallery, *(bottom)* Archaeological Survey of India, Government of India; **57** *(top left and right)* UNESCO, *(center)* Fogg Art Museum, Harvard University, *(bottom)* Consulate General of the Republic of Indonesia, N.Y.; **65** *(top left)* The Metropolitan Museum of Art, Eggleston Fund, 1927, *(top right)* Museum of Fine Arts, Boston, Marianne Brimmer Fund, *(bottom)* The Cleveland Museum of Art, Dudley P. Allen Collection; **71** Government of India Information Service; **90** *(top)* BBC Hulton Picture Library, *(bottom left)* India Office Library, *(bottom right)* Government of India Information Service; **92** Government of India Information Service; **96** United Nations; **103** Government of India Information Service; **111, 112** BBC Hulton Picture Library; **116** The Granger Collection; **123** The Bettmann Archive; **127** *(top, middle)* BBC Hulton Picture Library, *(bottom)* The Bettmann Archive; **130** India Office Library; **132** Historical Pictures Service, Inc.; **147** *(left)* Wide World Photos, *(right)* Culver Pictures, Inc.; **149** India Office Library; **150** Margaret Bourke-White/*LIFE Magazine* ©1946 Time, Inc.; **153** Culver Pictures, Inc.; **157, 158** Bettmann Newsphotos; **162** UPI/Bettmann Newsphotos; **166** Government of India Information Service; **168** *(top, bottom inset)* Government of India Information Service, *(bottom)* Keystone Press Agency; **187** *(top left)* Wide

World Photos, *(top right)* The Bettmann Archive, *(bottom)* Alain Nogues/Sygma; **189** Wide World Photos; **194** *(top)* FAO photo, *(bottom)* Philip Boucas/World Bank; **196** *(top left)* Robert Frerck/Odyssey Productions, *(top right, bottom)* Dilip Mehta/Contact Press Images; **200** Mimi Forsyth/Monkmeyer Press Photo Service; **204** *(top left)* UNESCO, *(top right)* Dilip Mehta/Contact Press Images, *(bottom)* Fuji Hira/Monkmeyer Press Photo Service; **208** Government of India Information Service; **211** Wide World Photos; **222** *(left)* Keystone Press, *(right)* Embassy of Pakistan; **226** Wide World Photos; **230** *(top left and right)* United Nations, *(bottom)* Embassy of Pakistan; **233** Robert Frerck/Odyssey Productions; **240** *(top left)* Black Star, *(top right and bottom)*, Wide World Photos; **245** Wide World Photos.

INDEX

This index includes references not only to the text of the book but also to charts, graphs, maps, and pictures. These may be identified as follows: *c* refers to a chart; *g* refers to a graph; *m* refers to a map; *p* refers to a picture.

A

Adi Granth, 95

Afghanistan, 2, *m*4, 6, 7, *m*120, *m*176–177; language of, 17; and Soviet Union, 223–224, 225, 227, 235, 237, 249

agriculture, *p*196; of Indo–Gangetic Plain, 7–8, *p*10; of Coastal plains, 9, *p*10; and Ganges River, 11, 13; of Harappan civilization, 30; during British rule, 134; in modern India, 191–193, *p*194; of Pakistan, 227, *g*228, 229; in Bangladesh, 243–244

ahimsa, 151

Ahmadabad, 9, *m*176–177

Ajanta, 70, *p*71

Akbar, *m*85, 88–89, *p*90, 94, 112, 125

Alexander the Great, 2, *m*32, 44–45, 53

Aligarh University, 143

Allah, 81, 83

Amritsar, *p*96; massacre at, 147, *p*149; Sikhs in, 185

Andaman Island, *m*4–5, *m*176–177

Andhra dynasty, 54–55, *m*56

Andhra Pradesh, 55, *m*176–177

Angkor Thom, *p*57, 61

Angkor Wat, *p*57, 61

Arabia, *m*85

Arabian Nights, 69–70

Arabian Peninsula, *m*56

Arabian Sea, *m*13, *m*56, *m*85, *m*120, *m*176–177

Arabs, 2

archaeology, 25, 28

architecture, of South India, *p*57; of Gupta Empire, 70, *p*71, 72; of Mogul Empire, 91, *p*92

art, Buddhist, *p*48, 49; of Gupta Empire, 70, *p*71; of Mogul Empire, 91, *p*92

Arunachal Pradesh, *m*176–177

Arunja, 37

Aryans, 25; spread of, 31–33, *m*32. *See also* Vedic Age

Asaf Jah, 97

Asoka, *m*32, 45–47, *p*46

Assam, *m*176–177

astronomy, 67

Atharva Veda, 34–35

Aurangzeb, *m*85, 92–93, 94, 96, 108, 112

Austrian Succession, 110

Awami League, 221, 238, 242

Aybek, 82

Ayub Khan, Mohammed, 220–221, 236

B

Babur, 88, *p*90

Babylonia, 45

Bactria, *m*32, 53, *m*56

Bali, *m*56, 60

Baluchis, 232

Bana, 69

Banaras, *m*32, 40, *m*120

Bangladesh, 1, *m*4–5, 14, 99, *c*101, *m*120, 131, 166, *m*176–177, *p*245; East Pakistan becomes, 221; government of, 238–242, *p*240; economy of, 243–244; population of, 245, 247; foreign policy of, 247–249; and India, 248; and Pakistan, 248. *See also* East Pakistan

Bangladesh Nationalist Party, 242

Bay of Bengal, *m*4–5, 8, 11, *m*13, *m*85, *m*120, *m*176–177

Bengal, 22, *m*120, 212, 238; and Robert Clive, 111–112, 113; and East India Company, 114; partition of, 143–144, 166–167

Bengali language, 17–18, *c*18, 218

Bentinck, Lord William, 123, 125

Bhagavad Gita, 35, 37

Bhartrihari, 69

Bhopal, *m*176–177

Bhutan, 1, *m*4–5, 6, *m*120, *m*176–177, 210

Bhutto, Benazir, 208, *p*222, 225–227, *p*226, 231, 236, 237

Bhutto, Zulfikar Ali, 221–223, *p*222

Bihar, *p*21, *m*120, *m*176–177

Bihari language, *p*21

Black Hole of Calcutta, 111

Bombay, *m*4–5, 9, *m*13, *m*85, 114, *m*120, *m*176–177

Borneo, *m*56, 59

Borobodur, 60–61

Brahma, 64

Brahmaputra River, *m*4–5, 8, 13–14, *m*120

K

Kabul, *m*4–5, *m*32, *m*85
Kalidasa, 68–69
Kalkin, 64
Kanishka, 53
Kanpur, 8
Kapilavastu, *m*32
Karachi, *m*4–5, *m*13, *m*176–177
Karakoram Range, 3, *m*4–5
karma, 38
Kashmir, *m*4–5, *m*120, 160, 167, *m*176–177, 188, 207–209, 234
Katmandu, *m*4–5
Kerala, 9, *p*16, 55, *m*176–177
Khan, Sayyid Ahmad, 143
Khymer people, 61
Khyber Pass, 2, *m*4–5, *m*32
Kirthar Mountains, 2, *m*4–5
Koran, 101
Korea, *m*56, 60
Kosygin, Alexei, 236
Krishna, 37
Krishna River, *m*85, 110
Kshatriya, 38, 94
Kushana Empire, 53–54, 55, *m*56

L

Laour Party (British), 164
Laccadive Island, *m*4–5, *m*176–177
Lahore, *m*4–5, 8, *m*176–177, *p*233, 235
land reforms, 121–122
land revenue system, 73
languages, *c*18, 20, 21–22, *p*21; Indo-Aryan, 17–18; Hindi, 17, *c*18, 91, 199–200; Dravidian, 18, *p*19, 20, 55; Sino-Tibetan, *p*19, 20, 21; English, 21, *p*21, 122–123, 124, 199–200; Urdu, 91–92, 218; and educational reforms, 122–123; borrowed words, 124; and social reforms, 199–200; of Pakistan, 218; Bengali, 218
Laos, 60
legislature, 149, 179
Lion Capital, *p*46
literature, Vedic, 33, 34–35; of Gupta Empire, 68–70
Lok Sabha, 178–179
Lucknow, *p*127, *m*176–177

M

Macedonia, *m*32
Madhya Pradesh, *m*176–177
Madras, *m*4–5, 9, *m*13, *m*85, 110,*m*120, *m*176–177; and East India Company, 114. *See also* Tamil Nadu
Magadha, *m*32, 44, 45
Mahabharata, 35
Mahanadi River, *m*85, *m*120
Maharaja of Kashmir, 167

Maharashtra, *m*176–177
Mahavira, 40, 43
Mahayana Buddhism, 47
Mahmud of Ghanzi, 81, 82
Malacca, *m*85, 87
Malay Peninsula, *m*56, 59, 161
Maldives, 212
Marathas, *m*85, 93, 96–97, 115, 119
March to the Sea, 155, *p*157
marriage, 102, 205; child, 123
martial law, 220, 224–225, 239, 241
mathematics, 67–68
Maurya Empire, *m*32, 45; Buddhism in, 44–49, *p*48; post-, 52–61
Maya, 38
medical care, 68, 201
Megasthenes, 45
mercantilism, 193
Mesopotamia, 27, 31, *m*32
Mogul Empire, *m*85, 88–89, 92–93; and the arts, 89–91, *p*90; language of, 91–92; fall of, 93; resistance to, 94–97
Mohajirs, 232
Mohammed, 80, 83
Mohenjo–Daro, 26, *p*29, 30, *m*32
Moira, Earl of, 119
Mongolia, *m*56, 60
Mongols, 86
monsoons, 9, 12, *m*13, 55
Montagu, Edwin, 146
Montagu–Chelmsford Reforms, 147, 149–150
Morley–Minto Reforms, 144
Mornington, Earl of, 119, 121
Mount Everest, 3, *m*4–5
Mount Godwin Austen, 3
Movement for the Restoration of Democracy (MRD), 224–225
Muhammad of Ghor, 81–82
Mujibur Rahman, Sheikh, 238–239, *p*240
Muslim Kashmir, 207
Muslim League, 143, 158, 160
Muslims, 97; and Tamil culture, 58; and failure of Buddhism, 66; invasions by, 72, 80, 81–82, 84–87, *m*85, 98–99; in Mogul Empire, 88–89; and Sepoy Rebellion, 126; and Indian National Congress, 142–143; united front with Hindus, 145–146; conflicts with Hindus, 156, 186–187, 208; and partition of India, 167–169, *p*168; in West Pakistan, 218; in Pakistan, 224, 231–232, 237; in Bangladesh, 238, 248–249. *See also* Islam
Mysore, 55, 97, 119, *m*120, *m*176–177

N

Nagpur, 9
Nalanda, 67

Nanak, 95
Narmada River, m85, m120, m176–177
nationalism, 76, 139; beginnings of, 135, 140–144; in World War I, 145–151
nationalization, 193, 195
Nehru, Jawaharlal, p166, 183–184, p187; language of, 21; and nationalism, 139, 150–151; life of, 152, p153; difference with Gandhi, 153–154; and Simon Commission, 154–155; and World War II, 159–160; imprisonment of, 163; on death of Gandhi, 169; and Indian Constitution, 175; and agricultural reforms, 192; social reforms of, 198; nonalignment policy, 207, 209–210
Nepal, 1, m4–5, 6, 115, m120, m176–177, 210
New Congress Party, 185
New Delhi, m4–5, m13
Nicobar Island, m4–5, m13
Nirvana, 42, 47
Nizam of Hyderabad, m120, p158, 167
"Noble Eightfold Path", 42
nonintervention, policy of, 119
North Africa, 163
Northern School of Buddhism, 47, 53
North India, and link to South India, 55; and Gupta Empire, 62–63; invaded by Muslims, 81–82
nuclear weapons, 197, 236

O
opium trade, 116
Orissa, m120, m176–177
Ormuz, m85, 87
Ottoman Empire, 145

P
Pakistan, 1, m4–5, 7, c101, m120, 131, m176–177; languages of, 17, 218; and Indus River Valley civilizations, 26–33, p29, m32; and Muslim League, 160; meaning of, 161; and partition of India, 165–169, 218; wars with, 193, 207–209; relations with China, 211; economy of, 217, 218, 227–231, g228, p230; women in, 217, 224, 225–227, 233; government of, 219–227; agriculture of, 227, g228, 229; illiteracy in, g228, 231; industry in, 229, p230, 231; and India, 234–235; for-

eign policy of, 234–237; and Bangladesh, 248. See also East Pakistan
Pakistan National Alliance (PNA), 223
Pakistan People's Party (PPP), 221, 223, 224, 225–226
Pamir Mountains, m4–5
Panchatantra, 70
panchayat, 75
Pandyas, 55
parliament, 178
Parsis, 100
Parthia, m32, 53, m56
partition, population before, 14; and diversity of languages, 22; of Bengal, 143–144; of India, 165–169, 218
passive resistance, 148, 164. See also civil disobedience
Pathans, 232
peasants, 114, 119, 121–122, 133, 134
People's Republic of Bangladesh. See Bangladesh
People's Republic of China, 209. See also China
per capita income, 190
Permanent Settlement, 118–119
Persia, 6
Philippine Islands, m56, 161
physics, 67
Plassey, Battle of, 112, 113
plebiscite, 208
PNA. See Pakistan National Alliance
politics. See government
Pondicherry, m85, 110, m120, m176–177
Poona, 9
population density, g203
population growth, g191, 192–193, 202; of South Asia, 1; of Indo-Gangetic Plain, 8; of villages, 14; Buddhist, 49; of Pakistan, g228, 232; of Bangladesh, g228, 245, 247
Portugal, trade routes, m85; Portuguese Maritime Empire, m85, 86–87; trade with India, 108; enclaves of, 209
postal system, 131
PPP. See Pakistan People's Party
president, powers of, 179, 180, 181
prime minister, powers of, 179–181
protectionism, 195
Punjab, 11, p16, m120, 160, m176–177; and British rule, 119, 120; and irrigation, 131; reactions to partition, 166–167
purdah, 102